Another Love

Another Love

A Politics of the Unrequited

Asma Abbas

LEXINGTON BOOKS
Lanham • Boulder • New York • London

Published by Lexington Books
An imprint of The Rowman & Littlefield Publishing Group, Inc.
4501 Forbes Boulevard, Suite 200, Lanham, Maryland 20706
www.rowman.com

6 Tinworth Street, London SE11 5AL, United Kingdom

Copyright © 2018 by The Rowman & Littlefield Publishing Group, Inc.

All rights reserved. No part of this book may be reproduced in any form or by any electronic or mechanical means, including information storage and retrieval systems, without written permission from the publisher, except by a reviewer who may quote passages in a review.

British Library Cataloguing in Publication Information Available

Library of Congress Cataloging-in-Publication Data Available

ISBN 978-1-4985-7675-8 (cloth)
ISBN 978-1-4985-7677-2 (pbk)
ISBN 978-1-4985-7676-5 (electronic)

For the beloved who looks back

Contents

Acknowledgments	ix
Introduction: Love Politics, Lost and Found	1
1 Spare(d) Fulfillments, Please: Love, Study, History	13
2 Undulating Love: Enfolding the Margins	35
3 Colonial Loves and Heimlich Maneuvers	59
4 Anticolonial Maps for Lost Lovers	87
Interlude: From Cosmopolitan Modernity to Necropolitical Austerity: Episodes in the Life of Capital and Colony	111
5 The Sanguine Subjects of Love and Terror	127
6 Love Stories as Dissensus: Aesthetics Out of the Postcolony	141
7 Materialists in Love	163
8 Invitations, Deferrals, and Refusals: The Many Hospitalities of Anticolonial Love	179
Epilogue: The Classroom, A Community of Longing	203
Bibliography	213
Index	221
About the Author	227

Acknowledgments

If love shifts how we experience times and spaces, where we are in time and space ought to explain why, how, what, and whom we love. And, given that most of us do not often choose where to find or lose ourselves, such love is closer to inevitability than will. Out of this banal proposition, this book irrupts, and these acknowledgments should span all those presences—most will remain unnamed here—that lingered long enough to turn spaces into times, and times into spaces, conserving each in the name of the beloved so we might unwill some ends that have already been written.

This book was kept over many years, in many places, in many times, and in many hands. It is no ledger, for there are those whom it trusts much more than itself to keep the ledgers that allow us a chance at willed requitals—whether in Karl Marx's feverish mockery and desperate yet hopeful condemnation of capital, or in Faiz Ahmed Faiz's welcoming of the Spring when accounts will be opened and questions will be asked, or in Walter Benjamin's or Leela Gandhi's attentive enumeration of ethical abundances drawn from within fascist and nationalist scarcities to counter curses aplenty, or yet in M. NourbeSe Philip's rescuing and remaking of Zong as if we could all yet be saved. It is not a journal, because its keeper was never sure who could be trusted with the litany of unrequitedness, and because unpossession has always seemed more tempting than records of experience as possession. Maybe, then, it is an attempt at imagining which books are, could, or should be kept, by someone who is more groundskeeper than accountant or archivist. In defiance of the law of value, it invokes rather than invoices, sits next to or behind rather than across, stands near without claiming, records but only to give repose to all it has room for—including flowers and photos pressed between pages, receipts repurposed for scribbles, remnants of *gota* to mark one's place, and the music that sneaks up to make sure we never run out of the little languages only lovers use.

The key site where the book was kept is Bard College at Simon's Rock, in the spaces of study, thought, construction, preservation, transformation, defense, imagination, reaction, creativity, agonism, exhaustion, and conviviality, that I have inhabited here with everyone I have been fortunate enough to hold the door for, break bread with, travel alongside, and defer finalities on behalf of. That some of us found each other here feels, on some days, like life itself, and on other days, like sweet revenge that rights wrongs. It is here that I have found words for my labor in relation to the possibilities and limits of institutions that impress on our selves in literal and metaphoric ways: the love and hope we bring to them, and the work we must do within them, when all space we must work with is always already an aftermath of something, cut from the same cloth as other spaces of a racial settler colony are, or else we are delusional. With its relative youth and its healthy ambivalence toward the project of the imperial University, this place has a shot at unwilling the ends these inheritances script for us. That is a good enough reason to tempt muscularities of thought to depart from those virile and hubristic ones within which so many institutions stay headlocked, unconsciously and irretrievably! This has informed who I have become as a thinker, reader, and teacher, and how and why this book has been kept, beneficiary of those insurgent, burgeoning, and fugal, motions that one would never expect from a little college nestled within the overbearing stasis and settlements that the Berkshires offers to so many. Those who make this possible every day are too many to name.

I thank those guardians of this institution who have enabled, trusted, and supported big and small steps of this movement. My fellow workers who care enough to look back and hold hands when it is most necessary for the soul, and who withstand our disagreements and shared desires in the spaces we occupy together: each of you is present in these pages more than you can imagine. I honor you and am here for you as you have been for all of us.

Scott Shenker's singular generosity and grace has given life to so much within and without these pages that would have been unthinkable and unspeakable without him.

Beyond the friends and keepers who have made life possible for me, this book's process also found its own home-grown interlocutors in Philip Mabry, Bernie Rodgers, Anne O'Dwyer, Valerie Fanarjian, Ian Bickford, Chris Coggins, Nancy Yanoshak, Wesley Brown, Gabriel Salgado, Jennifer Browdy, Brian Conolly, Sara Mugridge, Philip Shelley, Gwendolyn Hampton VanSant, Mary Anne Myers, and Brendan Mathews.

Many other spaces have held and guarded different turns of this project over the past eight years. I am grateful for the reading and writing I was invited to do at the Long Room Hub at Trinity College Dublin, the Faculty of

Social Studies at Masaryk University, the Social Justice Program at Union Institute and University, the Centre for Gender Excellence at Orebro University, the Humanities Seminar at Syracuse University, the Ontario Institute for Studies in Education at University of Toronto, the Department of Comparative Literature at University of California at Irvine, the University at Albany, Bennington College, the University of Katowice, Institute of Business Administration Karachi, and the Indus Valley School of Art and Architecture. The Love in Our World Conference at the University of Manchester, the Foundations of Political Theory Workshop on Political Myth, Rhetoric, and Symbolism, the Critical Theory Workshop, and the Hic Rosa Studio in Aesthetics and Politics in Granada and in Brno, allowed me to bring my pen, paper, and books, and think with others in different welcome interruptions of life as usual. This project finally found its closure in 2017–18 during the sabbatical leave from Simon's Rock, followed by a return to Brno (and near Ingeborg Bachmann's Vienna) as Fulbright-Masaryk Distinguished Chair in Social Studies hosted by the Department of Sociology. The Foundations of Political Theory, and the Politics, Film, and Literature sections of the American Political Science Association, the Western Political Science Association, the Association for Political Theory, and National Women's Studies Association, have made room for me to present my work, reactivate commitments to certain projects, and forge new relationships to intellectual production and academic performance. Brooklyn Institute for Social Research signals a revival of the very idea of shared projects, and I am lucky to share that space and think and teach in it. The Whitney Center for the Arts generously gave me space to write one summer. Kiran Abrar, Nada Raza, Nimra Bucha, Uzma Rathore, and Zerqa Yousuf smuggled me in and out of their homes so I could write a few half-sentences.

I have been a beneficiary of the kindness, generosity, and courage of those mentors, students, and colleagues who gracefully comport their exceptions to petty scholasticism and instrumentalism alike, as well as to the imperialism of the University and other incorporations, without giving up on imperatives of critique, study, and struggle by remaining answerable to someone other than themselves. So many of them graciously accepted my invitations as I tried to build spaces of intellectual hospitality and politics otherwise, by way of the Proseminar in Social, Political, and Humanistic Inquiry, the Materialism and the Colony conference, and now Hic Rosa Collective, a space for art, politics, and possibility *in the aftermath*. Thanks to Leela Gandhi, Gregg Horowitz, Thomas Dumm, David Adams, Adolph Reed, Kathleen Biddick, Elissa Marder, Alexander Weheliye, Simona Sharoni, Jana Vinsky, Jane Gordon, Lewis Gordon, Neil Roberts, Bonnie Honig, Fred Moten, Sunaina Maira, Susan Gillespie, Amitava Kumar, Lawrie Balfour, Lisa Guenther, Saidiya Hartman, David Rice, Auritro Majumdar, Denise Ferreira Da Silva, Rei Terada, Amit Baishya, Anna Agathangelou, Ania

Loomba, Suvir Kaul, Sherene Razack, Suvendrini Perera, Ameeth Vijay, Shari Goldberg, Tanushree Ghosh, Gabriel Rockhill, Rosa Medina Domenech, Vijay Prashad, Bill Mullen, Ajay Chaudhary, Suzanne Schneider, Ahmed Saleh, Omar Robert Hamilton, Bindu Menon, Marina Gržinić, Iva Šmidova, Eileen Joy, Larin McLaughlin, Ewa Macura-Nnamdi, Michał Krzykawski, and others who have made themselves available as singular conditions of possibility, just by being who they are. I am fortunate to be able to show up for political theory time and again knowing that I share that world, from near or afar, with Nancy Love, Chad Lavin, Samuel Chambers, Elizabeth Wingrove, Lori Marso, Laurie Naranch, Libby Anker, Cricket Keating, Torrey Shanks, Bill Dixon, Ryan Schowen, Andrew Schaap, Emily Beausoleil, Michael Shapiro, Kennan Ferguson, Anne Norton, Simon Stow, Smita Rehman, Heike Schotten, Vanita Seth, Nichole Shippen, Murad Idris, Paul Simpson, and Chris Voparil, who have offered feedback, camaraderie, wisdom, and guidance over the years. The seasoned transhistorical and transcontinental friendships of Barbara Alfano, Kiran Abrar, Nada Raza, Rehan Malik, Dawn D'Aluisio, Valerie Fanarjian, and Anne O'Dwyer make achy bones and hearts a delight to bear. Nancy Love, Kathleen Biddick, Denise Ferreira Da Silva, and Rei Terada have patiently parsed the world with me when it was at its most unlovable.

Joseph Parry kept this a book. I am grateful for his trust, confidence, and vision. Bryndee Ryan entered the fray and seamlessly saw this through to completion with care and kindness. Alden Perkins materialized it with patience.

Nusra Latif Qureshi generously shared *Days Dreamless II* (2003) for the cover. I am so fortunate to be in her company, and to have her art adorn this work.

The lives of my parents continue to signal the imperative of witnessing and of the ordinary partisanships of love and loyalty that allow many of us to wake up the next morning. I don't know anyone who embodies the dignities and indignities of unrequited love more honorably than them. I also don't know of an inheritance better than the incurable keeping of promises in the name of the beloved, with all the messes, joys, and failures appertaining. My bustling families in Pakistan and the United States—unflinching partisans of life, beauty, integrity, and justice—love and give beyond reason, measure, and proportion. Please feel free to blame all of them.

To you who remain willfully unschooled in the habits of foreclosure, ressentiment, the law of value, and overwrought self-possession, and come to reading in the name of another with a desire to release words from the meanings that kill, I owe my ability to inhabit any time at all. You know who you are. I am honored to be called your teacher.

To you who never asked me what I meant by love when I was writing about it, I owe gratitude for letting me be in it through all these years, and for believing with me that being is being-with. You asked me many other questions, and stayed with me in overlooked times and places and even took me to a few, all of which were far more essential and generative than the deadening inquisitions, fears, and doubts of all sorts of gatekeepers. I cannot name each one of you, but I am in awe of you as keepers of our shared anticolonial, communist, internationalist, and nonfascist love imaginaries, and of what you risked inviting into your life when we met and chose to give that radical acts we call reading, and listening, and hospitality, a chance. I am lucky to be with you. You make being in other kinds of love impossible.

To you who have been unflinching guides and companions in the aftermath that is always already a prelude, I am thankful for the promises you have kept and for those you didn't, and the spaces you have allowed to be preserved for something to happen. Here's looking at you, Hic Rosa, upstaging boring linear time and its litigious crises with your beauty and promise when we all get to be together, to grieve and hope at once. May the words kept in this book ward off the evil eye. That is why they had to be so flawed.

Thank you, Colin Eubank, Lucy Peterson, Lily Goldberg, Anna Poplawski, Ciarán Finlayson, Milo Ward, Stephen Hager, Anne O'Dwyer, and Valerie Fanarjian for clutching these pages in your hands at one time or another, and allowing them to imbibe your life-affirming love, attention, and brilliance.

Steve, I constantly feared that writing about unrequited love for so much of our life together would jinx us—either the universe would mishear it as a complaint, or the gods of linguistic idealism would feel invited despite what I feel about them. But, you have given me—indeed are—the abundance that underwrites the luxury to grieve fully, defiantly, and unapologetically for this world, and to have the honor of wishing otherwise, with you, for others. I am blessed to have you as an advocate to the universe so it hears better, for the sake of all of us.

Herman Melville, the feline mystic, and Zari, the trustee of the third word, have been stalwart cohabitants on the margins of time. In the constant dialectic of love and loss that came to be the keeping of this book, their presences are the most reliable and potent. Zari, I remember thinking I would finish this book before you were born, but so much dared to unhappen that I was afraid which completions might tempt which finalities. But then you arrived, and you show us every day what completion without finality is. Indeed, there is a love so utter, entire, and imperfect that one could not even wish it to be requited. I am humbled that you picked me.

A version of the Introduction appeared as "From the Love Studio" in the Feminist Love Studies Special Issue of *Hypatia: A Journal of Feminist Philosophy* (Volume 32, Issue 1, Winter 2017), published by Wiley-Blackwell. Issue editors were Ann Ferguson and Margaret Toye. Copyright Hypatia vol.

32, no. 1 (Winter 2017) © by Hypatia, Inc. Reprinted with permission of the publisher.

Chapters 1 and 2 excerpt material published as the entry on "Love" in *The Encyclopedia of Political Thought* (2014) edited by Michael Gibbons, and published by Wiley-Blackwell. Copyright © 2014 John Wiley and Sons, Inc. Reprinted with permission of the publisher.

Chapter 6 is a modified version of "In Love, In Terror, Out of Time," from *At the Limits of Justice: Women of Colour on Terror*, edited by Suvendrini Perera and Sherene H. Razack © University of Toronto Press 2014. Reprinted with permission of the publisher.

Mohammed Hanif, Kiese Laymon, Frederick Charles Moten, and Ahmad Saleh kindly allowed me use of their published work as epigraphs. Other permissions of use of quotes as epigraphs came from University of Minnesota Press, Hackett Publishing, Stanford University Press, and Seven Stories Press.

Introduction:
Love Politics, Lost and Found

The Beloved has become the only force in this world in dissolution that has kept the power to bring us back to fervent life.
—Georges Bataille, "The Sorcerer's Apprentice"[1]

Where there is no love there is also no truth. And only he who loves something is also something—to be nothing and to love nothing is one and the same thing.
—Ludwig Feuerbach, "Principles of the Philosophy of the Future"[2]

THE ADAMANT HEARTIST

When religious fundamentalists in Pakistan ran a "Say No to Valentine's Day" campaign in 2013, Sabeen Mahmud heartfully countered it with "Pyaar Hone Dain" ("Let Love Happen"). Two years later, she was killed in cold blood while waiting in her car at a traffic light, on her way home from one of the many fora she would routinely organize in an earnest bid to alleviate intellectual poverty in Pakistan—this particular one dedicated to state repression of the Baloch people, many of whom have been disappeared and killed over the years and whom no one talks about. Her killer confessed, after also being involved in massacres of minority Muslim sects and the murder of an American woman academic working in Karachi the same month, "We shot her for holding a Valentine's Day rally."

The battle in which Mahmud and her killers met had nothing to do with a silly corporate holiday, and perhaps it was not even the same battle for each. Remembering her friend, Nausheen Ali writes, "She was a *dil phaink*. She was a heartist like that."[3] For Mahmud, as for other casualties of these wars, love itself was the point of contention, their love against terror's soldiering in the name of some love. Two months after her death, her organization, Peace-Niche brought a number of Pakistani activists, musicians, artists, and writers together in what was called a "vibrant homage to the Pakistani spirit" in an art installation titled *Dil Phaink* at the South Bank Centre in London. *Dil phaink*, an Urdu phrase, literally refers to the manner of throwing your heart out into the world, or wearing one's heart on one's sleeve. After her death, more and more people recall Mahmud's fearlessness in the midst of death threats and general undesirability by both the state and enemies of the state, often invoking something she would say about fear being only a line to cross (or not) in one's own head.

Not far from this line is the murderous insanity of the Pakistan-India border which renders the madness of the inmates of the asylum in Saadat Hasan Manto's *Toba Tek Singh* the only credible claim to reason.[4] Someone always dies showing the world its unreason, and as we clear the dead from the land, it is often sadly those lines that get edified into concrete and barbed memorials, and become the stubborn condition of our existence instead of fading away into irrelevance to honor the dead and what they died for, in, and with, rather than what they died of. As one eulogy even put it, "Sabeen is being remembered for her fearlessness, but her friends say that what motivated her daily bravery was love."[5] Indeed, she died for, in, and with love, killed by someone else's fear.

LOVE AND GRIEF ON A GOOD DAY

It is a good day when someone at least acknowledges what has happened to Pakistan in the years you have lived in the United States, and where the destruction of that society as a casualty of the war on terror has paralleled a slow and steady assault on the psyche and a brutal domestication of your feisty confidence as an academic worker in this country. It is a better day when someone does so without you having to tell this story, for they have looked at you and the world enough, whether or not they know how every telling of that story also feels like an acceptance of, if not an acquiescence to, the humiliation and the barbarism, and runs the risk of sounding ungrateful for the love from this and that land and many in between that has held your heart and mind. On such a day, when you are not looking to those lands for any love because your someone did not need you to say or explain or apologize more, you can breathe differently, and the tense, cold, and aggressive block of time "since 9–11" starts to melt. And then you remember that the history of betrayals reaches much further into the past and into the indefinite future, that no state or society is ever a perfect victim except to arbitrarily validate its continuing crimes and power to script the ends of our love, that the home you left did not necessarily have more room for your pain or was not any less soaked with unrequitedness, and that no state-sponsored god or god-sponsored state was coming to save you.

How do you possibly tell the story of what happened while you were away? Of how two words—love and terror—came to enclose a whole minefield of hauntings, questions, thoughts, and feelings about the odd self-consciousness of consanguine inheritances. Of how you became able to apprehend the repulsions and the attachments that come with them, always wondering whether that is an inheritance specific to your religion, your class, your culture, your gender, your city, the colony that you left, or the colony in which you arrived. Of how those you left behind started to pronounce words differently. Of how the land of much sorrow and unacknowledged trauma, abandoned by all but capital, learnt to gaslight as some neoliberal nationalist positive psychology experiment with a developed distaste for all who "wallow." Of how fairly tragic Bombay gangster films began to offer more compelling arguments for love on the margins of time and space. Of how you came to be obsessed with narratives beginning with foretold death, complete or incomplete. Of how love happens on blurry thresholds between life and death. Of how you came to be allergic to pathologies and self-possession. Of how you thought too much about how women love men who kill, and what wives of butchers, soldiers, terrorists, and revolutionaries do with the smell of the blood. Of how you learnt to resist thinking about why someone would hate, or rape, or kill, in order to think of which wounds, deprivations, and prescribed loves fill those holes that cause the blood to be spilt in the first place. In each complaint a confession, and in each confession a question.

It is a really remarkable day when someone grieves with you, and does so beyond guilt, apology, corroboration, or exhibition, without you asking for it and, in a gesture toward a world in which we can be together, relieves you of being the exemplar, the exhibit, the exception, or the uninvited host. Then you say you believe no memory is bad if it came to be a memory, as you silently wish to go around picking pine needles from the hair of raped women you read about, or to sow the skins of tigers who keep tearing open their stripes, or to be the memory of kindness for those who hurt you that would make them stop. You instinctively feel that accepting the loves on offer as a way out of our conundrums is part of what brought us here, and you worry that rejecting those loves too loudly might leave none to go around. And then you find yourself writing about the love that makes a claim on you by mourning with you a scarce and austere world, not as an act of compensation, accommodation, or charity in the name of something out there, but one of freedom, mutuality, hospitality, even a kind of *dil phainkness*. An unreluctant abundance, the unaccursed share, of a heart eager to fall in love. As if all our lives and the meaning of our deaths depended on it. In being about such love, this book is about politics.

LOVER, OUTSIDER

In this book are ruminations on love given and taken, by way of its politics, lost and found. It is about the politics around or near which love lingers. Love is not the object for or instrument within this work, but a series of objections articulated on behalf of politics from spaces and times often deemed either antithetical to, cleansed of, or a relief from, politics. And, politics, I take to be the capacity to produce meaning in common and to make real which, when it comes to those who are either scripted out of reality, made insensible within it, or have not always mattered, is the capacity to make sensible and material what has been denied sense and immaterialized.

Presenting these thoughts may well be understood as one act of love, asking for a being-with in contemporary institutions of knowing and learning whose own forms of inclusions, affirmations, and love leave something to be desired. Quite often, especially given the collusion of much righteous liberal politics with its postmodern inversions, we are often left with stark economies of logos and understanding, passion and reason, self-possession and self-identifications, as if no one had thought of or experienced a love more fragile and yet more brave. In this economy, fidelity and integrity get maliciously interpreted as acts and relations *after* the boundaries of self and other have been affixed. Institutional politics repurpose this in order to unabashedly conscript desires and words in a way that labor, work, production—especially in Western academia—keep being drawn into a function of conserving only the life that is visible and legible in these structures. This feeds my insistent fear that what we see in terms of facile cruelty and xenophobia in this world is not merely "post"-traumatic or a consequence but a cultivated prelude to something else. What are the costs of continuing to slow down our racing hearts, minds, and souls always ready for departure, and of second-guessing our intuitions, just to accommodate ourselves to the methodological lethargy of hegemonic discourses, on the left and on the right, that turn experiences into categories and objects with their own unconfessed antipolitical moralities about living and dying?

Some of this has required overcoming a mix of banality and tongue-tiedness, most acutely felt around fellow workers with a clear object, fervent mission, and disciplinary home. This book exists because for each of those academic treatises, scholasticist performances of debate, and moralizing narratives, there have been those modes of attention, engagement, and fidelity, and the mediums and genres of expression amenable to them, which address imperial violence and neo-imperial destruction of lives not by "platforming" or reciprocating them, but by making room for the affective abilities that forestall premature reconciliations, forgivenesses, and optimisms on someone else's time, refusing conscription by another's fervor. Typically, these kinds of productions posit the unrequited as fighting not for loves that are already available but for those that are not; one trying to put that in academic language is bound to sound like either a bumbling mystic or a hopeless one. Add to these the many repulsions on a daily basis that make me think a lot about love, and a lot about how those I do not know but whom I imagine, have a hold on my heart more than those whom I often regret having comprehended. This disparate camaraderie tells me something about the acts of salvage and redemption in this moment, which entail acts of juxtaposition, acts of bringing oneself closer, acts of bringing other things close to each other, or at least overtures to impossible trust and intimacies, to see what might come about.

It is, then, a solicitous undertaking, born of struggles and a kind of consciousness that has come while being lodged within the production of knowledge and pedagogy, germinating in the kinds of spaces, physical and emotional, imaginary and real, that I have inhabited as a teacher and theorist invested in the space called "America" as home. With other devotions complicating the picture, it is not accidental that the question of love has become important only within the context of a posited home, and space has become important only when it invokes a likeness to home, or strives to ask of you what only home could and should ask. Throw into the mix the requirement of being a card-carrying participant of the forms of politics and initiatives that convert one's love into invisible, illegible labors of understanding and complication that are not always glorious or self-chosen. In fact, these burdens are quite limiting and inconsequential, not least because this labor is predicated on a status of outsiderness that brings home the nature and potency of institutions in which we partake as workers and representatives, versus those of which we are recipients and products. While I do not find these categories to be mutually exclusive, they certainly do mark different relations that forge our subjectivities in times and spaces.

In being about the role of love in the politics of the unrequited, this book commits many transgressions in trying to salvage acts of destruction out of love for those unknown or unmet, many of whom repel for their own attachment to destruction. Here, I ask my questions, if at all possible, with an aesthetic rather than a moral repugnance toward the violent and the sacrificial, since I know well that each often claim to act in the name of some love, and both are genetically connected to the forms of violence that pervade our lives in less extreme, more ordinary, equally potent, ways. Bourgeois liberals can only look good with these "radical" fanatics, and I say this not out of sympathy with someone who can kill, but out of an angry defenselessness at the fact that their regurgitations allow all those who have enabled them to go scot-free, to be forgiven, to be told repeatedly by those of us who did not blow ourselves or others up but were left to explain after burying the nonbodies of the dead, "No, this is not about you," that "This is us—we are the ones who could not get over your desires, your departures, and your abandonments." Instead, going back to W.E.B. Du Bois's painful quip—how does it feel to be a problem?—I want to see this problem, the becoming of which needs to still be dealt with, in light of the incessant, needy, arrivals of the everyday colonizers, their refusals to leave, and their continual demand for at once our hospitality and our evacuation. I believe that the problem of this love that I write about is all our problem, as inheritors of various murders, as victims or perpetrators, in postcolonial or imperial situations together. So, how can the onus of resisting this onslaught over our subjectivity, senses, and our ways of doing things be placed on just those who are the killers now (versus those who have killed us as their natural born right and never stopped)? This is the only reality in which we do find ourselves together with everyone else, no matter to which reality we feel ourselves to be outsiders. This is the only way we might be a *we*.

LOVE'S POLITICS: UNREQUITED INFLECTIONS

In a time when our loves feel conscripted and exhausted by what we often do not remember desiring, this book explores the form, method, and inflections of the experience of love within contemporary political life. I invoke the figure of "the unrequited" as a symptom of a brutally loveless yet effusively sentimentalized era, and also as an ineluctable yet very concrete normative space in response to the intensifying morphologies of war, crisis, empire, capital, colony, and terror, and the increasingly normalized internalizations of violence, austerity, imperialism, supremacism, purism, and fascism. Etched within this particular convergence of contemporary lived concerns are the instinctual, existential, historical, conceptual, material, and conjoined cartographies of two questions which brought me to this inquiry: one inspired by E.M. Forster asking what, if any, relation but that of carnality could be had to the colonized, and the other co-opting Frantz Fanon to ask what, if any, relation but that of terror can be had to the colonizer. *Another Love* asks that we look at practices of love and other material labors that yield and sustain the realities, the wishful impossibilities, and the confusingly destructive vitalities, of the lifeworlds of colonialism, capitalism, liberalism, and neoliberalism that unabashedly nourish each other with the death they produce. (In this sense, my use of the term anticolonial includes both postcolonial as well as decolonial engagements.) The unrequited is an occasion to think about what might, could, and ought to, still be expected of those of us who remain.

Re-apprehending and re-inscribing love in an anticolonial and materialist politics must learn from the histories of both, and at the same time see those histories as the imperfect pasts that will *still* refuse many of us refuge. This involves confronting both what is available and not acceptable, and what is not available and not possible. The imperatives and the modes of love available to and practiced by those on the margins—of societies, groups, institutions, systems, ideologies—change when the given, dominant, forms of affection, embrace, and belonging become unacceptable or even repulsive, even when they hail from textbook allies, even when love might be all the oppressed supposedly need. The question of love in our times is inseparable from the question of otherness and difference centralized in discourses of justice and democracy that opt for tolerance over intimacies, for neutrality over partialities, unless framed through abbreviating moralism. At such moments, love becomes the clarifying category in superficial debates for and against war, for and against inclusive, tolerant, inviting societies, and for and against peace, nonviolence, and overall affirmation. I refuse shortcuts afforded by love's abstract forms invoked in ethical and moral discourses, that at once elevate it but only by reducing it to a timeless, apolitical, essence. Instead, I approach love as that which makes present, an aggregate of desire and attachment, an emotion articulating a relation to time and space. Understood this way, love's different forms and performances, and its internal relations to other categories within dominant systems of organising life, signal shifts in historical reality in societies juggling various unending wars, trying to unwill many pre-written ends. Additionally, in relation to need or sacrifice, or as eros in its imagination of greater wholes of which we could be part, love is something in and with which we confess our complicities not only with but also against hegemonic notions of publicity, collectivity, and solidarity.

As is evident in our own time, the bland liberal democratic politics that shapes the world and struggles against the brutality of mindless fascism invariably turns out to be pernicious and reactionary. Confronted with friends who feel emboldened in their betrayals in the name of an order that might protect them, and who miss an opportunity even for their own sake to reconsider their preferred purities in the face of the unreliable mirages of fortresses those purities instantiate, this book believes in a fighting chance for a democratic reauthorization of politics, a radical co-authoring so to speak, possible only when we do not line ourselves up for that direct personal line to the Leviathan, but shake its arm vigorously enough to let its scepter fall on its own head. Both liberal democracy and what it is out to fix can turn out to be horrendous—and this is because they both miss the love that erupts in all trysts with possibility, in the beliefs, passions, and commitments, not consumed by or oriented toward the modes of desire nurtured under global capitalism. These missed logics of (be)longing and love can give us clues into past, present, and future, moments of rebellion, resistance, rejection, and redemption that are crucial to a liberatory and anticolonial politics in the name of a community and world yet to come. While such loves may be daunting and irreducibly other to us, we can find in the struggles, however failed and intimidating, something of a love that can still infect us, and create something different, even lovely, in the act of this infection.

CHAPTER OUTLINE

This book's move from the unloved to the unrequited as the subject of a materialist, feminist, anticolonial, and nonfascist politics pivots a rethinking of the topographic and metaphysical assumptions that underpin how we approach politics and who performs it and where, what qualifies as a political act, and who stands to yet be included and by whom. To facilitate this, Chapter 1 does the following: provides a conceptual map of suffering, hope, and love that could interpellate the unrequited as the subject of concern and politics; defines love in terms of both desire and attachment in order that histories of attachment figure visibly in the ways we desire today (and the other way around); and argues that love, not hope, is the appropriate double of suffering in a historical, materialist, and anticolonial account of political existence. It proposes that the study, and the politics, of love are interconnected, in a way that foreshadows the work of the subsequent chapters in articulating and performing imperatives of a political method that does not command objects but submits to them.

The temporal and spatial location of the unrequited is parsed in Chapter 2, by turning to the conventional contexts in which love's politics are invoked—whether to celebrate or to suspect—and showing that these celebrations and suspicions are, unimaginatively enough, always elaborations of the ethical demand of the presence of the other, and never as much as venture into politics and the political. Arguing that a politics of love is not and cannot be a mere extrapolation of the ethical and its certainties, and that we can and must do better, the chapter attempts an intervention on a plane that disrupts the foundational conceits of thinking about margins and the staple political desires and roles imputed to the other/outsider. Has the elusive desire to belong and relate in this lonely world actually led to more and not less presumptuous claims to knowing what others think and want? Why the turn to more grandiose and reductionist attributions of desire-as-interest and identity-as-interest the more those who feel entitled to this world seem to be losing control? Are other articulations of relations beyond epistemological certainties or merely epistemological uncertainties wholly impossible?

The unrequited is a dual critique of the methodological predilections of liberals (and of those left warriors who share with these liberals ideology as a form, structure, and habit for thinking about knowing and being and, just like atheists do with the idea of god as a shared fascination with the believer, will break other promises and elevate it to a common cause with them when the call to order is sounded): of the confident ignorance of taking the outside to be an extension of space and time as agreed upon by state, capital, and colony, as well as of the hubris that the desires and attachments shaping the margins are mere riffs on the desires and attachments that feed the inside and the center (itself based on the hubris that we know the latter too well, just because they are ours). Supported by philosophical idealism and transcendental empiricism alike, these topographies of representation, access, spatiality, distance, tolerance, and neutrality in liberalism hold discussions of marginality hostage by habitually domesticating and exhausting its insurgent potential. My argument for unrequitedness as an alternative framework (and not a standpoint) for marginality invites an aesthetic and political emphasis on presence, commitment, time, proximity, involution, and risk rooted in a materialism that is anticolonial.

The book then moves on to mapping the subject of politics in the context of hauntings of colonialism in our normalized ideas of love and requital. Chapter 3 maintains that the labors of suffering and love required to sustain the lifeworlds and institutions of our current oppressive systems are already indicated in colonialism, itself a discourse of desire, including the desire that produces a self as subject. The chapter argues that the relation between the colonizer and colonized (broadened to include new forms of colonizations and lives shaped by exclusion and marginality even when "at home") also brings into consideration a range of emotions and temporalities normally assumed to be at play in any fervent politics of solidarity demanded in this time. This chapter uses the lens of "home" to unpack the attachment narrative in contemporary leftist politics, and to illuminate the unhomely margins of space and time occupied by the unrequited by way of *fugue states*, the motions and stillnesses of refuge, exile, and fugitivity. These motions accrue their own maps. Chapter 4 tends to these by grasping at the loves that happen in the times and spaces that fall outside of the sensuous spatio-temporal schemes of global bourgeois life and idealist liberal philosophy. Triangulating love, time, and presence, it puts forth a reading of the epistemology and aesthetics that accompany the ontological deviances of subjects unsettling colonial loves in various temporalities, and an account of relations suggested in the figure of the unrequited that may help us deal with the foreclosure not of love but of life itself, and their mutuality, under occupations of all sorts. An anticolonial materialism takes a stand, via the aesthetics and politics of love, on the very demarcation between politics and anti-politics as an important aspect of the battle against continuing colonizations and the fascisms they concatenate.

Having conjured and located the unrequited as a subject of politics by reconsidering love, marginality, time, and the various registers of settlements effected by ongoing colonialism in the global postcolony in Part One, the book then turns to the objects and relations of love that articulate the politics of this subject. An Interlude turns to these questions to set up Part Two: What are the manifestations of the politics of unrequitedness when necropolitical austerity elicits a brutal consensus on one's own lovelessness and death as a kind of ticket to life on its terms? Which ends are already written in and out? Which judgments about materialist politics and method does this force on us? It circles back to Benjamin's trope of the historian as an unreciprocated lover in cosmopolitan modernity (discussed in Chapter 1) in order to reconsider our era and its modes of unrequitedness. It updates that conversation to offer a reading of the postcolony that anticipates the chapters of Part Two built around the aesthetics and politics of love in the interlocking temporalities of terror, necropolitics, violence, austerity, fascism—and solidarities to survive and counter them.

Each of these moments spurs an exploration of the interaction between bodies that love and "the political" to see what kinds of *needs* and *capacities* a materialist politics must be able to adjudicate in order to be true to a history of fulfillments, sought and refused, denied and granted. Chapter 5 returns to the questions of Forster and Fanon with which this inquiry began for me—that of love and terror in the ongoing colony—to approach the form in which the subjects of terror and love appear on the scene of unrequitedness; or how, for that matter, the unrequited appear on the scene of love as terror, and of terror as love. Chapter 6 takes up a range of contemporary fiction and film that juxtapose love and death, wondering if there are aesthetics that necropolitics assumes. In reimagining the imperatives of aesthetics wrought within but countering the modes of aesthetic production in necropolitics, it unpacks and critiques western, even contemporary Marxist, aesthetics as well as contemporary neo-phenomenological and biologistic empiricisms, to ask for an attention to the mode and relations of aesthetic production of the sensible. Chapter 7 returns to Chapter 1's proposal of the link between the study and politics of love, and highlights the relations between love, history, and materialism that, given the politics of subjects of unrequited love, furnish the necessities and imperatives to be considered in articulating a epistemological and political method for ourselves. Building on the previous two chapters and their identification of "dissensual" assertions in our stories of politics that may narrate particular subjects into being, this chapter meditates on the juncture of the body and the inception of "politics" to see what a materialist must be able to do, and what fulfillments she must withhold and spare, by raising the question of who confesses to whom—the body to the political, or the political to the body?

Chapter 8 takes up the challenge of relations the unrequited accept rather than shirk or abdicate, to ask what acquiescences, fervors, and refusals, are still available to us, and what is to be the basis of these judgments in this historical moment. The chapter returns to some examples of the invitations to politics in moments of "crisis," analyzes the dynamics that might render them unacceptable, and suggests elements that would be necessary to a politics that shifts the onus from the insistent and presumed hospitality of the unrequited and the marginal to a different arrangement of power in these relations of common desires, shared struggles, and solidarity.

I close with a letter.

NOTES

1. Georges Bataille, "The Sorcerer's Apprentice," in *The College of Sociology, 1937-1939*, ed. Denis Hollier (University Of Minnesota Press, 1988). P. 21
2. Ludwig Feuerbach, *The Fiery Brook: Selected Writings*, trans. Zawar Hanfi, 1st edition (London; New York: Verso, 2013). p. 227
3. Lois Parshley, "The Life and Death of Sabeen Mahmud | The New Yorker," accessed December 3, 2017, https://www.newyorker.com/news/news-desk/the-life-and-death-of-sabeen-mahmud.
4. Saadat Hasan Manto, *Mottled Dawn; Fifty Sketches and Stories of Partition*, 1st ed. (Penguin Books, India, 2004).
5. Parshley, "The Life and Death of Sabeen Mahmud | The New Yorker"; "The Assassination of My Friend Is Not Just a Personal Loss — It's a Loss for Pakistan," accessed December 3, 2017, https://mic.com/articles/116616/the-assassination-of-my-friend-is-not-just-a-personal-loss-it-s-a-loss-for-pakistan#.5AjC9i8X4.

Chapter One

Spare(d) Fulfillments, Please: Love, Study, History

What I do know is that love reckons with the past and evil reminds us to look to the future. Evil loves tomorrow because peddling in possibility is what abusers do. At my worst, I know that I've wanted the people that I've hurt to look forward, imagining all that I can be and forgetting the contours of who I have been to them.
—Kiese Laymon, "Black Churches Taught Us to Forgive White People. We Learned to Shame Ourselves."[1]

There are lots of people who hate dogs but care about the human condition; they care about children begging on the streets, or transgender people not getting jobs. Like them, I worry if it's O.K. to care about a mutt when the world around us is falling apart. Then I tell myself it's exactly when the world is falling apart that you should care about mutts. [. . .] Our classical poetry, religious and romantic, heretic and Sufi, is full of verses where a lover wants to be a stray dog living on the street corner of his beloved's home. Sufi poets have held dogs as a symbol of devotion and superhuman dedication. But even when the pious ones are crooning away about their desire to be a dog in the holy city of Medina, they can't stand a real dog when it happens to pass by.
—Mohammad Hanif, "Of Dogs, Faith, and Imams"[2]

They say that for weeks after Sabeen's murder, her cat Jaadu (magic) "would sit expectantly by the door of her house for hours every evening, waiting for a familiar footfall on the steps outside."[3] A couple of months after that murder, nine black lives were taken during a bible study session by a single shooter at a church in Charleston.[4] The first killer "shows little concern about his trial and punishment when asked about his future," "completely unfazed, laughing slowly," saying "We'll go to prison, but we'll break out of there. Then, we'll make plans." The second killer was taken for fast food after being arrested and just pleaded not guilty.[5] This chapter lays the groundwork for inquiry into a politics of those who wait in and out of love, sit at thresholds from which no one returns empty-handed, and whose hospitality to those who might take their lives is an answer to very different calls and claims to the ends of history than those who walk the earth with always already fulfilled promises of heaven and hell, instrumentalizing others and themselves, rendering the very idea of fulfillment sometimes morally and aesthetically unsalvageable. But that's just me.

LOVE STORIES

"Where is the love *for us*?" asks Chris Lebron after the murder of nine black Americans at the Mother Emanuel A.M.E. Church in Charleston, South Carolina in June 2015.[6] This question, for Lebron, is a spur to return to black radicalism, one of the two poles of black politics, this one associated with Malcolm X, and the other with Martin Luther King. What a strange question, and what interest does the *New York Times* have in maintaining this binary, I shrug petulantly: for one, when was this ever about the love one receives? The liberal story, which stays intact when we narrate radicalism as an attempt to invert it, cannot let go of the political subject understood as recipient or consumer rather than producer of politics—and of love, in this case. And the only manner in which African-Americans have been able to be subjects of the love, as Kiese Laymon writes, in the mode of existence and survival that got framed around the black church enabling and even forcing a kind of painfully intimate love for the white man over and against any love for oneself. So, when black people are producers of love, they get to keep shame for themselves, in a kind of non-primitive accumulation; centuries on from writing the body as its harvest, whiteness continues as the harvest of black bodies in this way. The issue of whether one does or does not receive love goes beyond, for someone like James Baldwin, the constructed polarity of ballot and bullet, driving home the fact that being only the unloved in this scheme reinforces the idea of a black subject who is imagined in a kind of transactional economy of this love, waiting for some to come their way, and at the mercy of being granted or denied something fundamental, like humanity. The story of this unlovedness changes if the unloved are not those waiting for love, or inscribed within religion's repetition of the secular liberal economics of affect. Something else has to be acknowledged, even made to happen.

Such a possibility relies on acts beyond agency and will that still shape subjectivity not as a lack of what is received but by way of what was produced and put out into the world. Being unloved has to be in conversation with being the one on whose backs this world is produced. The severance of production from distribution, in the case of love, suffering, "humanity," has to be called out and interrupted. For these bodies, the question of love, undisputedly inseparable from the question of suffering in society, needs to exit the enclosure of affect to which the economies of this world must limit them, so they are able to speak to different love, differently. So, it might no longer suffice to ask where the love for us might be: whose love are we asking for, and why? Instead, a declaration that this is our love is in order, and we might be confronted next with the question of what it might mean to confess the intensity and the force of our own love politically rather than moralistically or religiously. It might have something to do with these additional questions: What love is this? Why and how do we know what it means? What does it entail? What world is produced in that love? What other love is made possible in that love?

With the possibility of life and joy commonly staked on the requiting of actual and imputed loves, it is crucial to interrupt and revalue both the love and the meaning of requital. This is especially important when someone else's sense of requital—in this case, subscription to the expanding homes of neoliberal, neofascist, and neopragmatist love—depoliticizes and dissipates the struggles of those who are the arrogated recipients of this love (or conscripted in, through, or by it). It is also important to attend to the disparity between modes of love at work across instrumental alliances toward goals (the objects of desire understood narrowly) in common, and to identify and subvert the moments where notions of consent, consummation, culmination, and closure, are either attributed to struggles as a way of making them tame, legible, homogeneous, and unthreatening, or just demanded of them as a price for making a claim on this world.

Giving up on love altogether because we have only ever been particular objects of particular love, never having a say in either of those particulars, is not an option. If we are wholly subjects who love and love differently, and get to interrogate our love and those of others, then perhaps we might grant ourselves a break from the manipulative invocations of humanity, no longer caring to ask the naïve question of why we are not considered human, or why we are dehumanized. What do we want to hear in response, and what answer could we possibly get? And, what history could we summon as a witness on our behalf, when the very notion of the human has relied on the primordial extraction of the love from those who had no option but to give it? Holding on to love and choosing to decide its whats and hows, instead of giving it over in a gesture of defiance of the loves that have held us hostage, is a direct response to those who set limits on our love and on our terror, determining which is which. What else are we to do in response to this terror that keeps defining the possibilities of love, and to the forms of love that keep anticipating the possibilities of terror? Common to both these definitions is an understanding of requital that comes from a consensus on the logics of temporality and spatiality that work to produce a necrophiliac antipolitics of love.

The *story* of the unloved, conventionally told, is a story of the failure to become the object of love. As the unloved, the focal object is also interestingly the afterthought rather than the premise of the act or fact of love. (That, in itself, has nothing to do with being the object of love, but something to do with the story that is told, since in many mystical and devotional renditions what is loved is the premise of love.) In the same story, the unloved are made possible by their commitment to a meaning or value of the love they have ostensibly asked for or been deemed in need of, but supposedly lost out on. Once they have been established as the unloved, they are ready to be narrated, and out go all the negotiations with the meaning of love, and all the residual directionalities of love when we regard only those exchanges that we already know to matter.

The story of the unloved is a *love* story, however, if it is the story not of love ungotten but of love unrequited, in which subjects of that love are present as lovers rather than the beloved that they could never be. A lot rides, for me, on this hair-splitting between the unloved and the unrequited. The unrequited is a claim to a relationship that proceeds from the subjects of the love and returns to them, to fill out the meager outlines of subjecthood granted them within dominant narratives. Lack of requital is not invoked here as a moral or even empirico-positivist concept that captures something purely or only in the realm of deprivation, but as a category of experience. It is a character of life that is thrust on some of us more than others by societies that offer no intimacies, but insist on reifying notions of requital all the time. Importantly, for me, it is of the order of a relation to history, to the worlds it forces us to imagine, to the requitals it makes into habit, and to the requitals to which it makes us allergic—not out of messianic hope for redemption but out of love. Somewhat like Walter Benjamin's. In that way, the politics of love seeks not exceptions to it, but must be understood fundamentally from the outside of the outside, so to speak: the location not of the unloved but of the unrequited.

FROM THE UNLOVED TO THE UNREQUITED

In an essay titled "Aphrodite's Children: Hopeless Love, Historiography, and Benjamin's Dialectical Image," Chris Andre reads the figure of the historian in Walter Benjamin's work as a key interlocutor with Benjamin's meditations on love.[7] He argues that while Benjamin's discourse on love precedes the appearance of the historian, and while the latter can be seen as taking over from where love leaves off in the earlier works, there is a real analogy, first, between love and the writing of history and, then, between the production of poetic images and of history. (Both show us, perhaps, how love and poiesis might be related, not least by way of sharing a connection to writing/making/materializing history.) Andre reads Benjamin presenting, in his early works, love as a "particular form of consciousness" that suffuses the "essentially constructive method" in historiography or other poetic production, from the *Origin of German Tragic Drama*[8] to the "Theses on the Philosophy on History."[9] Andre writes:

> The thematic presence of love in Benjamin's early writing does not essentially contradict his later emphasis on construction, and these two sets of critical vocabularies and positions can be read as profoundly sympathetic. A comparison of the constructive elements of the "Theses" of 1940 with the emphasis on love and esoteric language in the "Surrealism" essay of 1929 (and the even earlier *Trauerspiel* [1925] and *One-Way Street* [1927]) forms not a linear narrative, not a story of the progressive development of models, but rather an image of the historian as a hopeless lover, an image figured through permutations of critical vocabulary.[10]

Andre traces this image of the lover back to "On Some Motifs in Baudelaire," where Benjamin speaks of a love in the era of cosmopolitan modernity—love that is always (1) what might have been experienced, (2) regrettable for having passed by, and (3) the object of contemplation for being both what could have been and having appeared only to disappear. Benjamin writes that, of this love, "[O]ne might not infrequently say that it was spared, rather than denied, fulfillment."[11] Andre finds this informing a conception of love as "a sort of heightened awareness that adamantly refuses consummation."[12] Interestingly enough, in this discussion, love also starts to resemble a prayer that does not quite specify what it is asking for, but where the act of praying as a relation to another and the audience it is granted overcomes the object desired in the prayer—a love for the beloved (God or other) on which Muslim mystic poets often insist. It is no surprise, then, that contemporary militant Islam violently shuns that insistence and takes to a literalism that has no interest in an audience with the beloved (God or other) but in the bullish and bullying clarity and enunciation of the supplication (to wit, the exacting Arabization of Urdu pronunciation in South Asia accompanying the invasion of Salafi and Wahabi Islam) that sees words as forced consummations rather than as overtures. (They have many undiscovered friends, it turns out, among even the soft positivists, disguised as realist social scientists who are worried about the world but have trouble reading or listening, in Western academia.)

There isn't much room for demanding redemptive poetics or interpretive deconstructions from Benjamin's historical materialist when contemporary culture brashly flaunts its barbarisms, and normalizes, even enjoys, its own brutal gaze on itself in a way that renders redundant those among us who were taught to read, write, and speak with lowered eyes, not out of shame or despondence, but in grace and generosity toward the unspoken and unspeakable. Rote historicism seems both sufficient to the task and a disheartening turn-off from history, when we sense: the unmediated scourge of anti-black thought and action as if we have lived even when and where we did not live; strange fruit inside jail cells; the unforgiven hospitality of women's bodies to order-conserving violence; the slow yet convulsive death of institutions that occasionally force one to compare ISIS militants to the austerity mafia on a rampage in the University; Islamophobia as if the armors have been hollowed out of bodies altogether, and all the trees bleed, in this extended Clarissa and Tancred dream sequence;[13] Europe's fascist xenophobia as well as Germany's imperial dispositions toward smaller, suffering countries in Europe as if psychoanalysis was always already Europe's confession; figures of great antipathy and ressentiment embodied not merely in the politician that Max Weber feared might emerge from the era of disenchantment and political humiliation when he gave his famous "Politics as a Vocation" lecture in 1919, but also in the German banker who incorporates neoliberal austere reason beyond the politics of scarcity or debt.

Not the fact of fulfillment but the general form of love premised on it, and the wider net of relations normalized in and around this form, emerge as the issue. Neither Benjamin nor the sufi poet dictate how love should happen or what it should ask for. Rather, they help direct our sight to the potential flaw or loss of only considering the love whose object and demeanor we presume to know, and proceed to derive confidence from knowing, where the object reassures us even as it renders us, the unreciprocated lovers, its "victims" (victims only because unfulfilled). Per the concerns of this book, this is how love becomes a proof of sovereignty rather than its absolute undoing or irrelevance which it could conceivably be. A different configuration and spatiality of relations between, around, and through lovers and the beloved might become possible, as might a claim to selfhood and human political relations that unsettles dyadic relations between lovers and their beloveds, and also the presumption about what political actors are attached to and why. The instituted separation—indeed, secularization—of ethics from politics keeps intact a conservative order of individual and state sovereignty as necessary, sufficient, defining, and eternal features of world politics. Even resistances to this order must first account for why they are not interested in those things.

With Andre and Benjamin, I find that the metaphor of *love spared fulfillment* speaks to the idea of unrequited love today. What sort of love does an era need if it demands a particular lack of fulfillment from those whose unreciprocated love or unlovedness concerns us? How would our answer change if the question of unreciprocated love in Benjamin and Andre is broadened to include love as both desire and attachment? The question goes beyond the kinds of love we will be okay with not fulfilling, to the kinds of love we wish would remain unfulfilled for fear of the kinds of worlds they might create or open up. It invites into consideration a love whose form (and not merely object or directionality) is different because it counters scarcity not by crossing the limits we never had a hand in setting, but by a kind of abundance that produces love in a different form that does not have to answer to those limits. Abundance is not simply what exceeds within a particular form, but what presents a different form, not merely content, in excess of scarcity. This is what also affirms the shift in analytical focus from desire to attachment, and then from the unfulfilled to the unrequited. While the unfulfilled adheres to a form already defined by desire, a kind of Aristotelian "perfect" act, the unrequited can flout or at least defer the submission to a given form by withstanding non-response, and relates to the other even in being denied audience. There is a gesture to another as the premise of love itself, not of love's fulfillment. At core, this is a gesture toward the very possibility of a world, not to its harvests and gratifications. The forms of love that can themselves be the abundance to counter austerity are those which attach rather than those that seek fulfillment or gratification, which work to bring closer, which experiment with intimacies and relations, and so might give us a chance at producing a world in which love might be possible. They also interrupt the urgencies that allow for certain forms to prevail, dominate, and pretend to become necessary, as if nothing else can be done. *As if nothing else can be done.*

LOVE STUDY: SUBJECTS, RELATIONS, OBJECTS

What does love study under conditions of its unrequitedness? How can it at once cease to be an object, and resist inversion into an idealized subject as the only way to survive? Against the purities, scarcities, redemptions, settlements, and requitals that make it a conscript of antipolitics of various kinds, love somehow continues to profess and remain a partisan to politics and its possibility, producing the world and often disappearing from it. When so much of that love is waiting to be spoken to, or called back from disappearance, the we and the I must make room for a forgotten you to be spoken to, heard from, grieved with, and offered a world in common. Even speaking as or for oneself in these conditions requires speaking to oneself, as if one were, just for a moment, the beloved, and not the accu(r)sed. This book's form and tone is an invitation to that moment, to a political method that counters the shared premises of racism, misogyny, fascism, capital, and the colony, lest our theories and practices claim further casualties: not even the beloved is safe from the wrath of that which seeks the final solution or last apology, encloses in words without excess, and squares away in smug, swift action, which is its own special curse.

The presumption that political acts of individuals and groups traverse a predictable and generalizable terrain of access and accessibility, or desire and desirability, has often surprised me over the course of studying and engaging with contemporary Western critical and political theorists. I am amazed at which foundations of human existence and subjectivity become non-negotiable, when, and at whose behest, in the turn of theory to politics or relevance, often in times of crisis such as these. Lines get drawn as a final patronizing act of conferring coherence to what is presumed incoherent and inchoate, especially by those who never had to prove their coherence within the order of things, since theirs is the order of things (and will often crumble at its very slight interruption). When we are asked to return to "the real world" and confess to it, it is not a wonder who flaunts it in their hands, bedecked with all sorts of presumed and imputed desires, all in the name of returning to a home that exists, when all is said and done, lest we might get completely lost.

While not cruelly unsympathetic to this desire, I worry that it has the whiff less of the love for another, more for a world in which one continues to be oneself. Fundamentally, it estranges—both in the sense of alienate and refuse to recognize—the love for a world where both ourselves and the world need to yet be found, a desire only those illegible, misplaced, dislocated, and immaterialized are familiar with. In being inattentive to the plurality of forms which people can give to their politics, it keeps the tried and tested forms in play, exemplified in the fact that the contemporary anarcho-populist ideologies of resistance that claim to depart from, but actually perfect and embody, the sabotage of liberal identity politics, feature the oppressed in the same predictable roles and subjectivities for a world that are bound to leave those people with nothing once this performance is declared over, or some new urgency tyrannises, like another kind of terrorism, like the financial crisis, like a climate catastrophe, like the presidential elections. Minimally, there seems to be a relation between urgencies and the presupposition of a form of love that desires fulfillment but does not investigate attachment (to one's imposed subjectivities, to objects of desire), on the one hand, and also who gets to declare the time of crisis and demand certain reliable loves to fill it, on the other hand. Unsettling this form of love and its presuppositions is imperative, not in the name of radical autonomy or the sovereignty we have known, but of a different collectivity, a shareable world, and a *we* awaiting confirmation.

To recall Stephen Dunn,

> *Beautiful*, I heard
> a spectator say, as if something inevitable
> about to come from nowhere was again on its way.[14]

LOVE AS SUBJECT

Love is what makes present and apprehends presence, even absence as presence. An intense feeling that serves as an adhesive for individuals and groups, love inheres both desire—understood as a movement and opening toward what one deems beautiful or wants to make proximate—and attachment—understood as a fastening, fixity, enclosure, and limit. As a natural or conditioned power, capacity, capability, force, attitude, or substance, love is articulated in the arrangement of relations within and across the time and space of bounded collectivities, and thus of significance to the nature and possibility of politics. A fully political reckoning of love as a concept requires grasping its endogeneity to judgment, its complex function as a precondition of political method, and its role in the genealogy of politics and political subjects as a morphing and transformative human power, capacity, and practice. Attention to the forms, locations, and functions of love is, thus, essential to the study of power, coexistence, and transformation at subjective, cultural, and structural levels.

I am not seeking to theorize, redeem, or reject the term "love," or to put it to use in a specific political project, or still to look to someone's correct understanding of it. Germane to this is the understanding that forms of love have a material history—so much so that they are not only consequences of, but deeply implicated in, the history of materiality and relations that is still unfolding. The core property of love, even romantic love, that is central to this meditation, is that embodied, coherent, and dissensual, relations to time and space ensue in expressions and acts of love—and that these not only happen to cross over into the political, but in fact systematically channel the aesthetic and the ethical into the political realm. Impressionistically, love converges pleasure, mystery, affection, and a draw toward what we deem beautiful (but is not equal to any of these alone, not allowing sorrow, intimacy, and repulsion to be easy antonyms to itself). With Jean-Jacques Rousseau[15] and the Romantics,[16] love is a feeling, a sentiment, and a passion, separate from more generalized categories of experience, not to mention one of the three "essentials" for Ludwig Feuerbach[17] next to thinking and willing. When thematized within an economy of production, creation, and need, desire is the objectification of love (in a Hegelian sense). What interrupts desire and what interrupts love are different things. Repulsion is not a discontent of love, conferring to love an element of the non-affirmative in the context of overcoming histories of hatred and resentment, especially where reconciliation becomes a fetish object.[18]

The confusions, clarities, and conditions of our moment force us to factor into our thought and inquiry a notion of love that is non-affirmative, yet not negative, somewhere between transcendent and fragmentary; that can actually grasp the emotion materially; that does not efface its ordinary politics or rationalize its aesthetics; that has space for the obsessive, the devotional, the fanatical, and the repulsive, without automatically conflating it with idealism and fascism; and that can interrupt the popular and acceptable conscriptions of desire and attachment in order to liberate other modalities of love, joy, hope, and their availabilities. These turns are required so that we may break a bad habit. This is the habit of well-meaning fervent ascription of certain kinds of love, as we celebrate the solidarity posited in the commonality and homogenization of stories with similar termini and unravelings. It is a bad habit because it ends up disregarding, stifling, and throttling much life and being.

The question of love is forced upon us not only in its absence or failure, but when being able to tell love from what is not love, to reject the bargains on offer, and to ask for any, more, or a different love, becomes a meaningful and liberating response to the austerities, scarcities, catastrophes, and crises of the time. This brings up the particular nature of love as objection in an age of austerity and the relations to time and space that are presumed in moralistic notions of love and render it apolitical or anti-political, whether in convoking the post-industrial multitude or the nation. Indeed, the discursive and ideological shift from scarcity to austerity as concepts with currency in global neoliberal necropolitics winds its way through and picks up force in a particular economy of affect and embodiment. The conversion of scarcity into austerity is mediated by contemporary capitalism's rebound into colony-style fascism, productive of new crises and urgencies that need recalcitrant counter-urgencies of love to oppose them, and a reclamation of form and time as if our lives depended on it. In austere times such as ours, when even friends are casualties to interiorized scarcity, love is not a luxury but a staple form of abundance, right next to history and memory, to which we must turn, as if our lives depended on it. Much to the chagrin of paternalistic truth-telling experts in the business of verifying human experience in order to save us from ourselves, a kind of defiantly need-based nominalism—claiming and naming as love that which someone needs to call love—is an act of materialist scavenging in the era of austerity, an admittedly twisted overture to the poetics of politics that Jacques Rancière finds even in the self-naming of the proletariat.[19]

Loving may be grasped as an action distinct from will or agency normally understood, as a distinct potency that is not merely an extension or distortion of other moral forces. This makes it worth exploring for its politics. To this end, both time and space need to be dis-oriented, so that our imaginations and understandings depart from the conventional topography of politics. This opens us up to the confrontations and propositions that happen in realms unfitting for a normalized (and normalizing) politics of survival and sovereignty, and produce variant political subjects. Not exemplary love, but love and lovers by example.

SUBJECTS BEYOND DEAD LOVE

For those who suffer the regimes of farcical, murderous, loveless, desire of "the other" that go by the names of colonialism, liberal multiculturalism, and neoliberal monoculture, love—*and not hope*—is the appropriate double for this suffering. Both love and suffering are experiences that are historical not just for producing history and making this world (even if what is made is a mess), but because their forms and contents are also historically produced. Globalized narratives of progress, redemption, security, salvation, or hope, as well as contemporary manipulations of love, affect, and community in various movements, easily pair with the globalized pronouncements of tragedy and crisis, building on a history of the domestication of suffering that produces victims with scripted relations to their suffering made legible and consumable in the general forms of injury and harm.

In *Liberalism and Human Suffering,* I argued that a critique of suffering in liberalism is even fundamental to a critique of labor in capitalism, labor (whose unit is time) itself premised on a certain understanding of suffering.[20] Capitalism necessitates our bodies and their time corralled within the experience of suffering in a particular way so that hope becomes a corollary of a certain political economy of suffering. When suffering is seen in this structural relation to time via labor as the ability to make present and bring to presence, then the relation between suffering and this "hope" pinned to a future moment becomes essential. Whereas hope is still an external relation to time disciplined within a liberal and colonizing ontology, love is the appropriate materialist double of suffering understood not as an object or material for a just politics, but as already insinuated in political method and subjectivity. The historical materialist account of suffering and hope in liberalism sought in that book crosses over into an anticolonial account only by considering what happens to the time of love in colonialism: disciplined into carnal desire for the sexualized object,[21] or into an imminently wounded or "failed" attachment to progress, that often ends in the self-destruction of the colonial subject itself.[22]

If injury is dead suffering, hope is dead love. Both liberal hope and liberal injury are idealized, ascetic, temporalities abstracted, respectively, from love and suffering. Hope is a domestication and commodification of love to match the domestication and commodification of suffering in injury and harm. These domestications of our sensuousness are ultimately primitive accumulations of time, unifying capital and colony. Hope and the promise of requital are to love as injury is to suffering. Love is different from hope because it inheres the possibility of requitals and not requitals. The mediatized deployment of hope is of a piece with the philosophical abstractions and political detachments intrinsic to optimism and nihilism alike. All these frenetic performances of homogenized voice and sentimentality are impossible without a dictated translation of, and relation to, suffering and love. Familiar ontologizing epistemes and moralities of life, death, peace, conflict, are deployed the moment anyone departs from these, rushing to re-equilibrate, re-appropriate, and restore the hegemonic sensorium.

As the not-good-enough victims have now become terrorists or potential terrorists, disloyal to the narratives of suffering that unfold in the minds of the good liberal and true fascist alike, it is analytically useful to see love as disaggregated into the attachment and the desire that lets people suffer how they do. How one is attached, and how one desires, says much more about how one suffers beyond a superficial, generalized, relation to the idea of deliverance from suffering. From working with the ways in which liberalism's quest to include ends up fundamentally misunderstanding, even violating, subjects' experiences of suffering by scripting their victimhoods, the performances of their injury, and eventually a pathologized subjectivity that sustains the fiction of the healthy subject of politics, the question of love gives us access to the supposed desire to which liberalism responds, and the attachments that it exploits, in performing these inclusions. When liberalism feels a little bit disoriented or stymied, it rushes to impute, name, and fill in the desire, in a way that ends up fundamentally domesticating love into a kind of abstract desire in a move resonant with that which domesticates suffering into harm and injury. What gets lost or at least obscured is the attachment. In contrast to the free articulations of desire and attachment with each other over time, the disciplining of time subsumes one into the other. It is thus that, in the fetish-form of hope, the desire as well as the attachment are indistinguishable from each other—so much so that adjudications of people's politics happen around whether they simply believe or do not believe in hope. This resembles the way in which the category of injury, learning from value in capitalism, destroys any traces of a relation to suffering by becoming the object that is suffered, and then assumes that no other relation to suffering may be had.

Beyond love in a relation with history— a relation that may be forgotten depending on what history is created, and as what kind of home or abundance it serves—is the question of love having a material history of its own. The ways in which we love are not the same over time, and what is deemed love at different moments in history is different. Certainly, what is deemed love within a particular moment in time also varies from one space to another. Claiming that forms of love have a material history (rather than just that love does material things in the world over history's course), and acknowledging their contemporary manifestations, is (unlike what happens in pragmatist understandings of history) not in service of sealing their form or fate, or claiming a pacific epistemic or ontic universality for them. Rather, it is by being a claim of what things could be and how things do not have to be, that (still) writing about (another) love is itself an act of love.

However, with all the crises and the calls to order around us, we could be tricked into thinking that a consensus around how and what we love has already been reached and announced, while some of us were busy unveiling the tyranny of generalized notions of humanity—and the accompanying hegemonic conceptions of life, success, health, injury, desire, knowledge—that never did nor will ever serve those who have been the premise for the formalization of the human to their own exclusion from (and now "humanitarian" destruction in the name of) that category. In turning to suffering and love as human capacities, I am not reifying any given idea of the human or a fixed ontology that might come with it. Instead, I am trying to show that such notions and ontologizing turns run the risk of doing so unless we keep the form of these capacities open (and free from the death grip of functionalist friends). It behooves us to counter ontological politics that proceeds from constructed, historical, and contingent notions of the human that pretend to be otherwise, by politicizing ontology in such a way that no consensual humanism can enter to neutralize or palliate without being met with a gesture to an agonism over the human itself.

SUFFERING TO LOVE: FROM SCRIPTS TO CONSCRIPTS

So, how have we suffered in order to love this way?

This question is a follow-up to what I read as Friedrich Nietzsche's exclamation in *On the Genealogy of Morals*,[23] "oh how have we suffered to suffer this way!" Following Karl Marx's "to be sensuous is to suffer,"[24] suffering here is sensuousness, not limited to pain, harm, and injury, but extending to the material that is given form in those categories and concepts. The question of suffering, thus, is central to the forms love has fallen into (and the forms of love we have fallen in), and to how and what we have wanted and been attached. A materialist critique of representation that I have offered elsewhere exposes the labor of making suffering matter that is overlooked or made invisible in discourses that begin with an injury but never stay with the sufferer, such as liberalism.

The ways in which we suffer and love index our political locations, defined as the spatial and temporal coordinates of our existence relative to the bindings of state, nation, society, and ideology. Beyond the fact that our political locations demand certain love and suffering from us that writes us as political subjects, our modes of love and suffering also index our political subjectivities. With regard to suffering, and reacting to modes of liberal inclusion and justice as fundamentally problematic at so many levels, marginal to liberal politics and ontology are those whose modes of and relations to suffering are incomprehensible, illegible, or effluent to liberalism. Beyond marginal forms of and relations to love, love is an action from the margins to begin with, inseparable from a certain relation to one's inclusion or exclusion in spaces and, indeed, spaces of time. Whether it is these locations that claim or purge us in the name of certain loves, or it is we who struggle to claim or purge them for the sake of some other loves, turning to the form and capacities of subjects marked by these locations is what brings politics back into the discussion of any of our numerous political conditions, from terror to austerity to crisis to fascism, even if only for a moment.

The world and its history are teeming with proof that there are capacities and forms of suffering that exceed the reach and subsumption of the liberal sensorium. Struggles against oppression subvert those patriarchal and colonial love stories in which we are seen as attached to our wounds, and desiring our own subjection. In doing so, these struggles propose their own organizations of affect, own redirections of desire, and own attachments (such as those to nation, freedom, equality, and more). If liberalism's scripts our injuries and wounded performances, it is our love that is being conscripted. For every representation of suffering in art and politics that seems to be harvesting an unrecognized labor of suffering, there are many more presences that speak of different configurations of that labor in the service of different politics. They often come through as attempts at a different kind of love, or at least as rejections of the rampant manipulation of affect and feeling. With hope as just one of those configurations, how is it that it becomes the consensus antidote, response, and attendant, to suffering, a sort of disciple (as in disciplined by it, or which disciplines it)?[25]

Love can then be seen as that which arranges and configures the labor of suffering. (Love, the labor organizer!) To fundamentally understand the work love does, we have to see it as organizing our attachments to our sufferings and those of others, our needs for witness and audience, and our overtures to intimacy and speech that inform any act of being sensed, any act of making suffering present. Indeed, even our closeness to suffering, let alone our attachment to it, is determined by the forms of love in which we engage. Love is what arranges (even decorates!), makes proximate, places things in relation to each other, not only to make meaning possible but also to grasp its impossibilities that then ask for new configurations and constellations. Love is the order of our labors, which is why in this moment any attempt to keep certain orders intact, remains such a loveless act, or an act that only sees or desires one's own survival. And, what kind of love is that anyway?

While love is what orders, it is not what adheres to an order. If ideological domestications of love and suffering kill both love and suffering, then we can witness the deaths that obtain in the declared orders of hope as well as no hope. Hope as dead love is love that has been ordered once and for all; the labor of suffering has been determined and managed from the outside. Its denials, in this frame, can actually give it a fetish character, attached to for its own sake, which is ultimately a subservience to someone else's preferred ordering of our labor of suffering. Materialist necessity, on this reading, becomes something that is on the order not of some objective or transcendental ontology, but of political provocation, organized by love. If what is meant by necessity is really a particular final or "perfect" arrangement of the labor of suffering, it corresponds to the perfect victim as someone whose relation to love and suffering has already been consummated in the act of defining a choice between of hope and no-hope (whether in the seeming polarities of Afro-optimism and Afro-pessimism, or of the worker with nothing to lose and a world to win, or of the homeless colonizer at home everywhere in the world) that removes all consideration of how people actually make suffering matter and exist as an act of and offering to life, as they continue to assess its meaning, in the midst of their own destruction. Whether or not this will all end well, or how the acts of politics can/not be shaped by the certainty of the unfolding, chastizes the labor of suffering and the love to produce perfect victimhood that is both complete and operates at exactly the level and terrain it is intended to by the oppressor. A perfect conscription.

So, whose scriptings of our suffering and conscriptions of our love will we resist, and how? And to which of those will we yield? Perhaps we must distinguish between, on the one hand, where we are demanded to be present, with the risk that entails (for everyone involved) and, on the other hand, where we are represented or asked to re-present ourselves, as disembodied voices asked to embody and appear on demand within a prearranged order of suffering, attachment, and desire. Here, form is crucial again; the forms in which we suffer and present our suffering are themselves informed by our relations to each other and the world that present themselves in our loves to begin with. Indeed, on this view, materialist necessity applies to material and content, not form; the form is where the politics, in some gesture to freedom, as the negotiation between necessity and freedom, lies.

Similarly, contra Georges Bataille's materialism, when the capacities to produce are fated to produce death,[26] in a way that accepts the discourse of "life" from the master (capitalist or colonizer), then what needs to be examined is not just how much love is produced, but its directionality, its form, its room for attachment. If the terrorist is in love, and the peacemaker also in love, what is it that makes love into what kind of cage and for whom? What arrangement of relations obtains, and for what poeisis does it provide the conditions of possibility? Ideologies and their eras that promise fulfillment on their chosen order, guarantee unfulfillment on every other, and keep asking for our love, deserve our rejection of the consolations—of pessimism and optimism, of ontology and taxonomy—that they offer. Unrequitedness, then, is a particular disposition to organizing the labor of suffering, intended to counter regimes of codified carnality, proximity, intimacy, sentimentality, and fervor.

LOVE RELATIONS

The relations—of belonging and discontent, of captivation and repulsion—important to politics are not only those between an us and a them, but also those that constitute and preserve the us as an us and the them as a them, and challenge these arbitrary lines and the affects they presumably contain. These are also the relations that might occasionally refuse to be domesticated into notions of alterity that are fundamentally epistemologically-driven, the forms of which are deemed beyond contention, and determined extra-politically. The sensuous realm and possibilities generalized in the contemporary consensual political subject in order to preserve these lines and feed our crises are not going to be our way out of any impasse of politics, indeed of being, in which we find ourselves. Questions of solidarity and commitment raise the issue of how paltry the analysis of relations between subjects and objects of liberal love may be if limited to dyadic identity, instrumentality, and affirmation as undisputedly good. Indeed, the commonplace associations of love with non-violence, peace, unconditionality, and idealism sneak in a moralism that a turn to politics must be able to navigate, and even momentarily put on hold.

Attending to the place of love in politics allows us insight not only into the possibility of actions that liberate or shackle, but entire lives that get shaped in the range of relations possible between the colonizer and the colonized, the master and the slave, then and now. These relations are not fixed in time but morph and grow, navigate need and desire, and require nurturing and sustenance, even and especially in the serpentine process of their undoing that takes decades, centuries, millenia. This is true for things we commit and attach to, and it is also true for what we seek liberation from; the prolonged and negotiated separation is another kind of being-together. This is especially important to consider in the present moment when we confront unseemly loyalties, and unexpected betrayals, many promises to never forgive or forget, and as many premature reconciliations that crumble quickly.

Not only do the wretched of this earth produce the world that continues to shrink under their feet, they produce the world as a world. The power to oppress and exclude is the power to deny this, and along with it the fact that the world is produced as a world by the insistent obligations, the tireless propositions, and the frustrated overtures, of those who alone iterate that a world is held in common and who insist on a world held in common by these relations. The world of the rich and powerful might recognize, but never needs to acknowledge, the relations on which it is built. The greater that austerity, the more the wretched generously detail exactly how and why we are related, and why there is a world, even if we want another. No one with the power or the ability to deny someone a relation ever made the world a world.

Besides naked oppression and injustice, even forms of humanisms and humanitarianisms that forget this fact are bound to replicate a fictive world in which we perform these roles of recipients and takers but never get to be the ones actually producing the world in which the idea of the human becomes possible, the body becomes an object, and so on. At least, we need to analyze our comfort in any natural point of epistemic departure, when the claim to a shared world or humanity as a given, as well as its impossibility, seems to come from the same place of forgetting who cannot but remember relations, who upholds them, and who sustains them. Even the act of dismantling the "natural orders" of inquiry and knowledge has to remember what must be discontinued, what modes of connection and relations were shaped and codified in liberalism and its versions of identity politics, and what sorts of emotions and affects conscripted.

I strongly deviate from critiques of liberalism and identity politics, and from calls for solidarity and alliance, that proceed without this history. I also take my distance from those studies that find our affect to be its own measurable thing as if can (or must be) delinked from who produces it and for whom—for that would be tantamount to ripping away the relations from the affect, a stripping of the only power the wretched are granted in this story, as far as I can tell. To study and write with subjects and objects of love is to attend to what matters most: not the love or the suffering which, once defined, affix and reproduce the subjects they need, but rather those who produce this world with their love and suffering and, along with that, the crucial potential to not reproduce it.

LOVE OBJECTS/OBJECTIONS

"Do not ask of me the same love as before," goes the titular refrain in a poem by Faiz Ahmed Faiz,[27] a poem that juxtaposes how courting the revolution and sustaining the beloved are entwined with each other, and what one love teaches us about the other love. For those of us raised in households where such tussles of love went absolutely unhindered and their dramas normalized in the name of yet other loves, our desires and attachments—relations—to what calls to be desired, attached to, and related to, is certainly shaped by seeing these loves fail, and these failures loved, both as claims to life itself. It is relevant to our times, as it speaks of an exhaustion that is also internal to, and not extraneous to, love in an age of austerity. The more "loveless" an era, the more someone is doing somewhere to keep the world going and any life possible in it against all prognoses. That compulsion looks a lot like love to me.

Useless, suggests the neoliberal optimist, decrying the wasteful romance of the failed and defeated. Melodrama, declare those who, in seeking to defend politics from the sabotage of sovereignty (a goal I share), legislate affective pieties and economies for a preferred non-sovereign politics with just the right pathology of desire and clarity of subject for the sake of epistemic comfort. Wealthy new-age realists of all cultures, faithful vanguards of the "concrete" against all "abstractions" (often a derisive synonym for thought), and confident that no revolution is possible, secure beyond measure the small measurable joys of property-ownership at the first sign of immeasurable loss (of love?). They would be quick to advise you to do the same. But, Faiz's poem undercuts these simplicities, and the twoness it speaks of is not a cleft of one love from the other, or the prying of the personal from the political, or the rationing of the same pie of love into different portions. If anything, the meaning of beauty, pleasure, what is sought in love, is expanded not shrunken. Love ceases to be a singular form across both romances, or the proverbial pie to be divided among different recipients. Love is made plural, and its many forms signify departures from abstract formalism, concrete economism, and their conservative normalizations of the subjects and objects of love. A shift in quantum follows a rethinking of form: the same concept of love shows itself to contain the many relations of and to love itself, the many modes of attaching oneself and the many relations to adhesion. It manifests in the varied intimacies that are inviting or risky, all in different measure to different subjects of love.

I bring up Faiz's juxtaposition not to gloss over the history of the common feminization of the object of revolutionary love (the mind races to Bhagat Singh's freedom as nubile bride).[28] That trope, on my reading, exposes that both the feminine and the love (and not just the feminine or the love) historically become something through that relation, and that it would be lazy to disavow the feminine and/or the love just because the poem, metaphorically speaking, must live on instead of being deconstructed and rewritten. Certainly, dominant forms of love and commitment that arise, nurture, and are cultivated, in a patriarchal, misogynistic, heteronormative, and statist space, are often proposed and affirmed in aesthetic formulations.

But, arguing for a poetics of politics, in which I follow Rancière, just as I follow Faiz and other poets of revolution, involves rethinkings and rereadings that run counter to the assumptions that: (1) the form called love is irredeemably impacted by its irredeemable object, and (2) that the relation between love and its object is singular and immutable. Otherwise, how might we be able to parse the relations and the adhesions that constitute the many problematic loves to which we are usually beholden: loves for nation, state, ideology that all have at least a violent if not genocidal provenance? Without parsing the relation and the adhesion in order to, for a moment, separate out the form from the object of love, we could not go beyond the knowledge that we die and kill for these (and other) loves, to ask the more pertinent and human question of the condition of the possibility of those matters of fact:

the how of loving that makes dying and killing possible. Alternate political locations in time and space get articulated and manifested in the utterances and assertions of love that constitute a given political subject.

Transformative love exists where its form and objects both are pried away from this provenance and the relations to space, time, self, and other that come with it. This is love that is a shifting form and compels other forms to shift; not a fixed form to be deployed to reassure a given order but one which dislocates the world and might push it to change. It involves negotiating our relations in time and space, and the attachments that we value: not only what is worth dying for but also what is worth living for; not only who will receive our love, but also what love we will accept and be presumed to be in need of; not only what love we will never be given but also what love we will reject. Perhaps ultimately a desire to make politics and love relate to and come closer to each other more honestly, not in the way we have known—where politics conscripts love and hence manages its economy—but rather where love as a capacity becomes an occasion for politics, inaugurated in this moment with a resistance to the presumed conscriptions of our loves.

So, when Prior, in Tony Kushner's *Angels in America*,[29] a companion of mine for a long time, asks for more life, he is also, or in fact, asking for more love. Those exits that I have always kept close to my heart—of Woolf's Septimus,[30] of Bachmann's Franza[31] or Ich,[32] of Benjamin himself on the France-Spain border,[33] of austerity-ravaged Greece, through windows, or against and into walls, or from Europe—are reminders that these exits are waiting to be redeemed by those who live on or stay behind, and that there are many of us waiting to redeem them. If nothing else, they ask us to hold off saying that these departures, whether spurred by one's own disgust with one's own desire, or collateral damage in the act of extinguishing it, are merely asking for some way back in. There is quite a community of those of us who have either exited themselves or inherited these exits, and who continue to promulgate other loves in these margins of time and space.

NOTES

1. Kiese Laymon, "Black Churches Taught Us to Forgive White People. We Learned to Shame Ourselves," *The Guardian*, June 23, 2015, https://www.theguardian.com/commentisfree/2015/jun/23/black-churchesforgive-white-people-shame.

2. Mohammad Hanif, "Of Dogs, Faith and Imams," *New York Times*, July 25, 2015, https://mobile.nytimes.com/2015/07/25/opinion/sunday/mohammed-hanif-of-dogs-faith-and-imams.html.

3. Naziha Syed Ali and Fahim Zaman, "Anatomy of a Murder," *Herald* Magazine, July 31, 2015, http://herald.dawn.com/news/1153209.

4. "Charleston Church Shooting: Nine Die in South Carolina 'hate Crime' - BBC News," accessed December 3, 2017, http://www.bbc.com/news/world-us-canada-33179019.

5. Naziha Syed Ali and Fahim Zaman, "Anatomy of a Murder."

6. Chris Lebron, "Time for a New Black Radicalism," Opinionator, 1434970944, http://opinionator.blogs.nytimes.com/2015/06/22/time-for-a-new-black-radicalism/.
7. Chris Andre, "Aphrodite's Children: Hopeless Love, Historiography, and Benjamin's Dialectical Image," *SubStance* 27, no. 1 (1998): 105–28, https://doi.org/10.2307/3685719.
8. Walter Benjamin, *The Origin of German Tragic Drama* (London; New York: Verso, 1998).
9. Walter Benjamin, "Theses on the Philosophy of History," in *Illuminations: Essays and Reflections* (New York: Schocken Books, 1988), 253–64.
10. Andre, "Aphrodite's Children." p. 106.
11. Walter Benjamin, *The Writer of Modern Life: Essays on Charles Baudelaire*. Edited by Michael W. Jennings. translated by Howard Eiland et al. (Cambridge, Mass.: Belknap Press, 2006), p. 185-86.
12. Andre, "Aphrodite's Children." p. 105.
13. See Kathleen Biddick, "Unbinding the Flesh in the Time That Remains: Crusader Martyrdom Then and Now," *GLQ: A Journal of Lesbian and Gay Studies* 13, no. 2 (May 14, 2007): 197–225. p. 198.
14. Stephen Dunn, "Always Something More Beautiful." *Poetry*, June 2015.
15. See Jean-Jacques Rousseau and Donald A. Cress, *Discourse on the Origin of Inequality* (Hackett Publishing, 1992).
16. See Irving Babbitt, *Rousseau and Romanticism* (Houghton Mifflin Company, 1919); Michael Ferber, *Romanticism: A Very Short Introduction*, 1st ed. (Oxford; New York: Oxford University Press, 2010); Jerome J. McGann, *The Romantic Ideology: A Critical Investigation* (Chicago: University of Chicago Press, 1983); Frederick C. Beiser, *Early Political Writings of the German Romantics* (Cambridge, U.K.; New York: Cambridge University Press, 1996).
17. Ludwig Feuerbach, *The Essence of Christianity* (Amherst, N.Y.: Prometheus Books, 1989).
18. Borrowing from Freud and Marcuse, and not limited to the realm of sexuality, is eros, signifying the life-instinct, the wish for producing larger wholes, connecting the desire for human freedom to sensibility and aesthetics. Those aspects of Freud and Marcuse that locate the desire for wholeness in a very individuated desire for being at home in ourselves are not very interesting to me here. What is relevant is the desire to construct wholes we can be part of, without necessarily having to tread the tiresome neuroses with which much of the twentieth century was beset—such as regarding the one and the many, the individual and the community, in the aftermath of Nazism and state socialism. This desire is inflected with a type of Jungian understanding of relation and interrelation, and by a species-inspired inter-sentience, as crucial to passionate or romantic love too. Invoking this intersentience, but also a Platonic understanding of thumos, love can bring together life and power rather than being rent between sex and power (as most post-Hegelian and post-Freudian philosophy, or, in general, contemporary thought too focussed on the individual-community rift is wont to do).
19. Jacques Rancière, "Ten Theses on Politics," *Theory and Event* 5, no. 3 (2001).
20. Asma Abbas, *Liberalism and Human Suffering: Materialist Reflections on Politics, Ethics, and Aesthetics*, 1st ed. (New York; London: Palgrave Macmillan, 2010).
21. To wit, "What relation but that of carnality can be had to the colonized?" (E.M. Forster).
22. To wit, Fanon speaking about the regurgitation of colonial violence by colonial subjects and the inception of terror as a relation proposed by the subject to match the violence of the colonizers.
23. Friedrich Wilhelm Nietzsche, *On the Genealogy of Morals and Ecce Homo*, trans. Walter Arnold Kaufmann (New York: Vintage Books, 1989).
24. Karl Marx and Fredrick Engels, "Critique of Hegelian Dialectic and Philosophy as a Whole," in *The Economic and Philosophic Manuscripts of 1844 and the Communist Manifesto*, trans. Martin Milligan, 1st ed. (Amherst, N.Y: Prometheus Books, 1988), 141–69.
25. Seeing love as the double of suffering allows us to identify this disciplining and conscription. Importantly, the double as a relation is a different one if we follow a materialist imperative perhaps beyond the binaries of the orientalist, Schmittian, or agonistic theses. Beyond discipliner, agent, residue, object, mirror, parasite, dependent, or manager, other relations of concepts to each other are possible: as friend, accompaniment, arranger, configurer, constel-

lator, communer, lover, (even stalker, attendant, lurker…), perhaps even just to pluralize ideas of being with, alliance, and solidarity, by more fully grasping the various undulating terrains of relations and their complicated implications.

26. Georges Bataille, *The Accursed Share: An Essay on General Economy, Vol. 1: Consumption*, trans. Robert Hurley, 1st ed. (New York: Zone Books, 1991).

27. Faiz Ahmad Faiz, "Mujh Se Pehli Si Mohabbat (Love, Do Not Ask)," in *Poems by Faiz*, trans. V. G. Kiernan (London: Allen and Unwin, 1971).

28. Ishwar Dayal Gaur, *Martyr as Bridegroom: A Folk Representation of Bhagat Singh* (Anthem Press, 2008).

29. See Tony Kushner, *Angels in America: A Gay Fantasia on National Themes* (New York: Theatre Communications Group, 1995).

30. See Virginia Woolf, *Mrs. Dalloway* (Mariner Books, 1990).

31. See Ingeborg Bachmann, *The Book of Franza & Requiem for Fanny Goldmann*, First English Language Edition (Evanston, Illinois: Northwestern University Press, 1999).

32. Ingeborg Bachmann, *Malina: A Novel* (New York: Holmes & Meier, 1990).

33. See Noa Limone, "Chronicling Walter Benjamin's Final Hours," *Haaretz*, July 9, 2012, https://www.haaretz.com/chronicling-walter-benjamin-s-final-hours-1.449897; Kevin McLaughlin, "Benjamin's Barbarism," *The Germanic Review: Literature, Culture, Theory* 81, no. 1 (January 1, 2006): 4–20, https://doi.org/10.3200/GERR.81.1.4-20; Walter Benjamin, "My Great Fear Is That We Have Much Less Time at Our Disposal Than We Imagined," August 2, 1940, http://harvardpress.typepad.com/hup_publicity/2015/09/walter-benjamin-last-letter-to-adorno.html.

Chapter Two

Undulating Love: Enfolding the Margins

LOVE ON THE VERGE OF POLITICS

In a recent and predictable misprision of the love of the margins trendy among the most righteous and self-avowedly superior inheritors of radically transformative thought and action that still unimaginatively pit a class universalism against a straw person of enclave identity politics, and do so generously on all our behalf, Vivek Chibber pronounced the love of the margins as passé, and as a distraction from real politics.[1] Having missed that enlightened boat, the site, for lack of a better word, at which many of my concerns in this work still happen to converge, is the political location of the outsider, the marginal, the pariah, and the other of politics made into the other for thought and the other of being. I happen to still be interested in exploring the counter-orderings of the labor of suffering that entail, and are entailed by, these locations. The unrequited is one inlet into the phenomenal and metaphysical imperatives of these locations in an ongoing anti-capitalist, anti-colonial, and anti-fascist politics.

In the way I see it, the unrequited's is a particularly different relation to the issue of exclusion than that which is presented to us in liberal identity politics and the marginalizations it sets out to reverse, and examining it may broaden the scope of both everyday redress and structural transformation that we must often seek together. The imperatives and the modes of love practiced by the unrequited may serve to index this marginality when the available forms of affection, embrace, inclusion, adoption, and belonging are insufficient and often unacceptable. When marginality is understood as already inhering a relation of love, we are better placed to appreciate different kinds of attachments, struggles, and desires that do not seek the culmination and requital imputed to them in dominant political narratives, and which do not always proceed from a decided and willing object of liberal affections. In this sense, unwilling and incompletely evolved subjects of liberal capitalism occupy a location beyond the notions of agency, the abject, the deviant, the victim, the heroic, or the miscounted, with a needful attentiveness beyond "our" experience of "them" or some generalized or merely historically accurate truth of their experience. The realms of these ordinary ethical, political, and aesthetic experiences articulate discontinuous philosophies in the very making and reinforcing of subjects in a social order of appearances and externalizations. They can and must force the process of inquiry and presentation to alter its demands—with due regard to what is not knowable and what must not be merely knowable, and what and who is made present, how, and for whom. It is with absolute regard for that which disrupts that we must learn to be—with even at the cost of knowing it. So, not just a new description of experience, but a new relation to that which deserves to be known and been with, differently than before. Because, as it is, it is just not working.

This chapter seeks to reframe the outsider, the marginalized, the alien, the pariah—characters at once placed on the borders of politics, and bounding politics as we know it—to see them as something other than Chibber's misattributed love objects, or the subjects of liberal identity politics reduced to a caricature often in tandem with a caricatural take on political economy that the first caricature is desperately trying to defend. I inherit, hence assume, conversations about the margins as sites of resistance[2] in order to think about the way in which resistance from these margins asserts a revision of the very topography and spatiality of politics, and also how those revisions may count as resistance to begin with, not to mention force a revisioning and remapping of politics itself. I believe something beyond the nominalization of politics—or its recognition as emergent from and embedded in certain locations—ensues as we attempt to comprehend anew the locations of politics, and the politics of location, revisiting and rearticulating the relation between motion and stillness, politics and location, metropole and colony, province and cosmopolis, refuge and fugitivity, outside of apolitical positivisms of standpoint theory.

THREE LOVES AND THE MARGINS

There are forms of love that institute the margins and those that dwell in them. There is the love that permeates the global liberal and neoliberal politics of diversity, inclusion, tolerance, democratization, human rights, bailouts, structural adjustment, and philanthropy, and fervently arrogates its recipients. Then there is the immanently legible and interpretable love of the recipients thereof which fits snugly with the kind of love on offer to them, making their struggles comprehensible as struggles for recognition, valuation, and possession as they are accommodated within the universalized liberal and capitalist logics of space, time, and desire. There is also the love that various political ideologies from liberalism to fascism assume when they posit solidarities among their various proclaimed subjects while only understanding them in limited ways: as projections of its own dominant modes of being body, person, human, non-human.

What these schemes uphold by way of these loves are the contracts of various sorts, economic, racial, social, and political, that map contemporary life with boundaries and thresholds that buffer our clumsy desires to gain entry into certain spaces. These schemes miss the love of those who go "unloved" therein, either as unidentifiable, unclaimed, or illegible objects, or as dissenting or deviant subjects, bending those boundaries and thresholds to make them into a world to inhabit. This love, whether as premise or as consequence of exclusion, inheres a fidelity to the time and the being that fall out of these spaces, by accident or by necessity. By resisting and rejecting the other loves on offer, this marginality is more than merely a frustrated desire for inclusion in the dominant configurations of space and time. The marginalized in this case have a politics because they love something else, and love differently.

The character of this marginality inheres a fidelity to the time and the being that fall out of these spaces, as it resists being a casualty to the happy unfoldings of the dialectic of recognition that, when all is said and done, often terminate in the death of desire itself. The unsated appetites of one side of the dialectic propel this exhausting farce of politics along with no regard to the desire that has been exhausted and extinguished. This goes some way to show that those whose desire fuels the dialectic of identity, affirmation, and recognition disregard the other's desire while still needing their labor. This dialectic's propulsions through time and space may not be as benign and philanthropic as we may think. Both the presumption that everyone falls in with such a "positive" dialectic, and the presumption of that positivity, need to be questioned, especially since the latter unfairly generalizes everyone's high enough opinion of themselves to accept being as an outcome of the dialectic's worldmaking work.

The dwellers of the margins invoked here are many. The margins of a liberal society identified not simply as minorities or protected classes, but as exceptions to the rule. The subjugated with "perspectives" that a good contemporary liberal conscience wants to accommodate. The categories of class, gender, race, nationality, citizenship, and sexuality come to mind right away, but not as competing quantum calibrations of marginality or oppression, or as bearers of some ontological truth with its own insidious path to purist discourse, but as difference that is both a phenomenological outcome of forms of supremacy and has to be managed by instituting a particular topography that marginal*izes*. Also important are intersecting and subjective messes of marginality as people navigate inertial and order-preserving political structures, *including* the order that reduces principles of action and political character that class, race, gender, sexuality, can be, to positivist sociological data. In this way, marginality is not merely a demographic or taxonomic social attribute but a relational experience of production, sustenance, and destruction, within which a subject is wrought as marginal, not only to spaces from which it is excluded, but also interior to the subject where that exclusion is mirrored or is duly inhabited.

We could think of moments where sheer alterity or difference gets to make an appearance within political space—especially when the "difference" is deemed recognized, dealt with, affirmed, and accommodated. Impressionistically, this invokes couplings of devotion and madness; the double-consciousness that empowers and exhausts; the navigation of schizoid dualities of a presence that is more determined by others' need; the inability to leave when the modes of accommodation are repugnant; the resort to kinds of imagination and romance that beset our inability to inhabit a given time in a given a space; the worry that the performance or lack thereof of outsiderness may come at a big cost. Insofar as marginality can be understood as a relation of preserving it through one's marginalization, without necessarily desiring that from which one is excluded, marginality is a relation of love, even longing, that problematizes possession and dispossession. Marginality, with the longing it holds, miraculously keeps intact, even produces, the space it borders, even though, and especially as, it suspends desire for what has been constituted by its own labor and love. Thus, the "unloved" in the schemes of politics mentioned above are actually the ones who love, and love in a way that is counted on but an account of which is never given. And if a political subject is formed in giving an account of itself in response to being hailed by a structure to which it will never be reducible, the absence of the account of the unloved is an occasion of its disappearance to which it must be present, resulting in the nullification or outright denial of its politics.

The marginalized can be seen as structurally located to apprehend the im/possibility (of language, desire, sensing, longing) in ways that posit love quite differently from those unaware or unattuned to the location's demands. Put another way, questions of trauma, loss, longing, nostalgia, desire, hope, etc., are inflected quite differently depending upon one's material location, thereby opening up or shutting down certain forms of loving. These locations reference not only the spatial and territorial expanse of the polis and other social and political institutions that are seen automatically referenced in the desire of the outsider, but also framings of time and temporality that accompany them. Subjects and subjectivities excluded from institutions of various kinds, or objects of various schemes of inclusion and integration within them, must be rethought more daringly: against the backdrop of discontinuous space and time (not merely an extension of "normal" space, or a continuation of time at the "center"), heeding the stillness and the motions that index various institutions as actively containing and shaping life within and with narcissistic, one-dimensional reference to themselves, welcoming the insurgent verification (instead of domesticating assumptions) of a shared plane of political existence.

The question of love, for those on the margins of certain landscapes, is not entirely separable from that of desire under neoliberal expansionism; largely because the relation to love that resists or evades objectification is irrelevant to those in power, and the performance of love (in service of the beautiful and the plural) on behalf of the marginalized ends up being a performance of desire (as stemming from need or lack). Moreover, the marginal subject subsists with promises of mobility made by those who are at once reliant on and resentful of this subject's relative inability to occupy space—as pariah, refugee, exile, fugitive, and so on. After all, the space which this promised mobility traverses is ahistorical, limited to dalliances with economic transactions of need and desire without regard for love, suffering, and their temporalities. Understanding marginality by way of love is a crucial element of any transformative politics rooted in the material experience of the outsider and within which this experience seeks some kind of redemption. Such politics has a different topography within which the margins appear on their own terms, and perhaps not appear at all. Those who are defined by the spaces that they have been written out of, and whose legibility is premised on their marginality to states, institutions, societies, and ideologies, are also often those who choose not, or fail, to abide by the modes of desire and fulfillment demanded of them.

INTERMATERIALITIES OF LOVE AND MARGINALITY

In narrating marginality through the postulate and experience of love, the figural and material natures of both love and marginality are retained, and the inextricability of experience in thought and sensuousness is upheld. Such a premise of interrelations is wholly agnostic and open-ended, allowing a co-existence and mutual constitution that leaves open rather than locks in (or accommodates, qua ahistorical phenomenology) the question of the history of desire in this relationship, and releases us from the strictures of a call-and-response dialectic that exposes the monotonous conceits of the subject's desire and its fulfillment. The experiences of love and marginality are not to be held within "finite provinces of meaning"[3] that can be captured as strict logics, for the attempt here is to show that the boundaries of the universes of these experiences are constantly merging into one another and "re-emerging as transformed fields of meaning" for political subjects.[4] The relation of these words to the uncontained parts of their suffered realities is enabled by their own status: in the case of love, as exceptions to love already known or validated as pathos or eros within our current sensorium; in the case of marginality, as excess of the normal discourse on subjects whose claim on space and time of a given society is safe, non-negotiable, and rooted in the basic affective, moral, and political economies of ever-renewing racial capitalism.

This is why love's intermateriality with the margins signals the methodological and normative bent of this prefiguring. Just as intertextuality can be defined as a confrontation "between discourse from different frames" that "effectively transforms the borders between the conflicting discursive universes," [5] my own taking up of intermateriality is derived in part from those actions in which the experiential boundaries or frames associated with love and marginality are "broken or made to overlap" and where the material experiences of each cut across the other.

In Julia Kristeva's discussion of intertextuality, a text has two orientations: one toward the language system of a certain society or group, and the other "toward the social process in which, as discourse, it participates. The text is constantly becoming the ground upon which the epistemological, social, and political reworkings of an entire era are put into play."[6] Probing the intermateriality of love and marginality would include things like: the manner in which outsiders experience love toward fellow "others" and to those on the other side of the margins; the orientation of outsiders to their experience both as desired or undesired objects within prevalent ideologies and as bearers of their own dismissed desires; the interactions between these subjects and the entire social arena in which this love enacts itself, their bodies becoming the sites, outside of normal time and space, where the epistemological, social, and political assumptions of an entire era, including the mapped terrains of inside and outside, are reworked.

In her reference to an *era*, Kristeva evokes history, memory, and consciousness at an individual, collective, and structural level. And if memory is understood as the space of time, the status of temporality in this schema becomes even more central. Intermaterialities negotiate memory and the present, the ghostly hauntings of possible and unrequited loves, the loves that are already done consuming us, the loves that have regurgitated us (a la Frantz Fanon), the loves that have been fiercely interrupted or deferred (a la Rabindranath Tagore and E.M. Forster), and so on. Intertextuality's mechanism is the lure of the absent in the present.[7] In this usage, intermateriality channels this into a method that historicizes form, and thus looks to various modes of love and suffering that are often neglected, forgotten, sidelined, even done away with, in societies that promise inclusion, intelligibility, and visibility in exchange for continued fidelity. These promises exact various compliances and forms of hospitalities from the excluded, without honoring their desire and love. If love can be seen (as I propose) as that which makes present, this intermateriality seems crucially reliant on love.

Perhaps this weaving of love and marginality resonates for some with standpoint theory, possibly also reminiscent of the consciousness of the worker as subject of history—as if, for instance, the marginal carry some more authentic, true, love. This is not my intention. Having spent a lifetime thinking about the privileged perspective of the outsider, whether in standpoint theory, or readings of double consciousness and the second sight of the seventh son in W.E.B. Du Bois,[8] it is important to see how this issue of the outsider is attached both to how the outsider is known and also how the outsider knows. I want to hold these pieces together and see what emerges. Relegating vastly disparate experiences and their differential resonances in people's lives to, and seeing the racial, gendered, economic differences as, just different flavors of the same *kind* of outsiderness fundamentally flattens the nuances of how these experiences live inside the subjects they produce. It is crucial to think about how knowledge on these various encampments on the margins looks, and how it corresponds to experiences of time that are erased in crass empiricism that turns experiences into territory, and quality into quantity.

In this regard, the plurality of modes of love ought to be acknowledged in order to reveal how liberalism misses or misreads the love and the intensities that end up only shocking or unnerving it, and disowns them readily by naming them fanatic, deviant, fundamentalist, or terrorist. And, when the love these systems extends gets rejected, they could benefit from learning what it lacked and where they must step out of the way—instead of, as they are wont to do, resentfully sidelining those whose approvals and willing subjections they sought with as much fervor.

LOVE MAKING AND UNMAKING THE OTHER: A BRIEF HISTORY

Jean-Jacques Rousseau's proto-Romantic elevation of feeling to a category separate from experience and reason (his disruption, thus, of the rationalist-empiricist epistemological debates of his time) holds the possibility of subverting the insularity of epistemic concerns from ontic and empirical ones. His emphasis on instinct is misread as a purist's deliverance from rationality and empiricism in the modern world; Rousseau's naturalism is far from ahistorical, thoroughly modern too, located within the enlightenment and its investment in the subject, even when it is contesting the imposed forms.[9] One such encounter happens in the *Discourse on the Origins of Inequality*, where Rousseau's critique of the modern subject is also a welcoming of it, reflected in the moment of intersubjective interdependence before private property (rather than in the state of nature). This is also, interestingly, the stage featuring teasers of romantic love.[10]

Between reason and crass empiricism, feeling likely stands for a simi-lar(ly) liminal status in relation to the self and its consciousness. It is probably owing to this potent liminality that Hugh Silverman claims that Rousseau sets the stage for the sex/power dichotomy with regard to love understood in the Hegelian or Freudian traditions.[11] This dichotomy may be understood thus: on the one hand, there is self-knowledge and a celebration of feeling that inaugurates the discourse on the limits of knowledge (whether derived from reason or experience, the mind or the body) in Immanuel Kant and the Romantics; on the other hand, there is the subject's insertion into the world and an assessment of the subject's limits in terms of its ability to bring everything within the sphere of will or power. In either direction, the focus on feeling (and imagination) as distinct from both reason and experience allows the subject to become objective or given to itself, either by the encounter with the desire that most fully expresses itself in feeling and externalizes it, or in the double of this move, a subject occupying itself better, growing inward. In the history of liberal modernity, these are complementary and mutually affirming movements.[12]

The relation between love and identity/alterity convoked in the shadow of Hegel and Freud is anchored within the double movement of the subject seeking its own objectification, recognition, affirmation, or evidence.[13] Affirmation is key to the subject thus imagined and sustained, paradoxically traceable to the modes of recognition through dialectical opposition that give us not only the role of desire in the dialectic,[14] but also an origin and journey of the self produced in and through it—as master, slave, colonizer, colonized. While the dominant logic of the dialectic is negation, opposition, and duality, the corralling of desire is nevertheless affirmative, sticking, and rather snug. The end of this story is called at the institutional fixing of our arrival at an identity, or when injury is deemed to have happened, or when love or trauma have been bounded as events. Moreover, these moments require constant affirmation, since we are supposed to keep arriving at the same destination. The entire dialectical enterprise produces affirmation conventionally understood, unless we actually think of the fact that the dialectic is one of production and re-production in the realm not only of *becoming* subject, but also of giving up that subjectivity and unselfing oneself as the slave, the victim, or the colonized. This undoing in and over time brings up those moments of desire that are more spatially intractable, less affirmative, and contain the materialities that either evade the dialectic—insofar as it already signifies or is a construct of spatialized time—or push it anonymously and wearily through time.

If power and love considered within the dialectic can be made to index also their unavailability and unrequitedness, smothering affirmation does not stand a chance as an accurate or valid leitmotif of our political existences. The effects of structural and power differences on the question of otherness—i.e., what kinds of others we become, and how marginal or threatening this otherness is—are important to consider when apprehending the struggles, procedures, and elements of subjectivity of those who are dispensable within, and not the preserve of, institutions and political capital. This may allow us to rehabilitate what is buried under the language of liberal multiculturalism, diversity, anti-discrimination, and liberal identity politics—the historical genealogy and morphings of identity itself—and to do so in a way that values this history over its terminus at identity. The reliability of this dialectic, whether in standing for the fluid imminence of recognition, or its absence, needs to be interrupted.

Important in this regard are three responses to the Hegelian dialectic that reconsider its designation of subjects and objects, its determinate affirmations and compulsions, and its ethical, aesthetic, and political substance. One is Emmanuel Levinas's,[15] rejecting the master-slave dialectic in favor of an ethical imperative to think of love outside of identitarian subject-object terms, preserving the subject through ritualistic repetition and replication across the ethical relation in an almost sacred way. The second is Frantz Fanon's writing of the ontological impossibility of recognition in a colonial context, the frustration of a desire for subjection that finally attempts to escape the Hegelian dialectic by exploding it altogether. And the third response is Theodor Adorno's counterpoint to the "positive" dialectic that also challenges the epistemological conceits of the Hegelian dialectic and insists on "preponderant objects" to whom we relate ethically only when we think outside of and in opposition to identification and assimilation.[16]

Alexandre Kojève's interpretation of Hegel's master-slave dialectic as a dialectic of desire present in both subject and object acknowledges the problem of the annihilation of the object by the subject, and subsequently, what was referred to earlier as the death of desire.[17] The end is inevitable, thinks Kojève— with an annihilating terminus of identity and the new synthetic affirmation, unless the alterity is preserved by feeding the desire of the subject for the object with an unconsumable other desire. This seems intriguing to me, and quite problematic in itself, a show of a kind of submission to the subject that hides behind a paternalistic rescue of the object who can now rejoice in its unmitigated alterity. This is because the premise of desire— need—in the Hegelian schema is unwavering. Even if the object survives in Kojève's wishful postscript to Hegel, the desire for another's desire and for other forms of acknowledgment gets sapped over time, exhausted by the neurotic addiction to forms of submission to another's desire, and to the perpetual gratification that gets scripted outside of one's own control.

Levinas has both a subject and an object, necessary for his ethical enterprise; the gesture of redeeming the object, propelled by painful liberal ascetic guilt, must ensue from a subject that we must not and cannot give up on. However, when compared to the dialectic, the interrelations are far less symmetrical or scripted. With Levinas, we take a step out of the limited but monotonous appeal to the mutual recognition of self and other inscribed within the dialectic, into a space of conscious intersubjectivity proceeding from the primordial subject, mindfully rejecting identity as a presumption, premise, or telos of this relation. In one way, identity is a non-issue for Levinas, for whom the dialectic retains relevance only insofar as he categorically undoes the conflation of need and desire in Hegel's subject. For Levinas, the subject may be as needy as Hegel's but is not the source of the desire; the subject responds to a desire that emanates first from the Other, this desire itself making the object into a subject. "There is no emptiness or lack to which desire is correlated; desire is the movement toward the infinite, a response to the other as Other."[18]

"For Levinas, desire is that modality of subjective being that brings us into a genuine relationship with otherness while preserving the other's alterity."[19] Since desire no longer stands in the way of the subject's survival (it is no longer need), and since it is not seeking culmination in consuming its object (because the object, in being the origin of desire, transforms into a subject not merely at the mercy of another's desire), its situation here is much less precarious than in the dialectic. However, desire does rely on a continuous production of alterity. This eros is "not desire in the sense that the two shall become one, a totality; rather, one desires the beloved precisely because the beloved is different from the self. Desire is perpetually aroused, as it were, since the other is the embodiment of surprise."[20]

All is well with the uniqueness and individuality of subjective experience in Levinas, premised as it is on the irreducible incommensurability between various existences and the ethical call to not violate it. This, incidentally, is a direct counter to the sublation of the ethical into the political in Hegel's dialectic. "Substance is realized as subject only by virtue of its having been mediated by the object of its reflection, that is, by alterity."[21] This insistent alterity goes hand-in-hand with the repetition and replication of these premises of subjectivity, giving us a categorical and seemingly universal form for various content. The self and the other never dialectically intertwine, epistemically or ontically, and this distance is the essence of ethical subjectivity. "To be in communion is not to be one in any transcendent or quasi-mystical sense, nor is it subjection to the greater will of the state. It is the ability to accept the radical difference of the other and to coexist in spite of the infinite distance or separation that will always remain between self and other."[22] So, while the result is an endemically pluralist political society by definition, the optics that seem to be prescribed in this relation of desire—and vulnerability in the (oceanic) face of the other—are no surprise to anyone who has read Levinas. I doubt if this distance in itself could withstand a critical scrutiny of complicity with the dominant sensorium. So, whether or not we claim identity and recognition, the sacredness of this distance that is unbridgeable in conceptual work does not cease to fetishize the newly apprehended and subjectified object.

To be fair, Levinas counters this charge of fetishism by claiming that his stance is "a-theistic";[23] that, in other words, it avoids the judgment—of history, of the World Spirit, of the state—that fuels and validates the dialectic. He identifies a stance outside of affirmation and negation, writing:

> By a-theism we thus understand a position prior to both the negation and the affirmation of the divine, the breaking with participation by which the I posits itself as the same and as I. It is certainly a great glory for the creator to have set up a being capable of atheism, a being which, without having been causa sui, has an independent view and a world and is at home with itself.[24]

What is troubling here, from the point of view of marginal and "lesser" subjects, is the fact that Levinas's extreme separation from and rejection of the political also allows him the license to pick and choose the forms of vulnerability he will heed—something entirely not a departure from the ideological proclivities of liberalism, when it comes to responding to suffering, injustice, and exclusion. With what does the onus of desire placed on the object correlate? Is it just another way of serving the subject who cannot legitimately get away with a claim of equality (without identity) and pathetic vulnerability in the face of someone who needs us to need their desire? From a frantic immanence of dialectical relations, we have only found a way to a different market that can feign its cleansing of politics. Like liberalism, it continues to affirm the relations it cannot take responsibility for, and sends us scavenging for the other whose desire we must first interpret as desire, and only then allow to matter. Levinas's subjects waiting to be called to their beloved are rather tense, unsuffering, quite liberal, in their makeup. While Levinas adequately challenges Hegel, the margins are still bearing the burden of heating things up, and needed for that reason—thawing themselves and us with them.

Thinking of those bodies that materially, physically—even in their own destruction—combust to fuel the colonial encounter past the ontological impossibility of reciprocity and recognition in the colony, Frantz Fanon rereads Hegel by encasing the ethico-political relation to the other within an unfulfilled desire for the dialectic itself. Between the white colonial master, and the black slave, it is the dialectic of recognition itself that is yet to arrive (and never quite does). What happens between the two—and Fanon gleans this as a colonial dialectic—is distinct from and does not quite qualify as a Hegelian dialectic: it does not begin with equal consciousnesses, and the desires of each are supposedly not speaking to each other in any way. (It is safe to assume that there is more than an accidental relation between the divergent or even asymptotic desires and the disparity in consciousnesses.) The white master needs the work and not recognition from something that is not even considered human, and the black slave cannot become subject qua black slave through his labor because it knows and desires subjectivity within this dialectic only in the form the white master has flaunted. Fanon imagines that the unfulfilled desire for whiteness that inheres within the slave is only compounded by the failure to successfully make whiteness into the product of his constant labor, as well as a lack of consciousness or desire for freedom that comes with the conferral to the slave of a freedom that has not been (physically) fought for. This desire that becomes an impediment to the attainment of freedom within a proper dialectical framework needs to be revisited outside of the question of the dialectic itself.

Fanon retrieves a colonial dialectic that falls short of the mutuality of consciousness and humanity in Hegel, but the problem here is that the Hegelian dialectic also circumscribes desire and attachment, and if becoming human will remain a project to be verified by that dialectic, then this is a love that is best spared fulfillment. Nationalist liberatory projects before and after colonialism that remained attached to the state (only to be deemed failures) exemplify the tragic insidiousness of the eventual ascendance into Hegelian recognition—and whom could *that* ever redeem given its own terms? Where I find in Fanon a tinge of lament at the Hegelian dialectic not yet being set in motion in the colony, I break away from his desire that that is even an unrequital of note. The being that is not yet Hegelian is a worthy space of unrequitedness, for the gestures to humanity that are not framed by the relation to the white master. That space of unrequitedness is not attached to just the object of desire, and is a space within which other ideas, possibilities, relations, and beings also germinate. The exclusive, exhaustive, and eventually destructive focus on attaining the white master's recognition of one's subjectivity has to be distracted, deflected, and inspire something else. The issue with this is the fact that there is an issue of attachment, and not just desire. What we will soon see Adorno being able to give up, the slave or the colonial subject cannot.

But there is more to be said, and Fanon's cannot be the final word on diagnosing the space of unrequital in the colony. More can be said for what the white master actually extracts from the relationship: not just labor but also a particular, even disproportionate, affective dependence and connection to the slave. When Forster enters into relationships with brown men and young boy-servants in Egypt and India which end in repulsive abuse when they laugh in his face, and white teachers punish black students for not answering back or looking at them, we learn that the master needs a lot more than work—unless the work can be seen as including the labor of desiring and affirming whiteness as proper premise and enactment of subjectivity.

The desire for whiteness is not an accidental part of the dialectic, or an underdeveloped exception to the dialectic of reciprocal recognition. The extraction of a particular kind of desire and attachment is needed by the colonizers to do the work they are doing. When Forster dresses up in Western attire to beat Kanaya, since per his benefactor the Maharaja of Dewas "violence ... was the only form of communication subalterns could understand," we know well that the master is not indifferent to the slave and who laughs in their face will get reduced to something, or swiftly put into their place. Whenever the colonizer's presumption of a shared world is denied or scoffed at by the colonized, it inspires violence. In my view, to counter Fanon's, this does not signal the unavailability of the Hegelian dialectic, but is well within its bounds.

There might be ways to disorient love in order to not feel caught in the trap of love understood as the desire for whiteness: if love includes desire and attachment, then it is best for us not to discipline them or presume a natural alignment between them in an undifferentiated way, and instead be able to see the attachment but not the desire as problematic. And, not that it needs to be said, but there *are* other others. A homogeny of desire is imputed to the colonized that allows for a kind of unrequited love, but also one that can only imagine itself being finalized by the destruction of the subject and object both. In what ways can we look at unrequitedness of the relation as a potential for imagining a decolonized relation to the other, including the women Fanon writes about or the resesentiment-laden masculinity of any chosen one that will find its misogyny or hatred toward differently marked subjugated bodies, as a convenient target to avenge the lack of love from the colonizer.[25] So, in that sense, being unloved is not only an injury—it might be a relief to those constantly extracted by the colonizer or by those avenging colonization—and does not automatically preclude injuring others. The dialectic becomes an attachment for the desire itself, congealing it. Decolonizing requires loosening up that relation, and disarticulating the desire from the attachment for new adhesions or orientations to become possible (or searching for evidence of those among the wreckage).

For Fanon the Hegelian dialectic is itself an unrequited love, and the experience of blackness is so shaped by desire for whiteness, that the only way to counter that love is through willing one's own negation. There is no capacity to detach from this relation of otherness since the world is built on the basis of that attachment. What Judith Butler calls the fraternity of Jean-Paul Sartre's white colonizers to which the preface of *Wretched of the Earth* is addressed, and the fraternity Fanon invokes writing the same book to his fellow freedom-fighters, certainly itself includes a homogeny of desire (and desirers!) imputed to the slave, and for freedom to be understood in exactly the way Fanon has. Here, the question of freedom becomes a particular way to hold the question of love hostage, but is not the end of the story. I write this knowing well what the conversion of freedom into a question of existence does to all the various dialectics that are sacrificed or cut short in the desire to attach to the Hegelian dialectic.

For Fanon, then, the question of love and the Other in the dialectical relation pivots around the (unrequited and) stubborn desire for white subjectivity and an attachment to the dialectic itself that forecloses or makes invisible or inferior other attachments, desires, and accountabilities to other others who exist beyond their instrumentalization into the dialectic only to consummate it by their destruction, writing the death of colonialism on and with their own bodies. This attachment to the dialectic snuffs out desires and attachments that do not align with the compromized desire for whiteness displaced onto the dialectic as a stand-in for it. I am interested in those unrequitednesses overwritten by the attachment to the dialectic that can only be decolonized by one's own destruction. I believe that there are anticolonial desires and attachments that do not always have to be tethered to the colonizer and its ways of loving, but are constantly sponsoring that tethering nevertheless, and need tending to their potentiality to suggest pathways literally sacrificed in the expediency of a national or revolutionary project's fulfillment. I am thinking here explicitly of Fanon's summoning of the bodies of Algerian women in "Algeria Unveiled," and also to the countless instances of overwriting other imaginations of liberation and emancipation (and sovereignty), and the acute abuse and betrayal of the same, in the narratives of winning freedom that won out over others to take their place in the hallowed dialectic of history. Ultimately, whenever existence becomes a unified and undifferentiated question, it disciplines the desires to be and not-be, and to be and become, sentencing those on the outside of being/not-being to a kind of non-being and non-becoming at once. The labor of the slave in withstanding death to build a life within it, the sorrow songs on the plantation, women and people of color in revolutionary movements who become mere means of expediency and asked to defer their own desire in the name of some crisis. These are all possibilities spurned or appropriated in the fulfillment and consummation of some desires, and fundamental multiplicity of anticolonial desire and imagination unified and totalized, in the inevitable synthesis of the dialectic of history, only because others remain unrequited (even though it didn't have to be this way).

In Theodor Adorno's return to the Hegelian dialectic, at stake is how what would or could (have) be(en) our intersubjective desires get displaced by desires that reduce subjects to objects to be annihilated with their own desire and attachment (which bodies they are, what names they carry, who they love, whether they desire the state) as weapons. Faced with the fascist impossibility of no account of their own desire or attachment able to redeem them, Adorno opts for rethinking the subject capable of this annihilation by suspending desire in order to detach, in the interest of potentially returning only in a way that would save something and allow it to be. In this relinquishing of "love" in the dialectic, then, Adorno forestalls an easy slippage into the anti-politics of the ethical by relinquishing desire as the desire-to-know and reserving the possibility of a kind of redemption of that (potentially transformed) desire at a later date only by detaching from it, on the condition that aesthetics might allow us to cast both desire and adhesion in terms other than epistemic.

With Levinas, Adorno takes on the Hegelian dialectic by upsetting its affirmative moments and working with the material this generates, proffering a version of independent judgment that, while not exactly a-theist, approximates the space that Levinas is reaching for. However, pace Levinas, Adorno does not give up on the dialectic altogether, does not evacuate the ethical and the political from each other, is more suspicious of the subjects of the dialectic even when they are supposedly behaving differently, replaces eros with beauty as an intermateriality, and offers negation as a more pluralizing force than the production of alterity through the sensorial and political machinery already in place. In Adorno's dialectical thought, subject and other are mutually constitutive and substantiate each other in their social and psychic existences. The reconciliatory negation of negation in Hegel's thought is culled, and the moments of identification given up to unlock indeterminate, unguaranteed, possibilities not for the subject but for the object that is allowed to be in its threatening non-identity. After all, whose worry is it that my nonidentity might be my non-being? Of interest, I suspect, are the potentialities that could evade the grasp of the capture that at once tames and values.

> Those who regard the thingly as what is radically evil; who would like to dynamize everything, which is, into pure contemporaneity, tend to be hostile toward the other, the alien, whose name does not resound in alienation for nothing; to that non-identity, which would need to be emancipated not solely in consciousness but in a reconciled humanity. Absolute dynamics however would be that absolute handling of the facts, which violently satisfies itself and misuses the non-identical as its mere occasion.
>
> Unbroken universally human slogans serve thereby once again to make what is not the same as the subject, into what is the same. The things harden themselves as fragments of what was subjugated; the latter's rescue means the love for things. What consciousness experiences as thingly and alien is not to be expelled from the dialectic of the existent: negatively, compulsion and heteronomy, yet also the distorted figure of what ought to be loved, and what the bane, the endogamy of consciousness, does not permit to be loved. Far beyond the Romanticism which felt itself as *weltschmerz*, as the suffering from alienation, hover Eichendorff's words, "beautiful stranger [Fremde: alien, stranger]." The reconciled condition would not annex the alien [Fremde] by means of a philosophical imperialism, but would find its happiness in the fact that the latter remains what is distant and divergent in the given nearness, as far beyond the heterogenous as what is its own.[26]

There is something nevertheless stuffy to which dialectics, whether positive or negative, Hegelian or Adornian, relegate us. This stuffiness is, ironically, of thinking about excess. If, on the one hand, the excess of the Hegelian dialectic cannot exist as excess, but must be understood, known, hammered into synthetic, uplifting categories of forms of resolution, then, on the other hand, Adorno gives us permission to saunter away from the dialectic, to be released from it, but to still pore and hover over it. Insofar as Adorno keeps us caught within the rejection of a regime of knowability, and hence the forms of identification that come with it, I want to take seriously his call to think about the "beautiful strangers" who incorporate a sense of the autonomous art object and a tentative peace with the conferred estrangement as hope for a deferred, inarticulate, and indeterminate reunion. This schema obtains from a space within the dialectic, or the choice to release it from our grip, knowing we can have it back. This schema does not factor in having no choice in this matter, in the case of those who are expunged from the dialectic, and whose abject removal from the realm of intelligible human history makes them act and love in certain ways. The form of autonomy that Adorno desires or values can be inflected differently if we start talking about the form of love as not disconnected from the sociality posited and imagined as the condition of the possibility, even of this seeming resignation.[27]

A concern, such as Adorno's, with the happiness of the subject, then, is certainly a concern with the happiness of other social subjects, and with the violence done to them by repressive social structures as well as by those whose own damaged condition is inseparable from their violation of others. Adorno thus reads like an anticipatory critique of Levinas's claim that only a guilty, accused, and unhappy subject can respond nonviolently to others. From Adorno's perspective, that is a prescription for repression and violence: violence toward other subjects and not simply toward the subject. It is important to recognize, in fact, that the first of these expressions—other subjects—has no place in Levinas's discourse, which is spoken entirely from the standpoint of the subject and its ethical interiority in relation to others whose own subjective experience seems, oddly, of no concern to this discourse.[28]

In Adorno's discussion of preponderant recalcitrant objects can be found gestures to forms of outsiderness that may be theorized without rendering them merely autonomous because unknowable, such as the work of art that resists any kind of assimilation, cognition, and intervention. (I shall return shortly to the question of the object that evades, eludes, and which entices the subject—that which lies between human and nonhuman—to mimic it.) A certain restriction to knowledge qua representation also pervades Levinas's work, whose notion of alterity remains too simplistically beholden to literality and opposing it in a specific spatio-temporal moment. Jacques Derrida's deconstructionist ethics—in his middle period, since his later works, like *The Gift of Death*, lie closer to Levinas on the issue of the absolute Other—offer a corrective to this limited sense of alterity by exposing the violence inherent to this non-interventionist affirmation of subjectivity, not least because it understands presence in a one-dimensional way, without bringing in the temporal and intermaterial nature of presence, absence, knowing, and not-knowing metonymized in its subjects. As presence, so love.

Moving forward from Levinas, Fanon, and Adorno, to more contemporary theorizations that struggle with questions of alterity in its idealist and materialist, individualist and collectivist, optimist and pessimist, ethical and political, formulations, the Freudian and Hegelian inheritances continue to suggest persistent correlations between otherness and love. In some ways, the ethics of alterity continue to conflict with the politics of love that has been called back into currency by many contemporary theorists in order to assuage the dread of the kind of love that impresses itself post-holocaust and post-state socialism.[29] One early example of this is Michael Hardt and Antonio Negri's fervent indulgence of linguistic materialisms to convoke the new bourgeois vanguard of affective labor in an unironic mimcry of the repulsive and virile aspects of Marx's praxical heraldries.[30] Hardt's earnestness in equating politics and joy and the desperate need to invoke a carnival at the drop of a hat used to be charming, but not without being slightly repellent and sophomoric. The need for affirmation, or the standpoint of affirmation, one might say, is also thoroughly embroiled in the linguistic sincerities of the West, especially liberal America, but also and increasingly Europe in grotesque mimicry of its favorite ex-colony, the United States.

Busy distancing himself from this discourse or even its more tamed, more ironic versions, but not without his own subtractive mathematical forward-lookingness, is Alain Badiou.[31] Badiou opens up the space for refusals in between the pathos of accommodation, inclusion, garish self-congratulation, and narcissism on the one hand and the legible, wordy, garrulous, equally self-absorbed melancholy on the other that characterizes both neoliberal western culture as well as global hegemony with and without domination.[32] In response to the neo-pragmatist vulgarity of the "multitude" and such, the line on alterity is inherited from Levinas by Giorgio Agamben (in his emphasis on irreducible otherness).[33] In response to Badiou's dispelling of pathos, Simon Critchley (among others) has argued for some restitution of pathos and the aesthetic.[34] The ultimate concern across the board remains ethical rather than political, thus driving a wedge between what each of these discourses can withstand. However, it is in between, one, the room for love as pathos, or love as at least attendant to pathos and desire, and two, the invocation of love as pure philosophy and truth-process, that many key issues of alterity and, eventually, marginality are raised. Love as pathos is related to the immanent differentiation in which Levinas invests.

Benjamin Noys, in his reading of Badiou, cautions the remedial mind-set that comes running in with more "difference": not too fast. He argues that it is important to take a look at this excluded pathos for what it contains, and to explore the attachments of the pathos, and through it, the reality of alterity, that Badiou is accused for having done with in his Platonic mathematics. It may be appropriate to ask here, following Badiou and Noys, "Whose micropolitics? Whose pathos?"[35] It is possible that pathos for pathos' sake occludes its actual self-serving nature, and keeps preempting a pathos that could disrupt. Left unindexed, the pathos can be repopulated, with needful refusals and with different kinds of abundances, rather than prescribed affirmations and conscripting, neutering, sentimentality. The discourse of marginality, and of relations between colonizer and colonized, can be reframed in light of this space that opens up, by keeping it from being too quickly and prematurely overpopulated by the well-wishing commitments of and to guilt, philanthropy, diversity, trauma, and easy sentimentality. In the spirit of Critchley and Agamben, then, I want to hold on to the non-heroic, but I do think that the everyday inscribes and is inscribed within structures that do not limit difference to a question of mere pluralism, and that our sentimental lifeworlds do not break down readily within new spaces and their new times. Badiou's disregard for the Other does not negate the space Agamben and Critchley want to retain, provided that this space, one, is not an excuse for the overdetermination of politics through ethics, and, two, is able to lend itself to reconsidering eros and pathos,[36] not only alterity but also marginality. These two requisites are, of course, related.

"If one accepts [. . .] that ethics under the rubric of alterity is an apology for this sorry state of affairs—'a spiritual supplement for incompetent governments,'[37] in Badiou's words—then it must equally be clear that something quite ambitious is required in order to stand up to it."[38] In averting the labeling of the question of love an ethical one instead of a thoroughly political and aesthetic one, one need only consider the fact that forms of marginality, even if not hierarchical, do differ when we try not to reconcile the increasing insouciance (in discourses of global mobility, virtual war, cultural homogeny, and geographical unboundedness) and increasing paranoia (in new imperialisms, occupations, security) about space to which are subject those who occupy staggered locations along real hierarchies of class, race, gender, and citizenship. So, perhaps these disparate yet synchronic locations need to be further examined for the kinds of politics and locutions of love that each of them suggests. Talal Asad's caution against the zealous fusion of the discourses of governmentality and security is pertinent here—especially when this zeal actually renders irrelevant the experience of those on whom the state continues to enact itself by law, geographical boundaries, and prisons, thus leaving them not altogether "evolved" enough to deem their condition the product of a deterritorialized society of intensity and control.[39]

The "spiritual supplement" that Badiou resents is, unfortunately, the stock not only of incompetent governments, but many fervent allies—those that may desire the same object, but where the celebrated commonality of this desire displaces the possibility of a more rooted commonality in modes of love. This actually displaces the potency of the marginal space and its inherent possibilities in relation to forms of love, longing, embrace, and haunting. This moment of coming together is also suspect in its ability to truncate the imagining of a radically anticolonial (decolonial and postcolonial) praxis that does not have to give itself over to ameliorist multitudes, but holds on to eros, pathos, and allows those on whose behalf one may feel these to actually matter, allowing a different understanding of marginality and marginal subjectivities to catalyze a different togetherness. This requires deemphasizing the ethical preponderance of love, affirmation, and otherness located in the subject who is a subject because she desires and because she loves—and closely regarding how this subject desires and loves. Addressing this *how* brings into focus those who are framed within the colonial space not merely as objects and subjects of desire and love, reconciliation, and affirmation, but those who are marking off their marginality by the modes of love and desire in which they can and do, and cannot and do not, engage.

LOVE AT THE MARGINS: AVERTING THE DEATH OF DESIRE

If there is something about the experience of marginality that can illuminate the experience called love, and if there is something about the modes of love that can show us something about the political actions we are filial to and configure for ourselves inside our homes on the margins, our courtings and professions of love must contend with its non-affirmative moments, with the negativity, with the non-acceptance, and with the failure of communication endemic to it. The time/space relation that constitutes the singular experience of love naturally shifts given how the margins are mapped and to what space or time their desire is beholden. The marginalized can and must be seen as marginal in ways other than just being outsiders to certain spaces; they are also, for better or for worse, outside certain relationships to temporality and love.

In understanding how love institutes and furnishes alterity and marginality, we are taken to the love that actually dwells at the margins and is what renders the margin a home of a different sort than those on offer to the more complete and consensual subjects of colonialism and global capitalism. In a passage in *Negative Dialectics*, Adorno writes on the post-Auschwitz possibility/imperative of being an unbearable discontent of liberal capitalism:

> Reflective people, and artists, not seldom have the feeling of not quite being there, of not playing along; as if they were not at all themselves, but a sort of spectator. [. . .] That which is inhuman in this, the capacity to distance oneself and rise above things by being a spectator, is in the end precisely what is

> human, whose ideologues react so vehemently against.[. . .]. Very likely human beings are without exception under a bane, none capable of love, and for that reason each and every one feels not loved enough. But the attitude of being a spectator expresses at the same time the doubt as to whether this could be all there is, while nonetheless the subject, so relevant in its delusion, has nothing other than that poverty and ephemerality, which is animalistic in its impulses. Under the bane living beings have the alternative between involuntary ataraxy – an aesthetic of weakness – and the animality of the involved. Both are false life. Something of each however belongs to a right désinvolture [off-handedness] and sympathy.[40]

The false life in this passage can be confronted with the fervent life that Bataille speaks of—largely because love can accommodate deferral, and closure not sought at all costs. At stake is not always or primarily even the mere survival of the self or the other, but of desire itself. This is where perhaps the desire for the beautiful stranger begs to be read not merely a draw toward beauty with the meaning of desire intact, but a love for it that is repulsed—unrequited, unkempt, homeless, and more—in its direction (and isn't any less love for that).

The passage importantly corresponds to Adorno's discussion of subject and object within his dialectics; it invokes the spectator and the subject as the two modalities that confront an object, the what and the where of the object remaining unaddressed, except in a claim of ubiquity. Of course, there is the claim that the subject is already object (in an inversion of Levinasian destiny)—and that it would do well for the subject to try to be more object, to mimic the object's "autonomy"[41] and incorporate it into the possibilities of being human alongside the subjecthood proclaimed within enlightenment unreason.

Those who seem suspended above time and space as framed within the dialectic and its reason reminds of the possibilities for those inactive, non-committed, non-Sartrean souls whose praxis resists overwrought fervor and complete indifference. While the pluralist ethic is compelling, what interests me more is the other to this praxis, one who confronts both the vigor of the involved, and the aesthetic of weakness, as objects of these modalities. These subjects, as objects to the central subjects and spectators, carry both the experience of this suspension above the logics of conventional dichotomies, and undergo them as well, not merely choosing among modes of praxis but straddling these as only the objects of liberal love can. These are, then, the marginalized to whom our stock political actors are either committed to or indifferent, at the same time as their own express desires and entanglements invoke possibly different logics not captured by these options. But, such resistant subjects (as in resistant to being certain kinds of subjects) are also resistant objects (who resist forms of objectification) because they are not always already the subject in the world of dialectics, positive or negative.

Adorno's gesture to suspension must be taken seriously, especially in thinking about marginal subjects who are not the mere inversion of the Sartrean "project," but who are the objects that lie between the spectator and the subject and are also sometimes both.

There is something about the false life that Adorno terms these modalities that reminds of a kind of compromised, if not de-ceased, desire. If understood in terms of the dialectic and a Kojève-inspired understanding of desire in the dialectic, then false life that inhabits and traverses the dialectic understood as a spatiality of time must have something to do with some form of contaminated desire. This contamination may be able to signal forms of love that resist the death of desire and at the same time emerge from it. In a sense, then, the human and the inhuman (the mortal and immortal in a different translation) in Adorno's passage are modes of love, and the space in-between where Adorno finds something "authentic," something that may scare in its contamination, may actually index the ontic marginality and the space of love toward which this book gestures. Perhaps, as inheritors of both Adorno and Fanon's unrequitedness, we need to figure out those forms of love and desire that make the inhuman more human, and the other way around. The substance of this in-betweenness, the lack of love, and the struggle for it, is what can be made central to a project of studying and attending to those subjectivities that are not reducible to the dualities or their quick resolutions posed by any of these thinkers. The aesthetic materiality constitutive of this space and time—and its embodiment in a subject suspended above the dialectic—must be examined by way of the actions of those who are themselves intermaterial to these realities—present in their absence on one hand, and absent in their preponderance on the other. Insofar as the Hegelian dialectic kills something through identification, the rubble of that desire materially produces other subjects, which is why marginal subjectivities to which a thorough analysis of marginality, alterity, and inclusion, must be devoted are marginal for their unreconciled, uncontained, unsettled relation to space as well as time. And, they are almost always in some kind of love.

NOTES

1. Vivek Chibber, "Why We Still Talk About the Working Class," *Jacobin*, March 15, 2017, http://jacobinmag.com/2017/03/abcs-socialism-working-class-workers-capitalism-power-vivek-chibber/.

2. Works such as: Alfred Schutz, "On Multiple Realities," *Philosophy and Phenomenological Research* 5, no. 4 (June 1945): 533–76.

3. Schutz.

4. Susan Stewart, *Nonsense: Aspects of Intertextuality in Folklore and Literature* (Johns Hopkins University Press, 1989). p. 48.

5. Leonard Orr, "Intertextuality and the Cultural Text in Recent Semiotics," *College English* 48, no. 8 (December 1986): 811–23, https://doi.org/10.2307/376732. p. 814.

6. Josette Feral, "Kristevian Semiotics: Towards a Semanalysis," in *The Sign: Semiotics Around the World*, ed. R.W. Bailey et al. (University of Michigan Press, 1980) p. 273; Julia Kristeva, "Word, Dialogue and the Novel," in *The Kristeva Reader*, ed. Toril Moi (Columbia University Press, 1986), 34–61.

7. Michael Riffaterre, "Intertextuality vs. Hypertextuality," *New Literary History* 25, no. 4 (Autumn 1994): 779–88, https://doi.org/10.2307/469373. p. 785.

8. W.E.B. Du Bois, *The Souls of Black Folk*. Edited by Henry Louis Gates, Jr., and Terri Hume Oliver (New York: W. W. Norton, 1999), p. 10-11.

9. Mark S. Cladis, "Redeeming Love: Rousseau and Eighteenth-Century Moral Philosophy," *Journal of Religious Ethics* 28, no. 2 (January 2000): 221–51, https://doi.org/10.1111/0384-9694.00045.

10. Rousseau and Cress, *Discourse on the Origin of Inequality*. pp. 39-43, 48-51.

11. Hugh Silverman, "Twentieth-Century Desire and the Histories of Philosophy," in *Philosophy and Desire*, ed. Hugh J. Silverman (Routledge, 2000), 1–13. p. 7.

12. Foreshadowing here the discussion in Chapter 3 of the colonial odyssey, a literary genre that grasps these moves as co-dependent.

13. Cf. Chapter 3. Each of these movements is a negotiation of subjectivity with space—inward with history and memory, and outward with the subject's reach and expanse in and across space. This makes it extremely imperative to remind ourselves of the spatial attachments of the modern subject, as well as the spatialized framings of time that enable the incessant homecomings or playful homelessnesses of the postmodern diasporic subject seeking imagined homelands (a la Salman Rushdie), or in the re-forging of cosmopolitanism in the new bourgeois ideal of transnational identities and alliances (a la Anthony Appiah's imaginary strangers or Maria Lugones' world-travellers) [cf. Rushdie, *Imaginary Homelands;* Appiah. *Cosmopolitanism: Ethics in a World of Strangers*; Lugones, "Playfulness, 'World'-Travelling and Loving Perception" in Garry and Pearsall, eds. *Women, Knowledge, and Reality: Explorations in Feminist Philosophy*].

14. Alexandre Kojève and Raymond Queneau, *Introduction to the Reading of Hegel* (Cornell University Press, 1980).

15. Principally, Emmanuel Levinas, *Totality and Infinity* (Springer, 1979).

16. Principally, Theodor W. Adorno, *Negative Dialectics* (Routledge, 1990). Discussion of the object's preponderance, pp. 183-93.

17. Kojève and Queneau, *Introduction to the Reading of Hegel*.

18. Brian Schroeder, "The (Non) Logic of Desire and War: Hegel and Levinas," in *Philosophy and Desire*, ed. Hugh J. Silverman (Routledge, 2000), 45–62. p. 61.

19. Schroeder. p. 45.

20. Schroeder. p. 59.

21. Schroeder. p. 48.

22. Schroeder. p. 61.

23. Levinas, *Totality and Infinity*. p. 52.

24. Levinas. p. 58-59.

25. My work and worry here is not an investment in proving or disproving dialectics as a universal heuristic or strategic device or diagnostic of objective material relations and their movement through history. I am primarily concerned with the shape in which our inherited understanding of relations of desire and attachment between subjects and objects within precarious political existence comes to us, and this (and not the dialectic) is what has taken me to Levinas, Fanon, and Adorno. That they happen to engage the possibility and impossibility of the dialectic is by no means accidental—both the relations and the motions at the heart of dialectics as method are supremely important to me—but the dialectic is not an object of redemption or damnation in itself for me in this book. I would defer to discussions such as George Ciccariello-Maher's *Decolonizing Dialectics*, Glen Coulthard's *Red Skin, White Masks*, and Patchen Markell's *Bound by Recognition*, on the dialectic per se, its entwinement with recognition, and the conditions of its relevance to ongoing struggles against capital and colony.

26. Adorno, *Negative Dialectics*. p. 191-92.

27. Some readers end up showing how Adorno's own redemption in the eyes of many a western philosopher happens thanks to his negotiation with Hegel—consoling folks performatively that not all is lost. Fred Dallmayr, for instance, regards Adorno as preferable and a lesson to confused anti-foundationalist thinkers like Edward Said because Adorno's vagrancy is kept in check by his pact with Hegel. (See Fred Dallmayr, "The Politics of Nonidentity: Adorno, Postmodernism, and Edward Said," *Political Theory* 25, no. 1 (February 1997): 33–56, https://doi.org/10.2307/192264.). This is personally very poignant for me, for I wonder if the unsaid terms of legitimacy of any real Other (Dallmayr, for one, proves that Adorno is in some ways really more "our" own…) are playing a role in whom I am having to address. I am not under the spell of the Hegelian dialectic—have no desire, above all, to appease Hegel, or to reject him. That the *non*-identity is still non-*identity* is a bit irritating, and not the frame for the problem I am pursuing. For this is not all it's about—and that forms of identification and knowing that come with a certain form of love can ever be beholden to, limited to, or seek approval of, these categories.

28. Robert Baker, "Crossings of Levinas, Derrida, and Adorno: Horizons of Nonviolence," *Diacritics* 23, no. 4 (Winter 1993): 12–41, https://doi.org/10.2307/465305. p. 20

29. Beardsworth, "A Note to Understanding of Love in Our Age."

30. Michael Hardt and Antonio Negri, *Empire* (Cambridge, Mass.: Harvard University Press, 2000); Dialogics, "Michael Hardt: On Love."

31. Badiou's attempt to theorize love renders it a philosophical concept, as one of four legitimate truth-acts. The former is the latter by since pathos and desire have been removed from it. (Desire exists separately, as executor of the ultimate form the truth-process takes, and other relevant disjunctive moments of gender, etc., are staged.)

32. Reference to the Subaltern Studies Group formulation of the notion of domination without hegemony on which rests the entire historiographic enterprise of the Group. The relation between hegemony and domination depends on where in the global cartography of neoliberal progress one lies. The question of hegemony without domination is also an open one, and can speak more to the increasing homogeny of forms of love and desire via prescribed abundances and deprivation.

33. Murray et al., ed., "Face to Face with Agamben; or, the Other in Love," in *The Work of Giorgio Agamben*, n.d.William Haver, "Queer Research," ed. Sue Golding (Routledge, 1997).

34. Alain Badiou and Simon Critchley, "Ours is Not a Terrible Situation," March 6, 2006; Simon Critchley, "Demanding Approval," *Radical Philosophy*, June 2000, http://www.lacan.com/critchley.htm.

35. Benjamin Noys, "Encountering Badiou," *Polygraph*, no. 17 (2005).

36. *Eros*, conceives of relations; and *pathos* feeling and sentiment. Mary McCarthy and Hannah Arendt are useful here, in their holding of an unsentimental politics. See Deborah Nelson, "The Virtues of Heartlessness: Mary McCarthy, Hannah Arendt, and the Anesthetics of Empathy," *American Literary History* 18, no. 1 (2006): 86–101.

37. Alain Badiou and Peter Hallward, *Ethics* (Verso, 2002). p. 23.

38. Jason Barker, "To Have Done with the Other" (Rhetoric, Politics, Ethics, Ghent University, Belgium, 2005). p. 9.

39. A critique of Foucault, but more so Deleuze; see Talal Asad, *Formations of the Secular* (Stanford University Press, 2003). Also resonant with Gayatri Spivak's strident takedown at the beginning of "Can the Subaltern Speak?"Gayatri Chakravorty Spivak, "Can the Subaltern Speak?," in *Marxism and the Interpretation of Culture*, ed. Cary Nelson and Lawrence Grossberg (Urbana: University of Illinois Press, 1988), 271–313. For more contemporary variations on the themes, pressing the urgency of bringing a global history of race and coloniality back into the conversation that has been evacuated of it even by Marxist thinkers of "Europe" such as Slavoj Žižek and Alain Badiou, see Da Silva, "Fractal Thinking," *ACCeSsions* 2 (April 27, 2016), https://accessions.org/article2/fractal-thinking/; Rizvana Bradley, "Poethics of the Open Boat," *ACCeSsions* 2, accessed December 4, 2017, https://accessions.org/article2/poethics-of-the-open-boat/.

40. Adorno, *Negative Dialectics*. pp. 364-65.

41. Such as that of the work of art in *Aesthetic Theory*. See Theodor W. Adorno, *Aesthetic Theory*, ed. Gretel Adorno and Rolf Tiedeman (Minneapolis: University of Minnesota Press,

1997); also, "The Autonomy of Art," in Theodor W. Adorno and Brian O'Connor, *The Adorno Reader* (Wiley-Blackwell, 2000).

Chapter Three

Colonial Loves and Heimlich Maneuvers

For years, Julian Sands and Helena Bonham-Carter stared at me from a poster on a wall in my room. It was the poster of Merchant Ivory's version of E. M. Forster's *A Room With a View*.[1] That room, with seven doors and two windows, lent itself to all sorts of strange soundscapes, vestibules into other spaces, no absolute exits, and no "view" to speak of. Perhaps I was too young to realize that those doors were exits. I was certainly not old enough to commit to the tyranny of aesthetic separatism or sensory puritanism that would pry away sight from sound, and both from imagination. Surrounded by all these spaces, in a panopticon turned over its head, I knew everyone could see me, but I could not see them, something that did not bother when the proverbial whole story seemed like a mosaic of remnants anyway. The poster, itself a picture of a window looking out onto Florence, was one of many more real portals, a potent angle on life and, in hindsight, a lesson about how spaces compel certain fixations and relieve us of others. Having excavated copies of *Where Angels Fear to Tread*[2] and *A Room with a View*, my relation to reading Forster was, in place of teenage romance novels, a keeper of love imaginaries. The European travels featured in *Room* came to haunt my trips abroad with my aunt who was a comfortably suspended subject between parent and friend. Romance seemed easy to ideate, and adopt, at the slightest provocation, when you were alone, in foreign lands, and often in a very Platonic or insanely abstinent way—something that suggests now that if I got the math right, I in Karachi in 1991 was like a much older Lucy Honeychurch in 1908 Edwardian rural England. That was my introduction to Forster and the universal promise of love, anywhere in the universe, where there was barely any difference between myself and the people in the book. Or, so I thought then.

I was quite a credulous conscript of Forster's expansive community of love, understanding, adventure, and redemption all at the same time. Maybe something even more interesting was revealed about this universality of love, and one's luck at finding it—contrary to popular claim, everywhere in the universe but *at home*. Maybe that was the lesson of *Room*; every other encounter and exilic harvest of homely love, worth stories never told, attests to that. I have come to understand differently, of course, after years of nonconsensual racialization away from that home, with insistent settlers encircling like vultures the unsettled and unconsoled lives tucked away inside these new homes—new not only for what they are, but also for what home must now mean and not mean—the fixations (of our desires) and fixities (of our attachments) that these homes compel or foreclose.

Gaston Bachelard's poetics of the space called home is indexed in my work here, informing my search for a minor poetics of home as if the colony happened. He writes,

> Of course, thanks to the house, a great many of our memories are housed, and if the house is a bit elaborate, if it has a cellar and a garret, nooks and corridors, our memories have refuges that are all the more clearly delineated. All our lives we come back to them in our daydreams. A psychoanalyst should, therefore, turn his attention to this simple localization of our memories. I should like to give the name of topoanalysis to this auxiliary of pyschoanalysis. Topoanalysis, then would be the systematic psychological study of the sites of our intimate lives.[3]

Exploring the kinds of loves that both produce and are bred within various spaces gives me access to thinking about the relations to desire and attachment that modern institutions, the state for one, require and foster for their own sustenance, rendering the question of love political in a different way beyond the ethics of permitted and forbidden desire and attachment among individual subjects. Modernity's fascination with, and ubiquitous and unprejudiced confidence in, the motif of home seems to indicate some of these dynamics that are naturalized and even primordialized in certain orientations to institutions, and then narrowed to certain choice institutions arbitrarily declared non-negotiable—such as the liberal state itself deemed a home built with and relying on certain desires and attachments—even when they fail to requite the love and labor put into them. I am curious to see if the loves that produce, and are produced within, these institutions have even a shot at breaking the closed circuit of this reproduction and annihilation in one. If there are indeed certain love relations and objects that animate colonialism and anticipate those pathological intermaterialities of love and marginality that shape life inside modern liberal institutions (and life on the run from them) in our wider postcolony, the universalized formation of home can be seen as symptomatic of these. Home is both an occasion to bring into view stubborn frames of love with a complex genealogy in colonial modernity that ratify political subjects of a certain kind, as well as a template for institutions the walls of which also mark the literal and affective boundaries between host and guest, insider and outsider, resident and alien, citizen and refugee, and so on. Read together, these yield a minor poetics of home (pace Gaston Bachelard) that may also give us insight into what is deemed *not* home, and into the (fugitive) homes on the move occasioned by colonialism itself. This ultimately allows us a return to the Other and the outsider by way of politicizing forms of love often misappropriated by a centripetal, walled, politics that cannot withstand the energy and the stasis percolating outside the home, on the margins of polities and societies, without distorting them to its own ends. Contextualizing our conceptual compromises with space and time in modernity that yield the object and relations of home as we know it—as I attempt to do in this chapter—is in the service of encountering the margins as not the binary opposite of home, but as a fugal, contrapuntal, recomposition of this motif, where entire logics of temporality and spatiality are disembodied and re-embodied, in order that life might still happen inside them.

HOME AND THE HAUNTS OF COLONIAL MODERNITY

The peculiar repository of politics that is *home* finds diverse but very persistent ways of conscripting our loves (for better and for worse). Its various locutions grant us access to the travels and destinations of political desire and attachment, sculpted into kinds of subjects who are deemed more valuable the more they see home as a pre-political or transcendental concept rather than a historical, contingent, and political one. Home as a motif within disparate political narratives—including nativist and colonialist, localist and globalist, capitalist and protectionist, declensionist and revivalist, nationalist and universalist, communitarian and communalist, legalist and humanitarian ones—can be brought to bear on contemporary politics of affirmation and inclusion within liberal and postcolonial societies, and about the colonizations, settlements, and marginalizations internal to them. Home is central to the mutual affections of colonialism and liberalism. When probed, it offers a grasp on the kinds of subjects, their desires, and their attachments that are shaped and harnessed by these systems, whether in colonization or dispossession or immigration or slavery, whether women or nations are domesticated, whether love or terror gets gated, and when the luxury of a spatialist or territorial mind-set—even in a liberatory mode—reeks of the blood and sweat of those who contend with the recalcitrant elsewhereness of life itself. I find it important to ask how marginal subjects negotiate the demand to be at home in the inclusions and accommodations granted them, as they belong to spaces with the possibility of desiring something that does not yet exist, where home is not something to be returned to—either because we remain in our homelands as residues of our genocides or because our homes that we left have been occupied by others or destroyed while we were gone.

The motif of home in colonial modernity and the motions that it stills and encloses reveal something about the dynamics and statics that are deemed extraneous to, or categorized as outside of or threatening to, these homes. Home's current forms are inseparable from movements that are normalized and pathologized, enabled and stilled, by colonialism and capitalism—effecting what hospitality, invitation, and inclusion come to mean (which becomes important later in this book). In this chapter's sections to follow, this premise facilitates attention to those motions that are expunged and those desires that are evacuated from homes thus occupied, as well as those opposing motions that seek different culminations and consummations. Far from valorizing a kind of voluntarism or notion of agency in relation to where we live, I want to emphasize that by deepening our understanding of and relations between these acts of homemaking and homebuilding, fugitivity and captivity, and occupation and accommodation, we might learn to think of the relation between necessity and politics in a different way. (Not only our desires for our basic needs, but also our less tangible actions in politics might stand to be re-understood, and the relation between need and love can evade pathology.)

I, then, turn to how this motif of home congeals in its dominant contemporary form out of the movements and travels of colonialism that employ particular understandings of spatiality and temporality, and what it then comes to hold and (with)hold that allows it to inform the state as we know it today. (In this frame, and in the departures that resist it, this motif might be able to suggest a fundamental connection between the nation-state and the settler colonial state despite other chasms of translatability). In seeing home via colonialism, we might be able to gesture to featured epistemic and ontic fixities of love—desire and attachment—as a way of bringing to light not only what is deemed home but that which is categorized as not-home, the unhomely, the margins, or the outside, and also to see logics that are suppressed by, or tear away from, the demand to engage with the desires and attachments normalized in the home, the nation-state, and other institutions.

HOME STATE

All modern nation-states are settler-colonial states. Far from intending to dilute or violate the power (in specificity) of the concept of settler colonialism, or trying to equate unequalizable loss at the heart of its reality in different contexts, considering this claim allows us to comb through some aspects of our very fundamental social and political desires that are tethered, and have easily fallen prey, to an ongoing colonial and now neoliberal politics (that basically generalizes and universalizes colonial desire for everyone to have) across various nation-states sponsoring the decided-upon disposabilities of certain populations. In the topography of this modern liberal nation-state, home serves as an object of desire or the location of love, the center that magnetizes whatever lies outside it as the space of unlovedness or frustrated desire. Colonial travels pride in their search for home, and allow the colonizer to be at home everywhere in the world; but that was a different home than that which is always available in the homelessness of slaves, exiles, refugees, or immigrants, who make places into homes they will never have. In this distinction, between being at home and making home (often on the margins of society), are found labors and loves that allow both the meaning of home and not-home to change.

Curiously placed among these figures are the colonial subjects who are made to think of home only when someone invades it and asks for their hospitality, or takes over their home wondering what claims they could have made that were too late—a home becomes an object only in being taken away. In doing so, the colonial subject perfectly emblematizes the historical nature of even the concern for home, and then foreshadows the homes built for housing the desires, say, of white American slaveowners that at once purify a language of interest (on behalf of home-dwelling white women) in order to seek the love of the state—white identity politics preceding any other kind of identity politics to follow—that continues to injure others in order to protect that home. This is especially ironic since those who get corralled into the love of the patriarchal state in this early moment, in this instance the hallucinating white wives of slaveowners that Hortense Spillers talks about as she works through the testimony of Harriet Jacobs,[4] forget the roots of the state in misogyny and the production of black and feminine bodies as premises of the violence that will be housed and secured in the state. This sexual contract, purified of its attachments to race, is an early instance of epistemologies of ignorance that keep the United States the home of the brave and land of the free, its endemic imperial violence at home and abroad still a source of shock or disbelief for many of its citizens. To wit, the simultaneity of imperial wars, nation-building wars such as the US civil war, and white women's movements that ardently bleach out their provenancial birthmarks from struggles where women's movements were struggles by and with women, tied to issues of racial injustice and slavery, and did not necessarily mean movements *for* women as if there was a category of that political subject of woman that was not wrought of the struggles from which exception was now being taken. Home becomes valorized as home not when home ownership becomes a plague in the United States, but earlier when the new nation is formed through the mutual recognition and desire between home and state in its fresh incipience and virility, nursed back to life by those who did not die (of slavery, genocide, or war). Home attains a political character in this context, beyond its materiality as an economic unit alone, as a space the becoming of which tells the same story as does the delineation of the body as body in early feminism, of the proto-civil war US variety. The home that the state reaches to protect and secure is the site of tragic displacement of the violence on bodies becomes the new enchanting object of opportunist flirtation or earnest devotion to match the fetish of home as the repository of epistemic groundedness and ontic integrity for the state and its desirous citizens.

Whatever its pre-political substance, it is naïve if not irresponsible to see the concept of home as pre-political or ahistorical, a common practice in normalizing and domesticating certain aspects of our political existences. The home that is able to serve as the center, origin, and locus around which the nation-state wraps its publicness, cordoning off not only the space of politics but also the space of all-those-things-that-will-seem-extrapolitical, comes to contain all sorts of conceits regarding family, society, and sociality. These elements of its meaning and extension are to be best understood through the travels that produced home as that kind of space, to an illuminating instance of which I now turn.

BE STILL, MY HEART: LOVE AND THE COLONY

Forster's writing is framed in travel, his own and that of his characters. From *Where Angels Fear to Tread* to *A Passage to India*,[5] either a journey frames the novel, or someone in the novel, as in *Howards End*,[6] exemplifies a bringing home of imperialism, into the domestic space. These novels involve travel, the promise of finding something very real in a place that is away, in each of the earlier cases, Italy, the then, and more reliable, Other of England. Some of the novels are more light-hearted than others, but show their ambivalence about modernity without giving up its luxuries—a classic trait of colonialism itself—and play out the cultural conflicts in a half-hearted liberal apology for the same. Right in the first novel, the English are admittedly the race of inexperienced angels who are rushing into spaces of love, passion, desire, mystery, secrets, illegibility, disorder, where smarter angels would not. The casual cultural conflicts, and the playoff of the conceited binaries of reason and emotion, passion and restraint, mind and body, mind and heart, masculine and feminine, etc., for which the Mediterranean is the site, are just about enough: *for now, right here*. The Mediterranean serves as the site for romance, and also for the remedy of the disenchantment of modern civilization, and a recovery of something lost. In *Angels*, true love remains found but impracticable, meeting a tragic fate at the hands of the English who want to control everything, redeem all failures on their own terms. Colonial spaces such as India up the ante a little bit, stripping the colonized of a language of loss to begin with—since they were, technically, *still* at home.

In about twenty years from the publication of *Angels*, Forster travels to India and North Africa multiple times, and publishes later novels and other writings on India. *Passage* is clearly not his only work that broaches in some rudimentary manner the question of relations between the colonizer and the colonized, and between the traveler/the seeker and those with secrets to tell, love to give us, and invitations to whisper. While Italy's resistance to the English is tantalizing and ultimately reassuring, the attempt by England to enter India results in England "being worked into its pattern and covered with its dust."[7] India is muddle without solution. Colonialism, in this way, enacts not only a nostalgia for wholeness that was or wholeness that is outside of enlightenment, but also the power to act with reason on the spaces that are yet to be brought into history. Thus, the paradox of colonialism: the need for the other to be created in one's own image, and the resistance to this mirroring as threatening, where the terms of this psychotic dialectic are set by the ones in power that could remind us of the white master in Du Bois.[8] England has somewhat gotten ahead of itself seeking itself in India. There is something deferred, almost impossible and unlocatable, about the appeal that India holds in Forster. This is exemplified in the "not yet," the "not here," that the narrator utters on behalf of both Aziz and Fielding.[9] With India, Forster himself goes too far, treading where the inexperienced angels should have feared to tread. Where the interaction reveals a fundamental failure of the encounter not between man and man, but between man and god, it reveals something about all of us, and destroys the romance of it as well.

Forster's *Passage* is an example of what David Adams calls a "colonial odyssey."[10] This particular genre in colonial writing curiously synthesizes the novel as a modern form, the form of expression of modernity, hence of modern colonialism, with the epic as an ancient form that brings space into language, and tells of the journey that circles back home. In doing so, the colonial odyssey consciously mixes the interlacing of the journey inward with a journey outward. The colonial odyssey, like any form of writing, authorizes a configuration of space and time. In the ancient epic, travel is spatial. Time is explicit, but barely essential to the core of the unfolding; the notions of time prior to modernity have a certain partiality to wholeness, where time circumscribes space, and what we have is a situation where this circumscription renders time irrelevant. The epic is, hence, ahistorical. On the other hand, in modernity, space is temporalized; travel becomes a temporalizing practice, and in novels, is brought home, made inward.[11] When secular time becomes a presupposition, there is no need to theorize it (similar to modern discourses such as evolutionism that explicitly talk about time, but are atemporal). This secular time promotes a scheme in which not just past cultures, but all living societies are irrevocably placed on a temporal slope, a stream of Time—some upstream, others downstream. Think: civilization, evolution, development, acculturation, and modernization. A colonial odyssey is, thus, a strange mixture of spatialized time and the temporalized space composed of decomposed time; the genre augurs a unified subjectivity and reconciliation toward which we are all moving. Thus, time gets arranged linearly, then broken up, and then composed into a unified subjectivity. Travel, thus, is a temporalizing practice.[12]

AT HOME IN THE COLONY

A look at colonialism and capitalism and their role in inscribing a relation between being at home, being found by oneself, arriving at a destination, and finding love, is fairly crucial—not to mention that home and love find *themselves* through travel and territorial relocation. The material history of this transformation runs parallel to the world spirit manifesting itself in the becoming spatial of time and history, the template of this journey generously and unexhaustingly provided by the odyssey, relived time and again in the search for itself that love inaugurates. Love's colonial elements, in its colloquial fidelity to notions of possession, property, conquest, violence, and surrender are well-documented: from the double of enslavement and liberation that the subjection to love promises, to the entire third wave of feminism trying to articulate what it may mean to get or run past colonialism, and why we will our own subjections. It isn't merely that love is colonizing, but that colonialism itself *is* love. Love is where one finds oneself, and this search is emblematized in colonial discourses of travel and arrival.

"When the structures made for man by man are really adequate to man, they are his necessary and native home."[13] There are two types of homelessness featured in colonial odysseys, having to do with the issue of marginality. In one case, the interior is too small as compared to the outside world and hence idealizes the world outside; in the other, the interior is too big and easily disillusioned. In doing so, they capture the fact that colonialism is both too little and too much for the European subject. In that scenario, then, how must we interpret Forster's own marginality in England, his colonial pathology, and the resolution of the two? What form of romance, and what form of love, is being sought here? And, what can we find in Forster by first linking this desire for intimacy, love, friendship, and home to a political subjectivity, and then by linking these to structures that shape and sustain this subjectivity?

In Forster's writing, one sees the manifestation of the metaphysical homelessness of the colonizer's world, to which colonialism is a response and also a fix. *Passage*, remarkably, links metaphysical homelessness directly to political invasion. The unresolved malaise embodied in India is a treacherous invitation for British Imperial rule:

> How can the mind take hold of such a country? Generations of invaders have tried, but they remain in exile. The important towns they build are only retreats, their quarrels the malaise of men who cannot find their way home. India knows of their trouble. She knows of the whole world's trouble, to its uttermost depth. She calls "Come" through her hundred mouths, through objects ridiculous and august. But come to what? She has never defined. She is not a promise, only an appeal.[14]

Forster transmits this search for salvation, and for home, from the terrestrial to the metaphysical realm, showing how he at once displaces and expands the notion of home. He writes that *Passage* is "[c]oncerned with the difficulty of living in the universe; the book is not really about politics, it's about something wider than politics, about the search of the human race for a more lasting home, about the universe as embodied in the Indian earth and the Indian sky."[15]

Forster's deterrestrialization of the question of love and salvation is no improvement on, but only indirectly validates, the very terrestrial, material structures of colony and empire. The "failure" at the end of *Passage* (which is central to my discussion in Chapter 9) has everything to do with his power of displacing, arbitrarily, the question of love and conquest onto the heavens again, as a move that repeats the earlier displacing of time with space, accruing to Forster one more exit via this abstraction and fetishization.[16] The very claim that *Passage* is not a political novel, but one about humanity in general, is just such an exit. In this move, Forster completely reasserts himself as the arbiter of love, home, and belonging. If Fielding cannot have what he wants, then he will displace this possibility on to another time and space, and he will find it in the Mediterranean, whereas Aziz is left with his equivalent home of Indian nationalism.

Passage flirts with and rejects the dream that colonial travel offers a rejuvenating antidote to disenchantment. But, where is the wreckage? At the height of orientalist rhetoric, a number of educated Englishmen discover India and romance it, where nothing less than their own story is at stake in how India is narrated. This is why questions of exile and displacement are bound up with the wish to disrupt and displace our current accounts of ourselves, to be legible in a different manner, and to be composed of different things. Perhaps there is something about *Passage* that forces Forster to end the story with a failure—a failure that shows why this search for home and identity is something that plagues the white man a lot more than it plagues the Indian. Even this "tragedy" can only be explained if we find the respective homes Aziz and Fielding have found to be irreconcilable in this time and space, and thus forbidding of true friendship between them. All of this happens with no regard to the fact that the disillusionments wrought of a search for a certain kind of home—of inscribing home as comfort, as end, as destination—that underpins forms of nationalism are products of colonialism. We are still spitting these homes out of our systems, as Fanon would put it in the context of the Algerian war of independence (even if he does not see the white master's involution with and dependence on the dialectic of recognition).[17] And then there is Fielding, whose frustrated wishfulness and newfound realization of having gone too far allows him to discover the limits of the possibilities of friendship, where Italy now becomes an ally close-at-hand. Unsurprisingly, the narrative does not follow Fielding all the way to London; in Forsterian terms, his nostos is complete by the time he reaches Venice, and the Italy that promises him a home he should have just been content with before, and a boundary he should not have crossed, also flexes its fascist imagination: home without history, history as home. Nonetheless, for present times, Forster stands prescient of all that Europe, for all its elephantine memory, is able to excise at will, all that it is able to forgive itself, largely because it alone is both judge and jury.

At-homeness continues to be a key trope of the liberal project, and inheres in the reactionary nationalisms that the colonized spew in response to the originary supremacist "identity politics" of the colonizers. The discourse of home and security, and the meanings of attachments that abound in this are different given one's location in the colonizer-colonized matrix. The colonized are not only left to take care of their subjection but have to bear consoling the colonizer whose hope of recovering lost meaning through geopolitical domination can only lead to demonic madness and deepened disillusionment. This manifests itself in colonial odysseys as a wish not merely to desert home but to expand it, reflecting a desire to be at home everywhere. (And, in a faithful incarnation of the pathetic and loathsome Odysseus, to destroy it upon return; I find his being recast as a refugee in contemporary narratives of Europe a protracted pathetic fallacy beyond bad faith.)

And what home is this? It is a place where the meaning of experience is fully immanent, where the totality of the world is fully accessible to the subject. At what cost will this be wrought? Both liberalism and capitalism embody the need for new content to confirm universal epistemological claims that become necessary amid modern age's loss of hold on totality. There is an unabashed search for makeshift homes with which colonial modernity attempts to compensate for this loss, the sort of homes provided by romance, nationalism, imperialism, fascism, or certain enlightenment teleologies. Any such home, in claiming to offer a lost or not yet had plenitude, opens itself to the critique or attack of those who feel either suffocated or excluded, or who are otherwise disillusioned with the claim.

Identity as understood by liberalism is one such home, something which marks, for liberalism, the final containment and closure of meaning, a readiness to be indexed and referenced, and an availability of a surface to act in place of depths. Certainly, identity in this way can also be understood as scar tissue, something that is in place to protect but in turn inhibits movement. At the same time, it is constituted by motion and movement, and not the stilling implied in those categories which, in their willful conclusion of meaning, also wishfully assume that the fronts both of desire and betrayal are done with, completed, ready to be moved on from, or that the final battle has arrived. How do our needs for a home for our desires and attachments change when at stake are not the wrongs that have been done, but the wrongs that remain to be done as much as those that are happening now?

NOT HOME IN THE COLONY

Rabindranath Tagore's hybrid stances, and the distance from M.K. Gandhi, on the question of nationalism and the Indian freedom struggle, are well-known; his politics is often swiftly summed up in the notion of liberal cosmopolitanism, and taken to mirror the West's idea of itself especially in the forms of the dichotomies with which Edward Said has credited orientalism.[18] Tagore is regarded for his self-image of poet-politician that, in its rejection of vanguardism and paternalism toward the poor, offended both socialists and nationalists alike and ultimately has been held culpable of a kind of poetic transcendentalist quietism. Then there is his actual politics, bold enough to suspect an ideology that prognosticates, with Gandhi and the communists who ratified the nationalist and communalist trajectory of partition, a way through war to peace, from nationalism to inter-nationalism. In Tagore's work, home is something that refuses to be the key presupposition and premise on which one's struggles with the outside would be waged. This is why he is part of the story I am trying to tell: within some of Tagore's writing, I find clues to the problematic of home that nationalism or cosmopolitanism do not solve, but which, in its messiness, allows us to turn our gaze to other kinds of freedom struggles that have not settled the question of home and what lies outside of it, struggles that got overwritten by the ones we have been forced to accept as somehow more our own. These filial, known, and affirmed struggles are those that presuppose acknowledging and identifying with a piece of land as home—no less a home with a shape and reality born of the lines and dimensions on a map gifted from the colonizer himself. Perhaps my implicit politics of negation, rejection, and objection in relation to our inherited spaces of and to desire may be too jarring to the reader. But please bear with me. I have a long way to go.

Tagore's *Ghare Baire (The Home and the World)* is not an unusual story.[19] The novel's title is better translated as home and outside. The "world" is not present in the Bengali title, at least not already to be interpreted as the other to home, especially when one looks at the character of spaces in which this book is set. For someone like me who spent most of her adolescence in a room with seven doors and two windows, even the outside of home has so many ironic and puzzling referents—is it the outside of one's room, is it the fact that the outside to the home is still the courtyard, or is it the outside of one's immediate consciousness? My own imagination in this regard is reinforced by a cinematic adaptation of another of Tagore's stories, *Chokher Bali* (*Sand in the Eye*),[20] which inserts an aerial view of an old wooden staircase as the frame for the opening sequence of the film adaptation, bounding the scene physically and cinematographically. The film begins with sounds permeating this space, including the Aza'an in an era surrounding the Crown's first attempt to partition Bengal in 1905 (which was to become an unsuspected trigger both of communalism and of political parties that were to be key actors in the eventual freedom movement). Later on, the home is revealed as a complex of pathways and many internal walls and screens, where the expulsions and expungings are all interior to the boundaries of the home itself, and allow an understanding of the world outside by confusing the presumed pathologies of interiority and exteriority, mystique and exposure, intrigue and transparency, introversion and extroversion, reclusion and rebellion, common to the "West."

The romantic reading of Tagore that sees him as staging a grand battle between the forces of progress and reaction, the east and the west, nationalism and cosmopolitanism, seems to lose traction the moment we start to figure out that home is not an antithesis of the world, but an outgrowth of the world, and the space where the world's denials and promises are forced to take form by inhabiting and interacting with us—the boundaries are not so strict, and at least not defined by first defining home. This can be seen when we acknowledge colonialism as lifeworld: home is one among various spaces where the lifeworld manifests in the everyday life of its subjects and the location where subjects interact most immediately with the colonial framing of time and space, whether to adhere to it or to reject it (in love, madness, sleep, etc.). Home is the dual space: where one returns to (be) oneself, and which at once contains one's not-at-homeness. In that sense, home is not the negation of the world outside, but the container of its potentialities, and the trapper of its insurgencies, regardless of what someone said it ought to be.

Here, I am alluding to Freud's *das Unheimliche* (literally, the unhomely) with its clustering notions of the uncanny, of haunting, of present absence, and of absent presence—importantly, home already being a complex repository of its own others.[21] The word invokes a sense of strangeness, mystery, the occult, and an unfamiliarity that is unsettlingly familiar (sort of treading the terrain of a phenomenological understanding of Marx's early notion of alienation, which always brings to my mind ghost limbs).[22] The Unheimliche allows time to be reinserted into this architecture. Freud writes that the uncanny is "in reality nothing new or alien, but something which is familiar and old-established in the mind and which has become alienated from it only through the process of repression."[23] Repression is already a temporal notion, in the sense of memory's various blurred edges and the parts of it that become unfamiliar over time. Interestingly enough, Freud also invokes F. W. J. Schelling who writes of the Unheimliche as "Everything [. . .] that ought to have remained secret or hidden but has come to light."[24]

This connects to the etymology of "the uncanny" itself, (a word into which *das Unheimliche* is translated) in "to know." If we see the spatialization of modernity to be connected to its modes of systematizing and organizing humans and their pursuits, then home lurks as a space of immanent familiarity and knowledge. But the uncanny interrupts that, without completely severing this relation to knowledge or, better, to "sense." Just acknowledging this makes room for other modalities of time, space, and knowing, that may ensue from and constitute beings that are external to the dominant modes. The dominant modes are organized by the spatial conceits of a politics centered on the state, and invested in spaces only as an extension of the space thus configured under the modern settler, colonial, capitalist, and liberal logics. Here, Freud himself is helpful, when he writes of the native as being the opposite of what is familiar. And we need not assume, regardless of what Freud intended, that this familiarity is only calibrated in relation to an established knowing subject to/for which the native is object. So, perhaps there is the possibility of those imagined and desired spaces of home or its outside to be spaces for an unsettling unfamiliarity to oneself, and an establishment of relations of love and desire on other premises (and promises) than those of knowledge and possession.

This is why, alongside discussions of spaces in which one does not feel at home, must emerge a serious account of those spaces whose homeliness one resists and those homes that were destroyed before they could raise the question of homeliness except in their withdrawal. Our "complaint" cannot just be (construed to be) about those who do not love us and whose love we desire, but those whose love is unacceptable and whom we cannot love (ever or anymore). Colonialisms and various forms of displacements of populations exemplify how those who are in these homes are also the ones who are written out of them or who inhabit a different temporality in that space. The Unheimliche brings out those aspects of memory and experience that struggle with the kinds of spatializations and sedimentations under which conventional psychoanalytic theory has placed them. If time is liberated from this repressive regime, which I believe Freud himself does not quite know how to desire or do, perhaps there is a possibility for redeeming the unhomely for those who might be inside spaces but out(side) of time, especially the time of home. What love happens in which homes? What is the notion of love that inhabits those spaces, and indeed, inhabits the marginality, and the estrangement of someone who was best kept hidden or who was not supposed to be revealed or known? Enter the pariah? To recall Hannah Arendt here,

> "Qualities which one cannot govern are faults," gratitude, excessive attachment, is the typical vice of the pariah, who feels obligated even by a casual word, an almost unintentional gesture of friendliness, because he expected nothing of the sort from the world. This longing to be grateful would be only a fault if it were not accompanied by another trait equally characteristic of the pariah: what Rahel called "too much consideration for a human face." This sensitivity is an emotionally exaggerated understanding of the dignity of every human being, a passionate comprehension unknown to the privileged. In a society based upon privilege, pride of birth and arrogance of title, the pariah instinctively discovers human dignity in general long before Reason has made it the foundation of morality.[25]

HOMEMAKING THE WORLD: THE HOSPITALITY OF THE PARIAH

In *Rahel Varnhagen: Life of a Jewess*,[26] Hannah Arendt offers a case study of the politics of space and the spaces of politics, foreshadowing much of her normative struggles with the promises of politics and the spaces that invite or permit them to be made, even if not fulfilled. In this book, history becomes an interlocutor, an actor, a co-inhabitant of spaces with us; from salon to home to cities with lovers, Rahel lives, unwrites and rewrites herself, only to reach the ultimate conclusion that some of these spaces engulfed her labors and could not reciprocate or redeem her presence. Right in the first paragraph of the book, Arendt writes about Rahel: "It had taken her sixty-three years to come to terms with a problem which had beginnings seventeen hundred years before her birth, which underwent a crucial upheaval during her life, and which one hundred years after her death—she died on March 7, 1833—was slated to come to an end."[27] Arendt's use of the word "problem" is telling (and importantly amends the more generalized philosophical and political convention of using the term "question"). In her preface, Arendt refers to the "Woman Problem" ("that is, the discrepancy between what men expected of women 'in general' and what women could give or wanted in their turn, was already established by conditions of the era and represented by a gap that virtually could not be closed")[28] and confesses that her unwillingess to try to read "into" Rahel more than Rahel could, in some ways, read into herself, was the reason she was not taking up anachronistic issues of liberal gender-as-identity politics. In both situations, though, the framing of the question as already a problem is already a political step, and there are continuities to be found in the two "problems" Arendt notes. It is important to also note Arendt's reference to the "end" of the problem in 1933.

What end? One takes heart from such a phrase, since it is clear that Arendt talks about the end of that problem being the beginning of the "solution," and one which would end up being cast in exactly the terms in which Rahel's body and being had refused to regard themselves, and the spaces in which they lived, became, and got undone, however unrequited. Rahel accepts the impossibility of being herself, but has also not come to understand the space of Germany as a space that needed to be courted as mere territory, and she was not to be the one to begrudge those spaces any denials of love and requital by those who were perhaps even less able to make those spaces their own (but still to whom the spaces had given themselves). Rahel decides there would be no way for her to assimilate and still continue to be, and she chooses to not give up her "special misfortune."[29] Nevertheless, in an act of disappearance and erasure much less dramatic and much more verbalized than the women of Ingeborg Bachmann's novels, for instance—who disappear behind the interior walls of their homes, or bash their heads against the exterior walls of the pyramids to die of concussions—Rahel accepts that, despite all that she may able to produce and bring to those spaces, her labors were to bring no love back to her. This particular form of claim on spaces ultimately does not materialize, the forms of possession that are claimed and made are not going to be sufficient, and ultimately we are invited to understand that other dynamics not reducible to this struggle over territory are happening. Add to this the slowness of the spaces themselves in coming to a realization of what they are up to, evident in the fact that Rahel dies a hundred years before the "problem" has come to its "end" (both as terminus and as completion) and Europe resets its clocks. The question was, then, either no longer or perhaps finally completely of space, both of those being really the same thing. Idealist subsumption by capitalism's occupation of time that has been spatialized by communism, and by colonialism's occupation of space by displacing their time with history—and the seamless, often cyclical, translations between the two that produce the idealist absolute as an object of desire—also pave the way for fascism. She writes, in her own adamant ambivalent love, "It is through love of the world that man explicitly makes himself at home in the world, and then desirously looks to it alone for his good and evil. Not until then do the world and man grow 'worldly.'"[30]

I cannot help but connect this to how Arendt's notions of political space develop over her own life. She explains and normativizes the space of politics as comprising of multidimensional areas of the creation of life in common with others. This space is "outside" of, and enabled by, what remains (in my reading of Arendt) a fairly uninterrogated (but not glorified) economy inside the home, better understood when placed next to her argument for spaces of individuality, privacy, and thought, that work, at best, symbiotically (but often parasitically too) with politics outside. I would like to read this more symptomatically. It is worth probing when it is that we wish for spaces outside of the home, or for homes outside of politics. If it is the case that the labors inside the home are key to the labors outside of it, we must acknowledge these as different labors. Thus, the state ascending to become the form in which the labors of politics get consummated is a historical and contingent act, and not a normative necessity (like it becomes for Arendt). Could Arendt, then, have mistaken Rahel's deferred redemption as materializing in the state as we know it (and as Rahel did not)? Could this be an act of endorsing, in one arbitrary redemption among many possible, this particular challenge of history called the state as a space on which we can/do/must rely for its premier power in granting humanity and life, and defining the possibilities of both? I think Arendt may have, despite herself, read history back into Rahel too much. She has perhaps deprived Rahel's of its rough, frayed edges with trailing threads by neatly packing it into an affirmative relation to the known spaces of politics.

When Arendt brings in the state as an absolution and as an idealization of the space between us in which she sees politics erupting (and in doing so settles the question of space despite herself), she ends up raising the issue of home and the outside. In her story of Rahel, Arendt makes an astute observation about the ways in which history makes demands on us. She accords a kind of subjectivity to spaces and times, a post-Adornian move if any, that allows us to render these spaces and times, animate, live, multiple, and autonomous—intersubjectively produced and carrying parts of us in them. This allows for history to be more than a marker, and for spaces to be more than origins, termini, and destinations. I want to bring to our understanding of margins just that kind of vitality, to allow a turn away from the question of space as premise and presupposition. This would be a challenge Arendt cannot quite manage by herself when she makes the state the key space—among the spaces in between us she deems necessary and peculiar to politics—that accords people the humanity to produce politics in common. Inspired by an early Arendt, we can bring in space as an inter-actor and interlocutor, and along with reintroducing temporality as one such actor, cross into a more materialist, more plural, and undulating understanding of our locations. Space, for that matter, need not be reducible to only text or only context, or validated only as object of inquiry and romance for us as active or passive subjects (as in Bachelard's poetics of space).[31] It is not a question of space versus time in some merely analytical sense, but the life afforded to or kept from these in our analyses, especially when our methods turn time and the body that lives in it into spaces that are more definite, readable, measurable, mappable, containable, and conquerable.

TIME, LABOR, VIOLENCE

The incessant spatializations of modern life and discourses of security, on the one hand, cover over the violences of home, and on the other hand, allow for a form of dissipation and a retreat that nevertheless becomes important only in a society—a liberal capitalist one—that allows us to "choose" home as the space to be oneself, of where we live. A politics of creating a life in common suddenly feels both necessitated and hindered by the walls of the home, and walls of the polis itself. The space of home is one that is always already defined by a defense of our own temporalities and becomings against structures that control us by controlling what happens to time in those spaces. At the same time, home becomes important as a space to be when one is marginalized, pushed back, domesticated. In work on domestic violence, for instance, attention has been drawn to how misconceived and violent the conventional apotheosis of home is, in classic works such as Bachelard's, to those whose suffering is kept in this place called home.

In "The Apotheosis of Home and the Maintenance of Spaces of Violence," Joshua Price forces us to interrogate the romance of home.[32] He draws us, not unlike Arendt, to the labor of the production of those spaces, which is to say the production of time that deeply links home to love and hope. Price offers a counter-narrative to the edification of home as the space of safety and to its association with glorious attributes of growth, development, and becoming. He punctures this conceit and seeks to somewhat complicate this allegiance by looking at the bodies and other matter that populate the home. While my interest is not merely in wanting to see safe spaces as "actually" unsafe ones (and I sense neither is Price's), the critique goes beyond the discourse of violence into broader aesthetic and sensual concerns. Price takes on two different approaches to home: first, he asks about who constructs home as a space, how, and for what purpose; second, he challenges the presumptions of safety and intimacy (and in that sense, an easy discourse of desire, privacy, comfort, and immediacy). He accepts that home is a place that one rather not leave, or is kept from leaving. Home can inspire different feelings for different inhabitants, and the politics, senses, and sensualities of home are as various as those of any other. Moreover, if we expand the notion of home to include desires we enact at a distance from home, and for home, it is clear that there are those for whom home will mean something completely different.

Affirming Price's attentiveness to the production of home, the insides of the home become more available to vision, and staked in every "worldmaking" that happens outside the home and the other way around, is the labor that produces it: not only how home produces safety, but how home as a motif itself is produced; and what is produced as the effluent of home, the outside, the world, the margins. The odyssey for which we all stand conscripted in different ways by even our most fervent allies, and certainly by our opponents, itself stands to be interrogated: narrating our departures and returns must involve making the act of ideological homemaking or domestication central to any understanding of what people are striving for, and to the imaginations of homogeneous spaces of safety and security at hand. How many of us are harnessed to produce time in such a way that it then needs this home . . . away from claims on spaces outside of this home, in the "world"?

TOWARD A MINOR (COUNTER) POETICS OF HOME

If colonial travels and fantasies thereof configure space and time in a way that corroborates the modern idea(l) of home, it remains to be seen which movements, stillnesses, attachments, and desires, reside in an anticolonial conception of home and hospitality. In political space and time, stasis and motion occasion each other. In our context of increasing statelessness—and its association with both disposability and criminality even as the "refugee crisis" erupts in a world order shaped by some hegemony of humanitarian reason—this dialectic between stasis and motion has become stilled, retarded, contained, reversed, disoriented, or irreparably distorted.

Taken in multiple and broad senses—literal, physical, geographical, biological, metaphorical, fantastical, psychological, ideological—home as shelter, location, enclosure, refuge, rest, front, destination, normativity, settlement, can help us think about the margin as the space of exposure, exclusion, exception, exile, excision, itinerance, disturbance, refraction, because it allows us to ask, among other things: Is home the place to depart from or return to, and for whom? Is home "political" because it is the place of labors that build a politics out there, or is it what all the politics out there are seeking to establish? How is home politicized differently depending on where in society we are located? What sort of home is the margin, then? How can and do the margins disrupt the dominant ideological motifs, economics, and poetics of home—when our lives and politics ensue in either an unprincipled expulsion from our homes or in a principled negation of the homes on offer to us? When are we obligated to submit to or subvert the containment and channeling of our labors and loves that has become the condition of membership of state and society (that often need us more than we need them, contrary to what we are told)? It is necessary to remember the connection between the colonial desires for home, the odysseys which necessitate and produce them, and the center-margin discourse—just so that we know how and in what compositions their opposition moves and settles. They contain those desires that are evacuated when homes are invaded, and which have to find other forms of dwelling and travel, stillness and motion, and thus suggest consummations of the desire for home other than the state and nation.

Without the settlers who build homes, or those who take away others' homes while others have left their homes thinking they would be right back, home would not be an issue, and the margins not an aftermath. In this moment, I want to invoke the margins as the spaces of counter-settlement or unsettlement that proceed through logics that run counter to, and at once contain and adumbrate the polis if we are to see it as an enclosure. The margins which border/outline/contain the triumphal text, become locations and lifeworlds, by virtue of the desires and attachments that they enfold. In the instance that the love in and on these margins (not love *of* them) speaks to fixations and fixities other than the nation-state or the settler colonial state, and does not seek re-enchantment of life through it, it is at once disregarded by and threatening to the polis iterated through occupation, colonization, and liberalism and the affective economies they each institutionalize. This requires, first, establishing, containing, domesticating, encapsulating, stilling, and creating as exceptions, the motions of politics so that the only love and fidelity that counts is that which repeatedly confesses and reproduces the hold of existing institutions on us.

The same political and discursive move that institutes home is what seeks to organize the margins of the polis, but this administrative fantasy's biting of its own tail—when confronted with the resistant materiality of the excluded that does not always give in, consent, or desire or die on demand or per plan—saves the idea of home from being irreparably flawed or fundamentally unjust in and of itself. These intransigent motions and stillnesses allow us to see beyond the oppositions—between home and the margins, the private and the public, the inside and the outside, the unities that have been sundered to produce dualities that nourish someone else's murderous and order-conserving dialectic—to their interdependence. This means seeing not only how the margins are the aftermath of home invaded, colonized, settled, but also that the work at the margins can and does reconstitute the homes that they were kept from as well as modes of hospitality they conjure.

The homes imagined by anticolonial nationalisms desperately need to conspire with the homelands disappeared discursively and physically by settler colonialisms. A critique of the nationalist and proto-fascist nativist imagination has to center on the nation that offers itself as the site of the state's murderous reconciliation of its spatial/territorial with its temporal/historical boundaries that oversees the transition from colonialism to fascism to humanitarian war. This critique also offers a path to decolonize the idea of home, and stave off colonial modernity's heimlich maneuvers awaiting us at every turn to domesticate and "neutralize" our politics. Our spaces might let go of some unwanted burdens and curses, and the unheimlich of the margins might be liberated as a possibility for all those who have been exiled, banished, disappeared, or handed a mortgage destined for foreclosure.

To reiterate, home becomes an issue when it is sought and taken away, at the same time as it becomes a space where desire can be stilled, located, domesticated, appropriated, and primitively accumulated. This concurrence sheds light on how many literal and figurative homes are built with the labor, and made liveable with the hospitality, of those who will be kept out of them, or asked to leave, or will be reminded sooner than later with whose permission they get to live there. These twin functions of spaces are historical and political: any political space is bordered and contained by the margins, and what keeps it tethered, stable, and "settled" are those things that allow the centripetal force of attachment or adhesion, for instance, to be equal and opposite to the desire that seeks to cut loose and follow its own motion, logic, and law. So, modes of attachments to home, nation, ethnos, demos—to the time and history disciplined in these topographical formations present a countervalence to the insurgency of the margins and the underground. We are deluded into believing that our desires and attachments are naturally tropic toward that center rather than that which looks outward, and is ready to break away. The margins that are meant to show us the way to settlement and state, to property in rights and citizenship, look remarkably deformed by constantly having to shrinkwrap the polis to still the natural motion—of decay or liberation—of matter.

In this way, home, as a metaphor for state, nation, institution—of that which domesticates and contains—becomes a mere motif, which seems more ample, powerful, and incontrovertible the more it is extricated from the fugal compositions of political subjects that constantly depart from, counter, extend, and transform it in face of much resistance. As such a motif, it stands for the orientation and the content of political desire wherein it is both the source of society, but also an escape from it. It is what becomes shaped as a frontier, a place behind which to privatize politics. The domestic space becomes the space of desire that is held within, in reserve, supposedly supplying the material, but is actually produced through the work and slavery that exists outside it. It is produced when that labor is tamed, but is never able to give a home to those who labor in it.

It does turn out, then, that the woman who ultimately is seen to be wrapped within the *chadar aur char divari*[33] is a historical consequence, not precedent, of the home produced as the space which would allow different kinds of exploitation to happen inside and outside it. In both Atlantic slavery and British colonialism, the home becomes a project in symbiotic relation to war and slavery. It also accommodates the desire that can then desert other struggles to seek consummation with the state or other institutions whose cruelty and wars promise will keep the home "safe." From colonialism to the contemporary global postcolony, the illegality and "anti-humanism" of certain rituals, traditions, practices, professions, seen as "immoral" or "barbaric"—and threatening to the "family values" embroidered in the "fragile social fabric" that needs our love and care—produces capitalist afflictions of domestication, dependence, and disposability. These afflictions never save those they are supposed to be saving. The "chosen ones" are relegated to even further indignities and more savage death sanctioned by the legalized murder by the "secular" colonial (and postcolonial) capitalist state.

So we get the discourse of "way of life," and of the privatization of bodies and sexuality, rights to which invoke the state and other institutions to act in their behalf. Domestication is deemed security, and love equated with "gentler" emotions that allow the state to be cruel on our behalf—either protecting "white women" from "black rapists," or "Americans" from "Muslims." In this functionalization of love, and instrumentalization of our ability to locate, express, and understand it, a relation of intimacy with the state begins to stand in for the love. Consequently, whatever stands outside of these transactions of "love" is deemed to be marginal, pent up with the desire to be taken in and owned by the state. While we are framed by this history of misappropriations, the misprision of these margins stands to be corrected by understanding the desire that does not follow the scripts written for it, and the attachments that warp the margins because of the weight and impact of the existences it embraces and holds.

With the motif of home ensconced within many different compositions of politics, departures from colonial modernity still carry riffs on it. In this context, the idea of the fugue in relation to the marginalized, the homeless, the outsider, the pariah, the refugee, and the fugitive, can highlight both the contrapuntal extensions on this motif of home that depart from it and form new compositions often out of necessity, as well as depathologizing the psychiatric concept of *fugue state* to release some other logics of identity, being, inhabitation, questing. These motions offer a way to think about the homes we see and depart from, of the stillness and ends of politics, willed or unwilled.

Fugue States

While everything was falling, she stood still protecting us with her shawl.
No worries, she said, when a house dies a small flower blooms out of it, you can plant it anywhere and it will grow into a new house.
We thought it was one of those things that my mother invents to make us feel better. But it wasn't!
A flower grew out of the ruins of our house!
She told us: you should surround it with love until we reach our new shelter, otherwise it may die.

Some people hung the flower close to their hearts, some hugged it and some kept it warm in their hands.
But me and my brother, played music to it, the whole way.

I wasn't sure if our music would save the flower, because my brother always mixed up the melody. But it stayed alive.
When we arrived to a safe place, people rushed to plant the flowers. Houses started to grow one on top of another. Forming a tree of houses. A beautiful one.

Our new city loved our music. The houses danced with our melodies as trees would sway in the soft wind. Even the sky would light a star with each stroke on our instruments.
One day we noticed an old man arriving in the city. His flower didn't grow a house, instead, it grew into a music shop. There was a beautiful oud. We instantly fell in love with it.
So we started running to collect metal scraps. We piled them together and waited. Soon we realized that a big pile of them would make only a small coin.
My mother said: sons, be satisfied with what you have. What you see is not what you see. The trees are not trees and the sky is not free.

One day, my brother found a big piece of metal stuck in the ground.
He said: it may be heavy enough to buy the oud.
We pulled it together, each with one arm.

My mother used to say, there are evil metals grow in the ground, if you touched them they would shout at you and kill you.
We thought it was one of those stories that my mother invents to scare us from leaving the house.
But it wasn't.

The evil metal took an arm from each one of us.
But we sat next to each other and played the oud, each with one arm.

Our melodies made the kites fly higher.

—Ahmad Saleh, *Ayny: My Second Eye*[34]

So narrates one of the two brothers in Ahmed Saleh's award-winning short film *Ayny* (*My Second Eye*). From homes that die and turn into flowers that will bloom into homes wherever we stop to plant them—provided they outlast the travel—the story ostensibly set in the settler colonial context of Palestine translates into numerous other contexts in which home is what gets destroyed and also carried with us and nurtured with the promise of an elsewhere—of context, economy, and architecture of desire and inhabitation very different from the one that was demolished. The image of a dead home that lives in a flower is not a wishful consolation for the destruction of homes, speaking to the living substrate that remains even when the house no longer exists. In *Ayny*'s narration of both the flight and the respite, the movement and the stopping that yields refugee camps, the flowers metamorphose into houses that sometimes arrange themselves into a beautiful tree. But, let us not forget the mother's caution that nothing is what it seems.[35]

Saleh invites us to witness the movement of the unheimlich in a way that grasps dispossession and displacement a little differently; the flower emerges not in place of the home (since that will be something else), but out of it, inheriting its essence. And so the flower and the home are genetically connected, different in form, their movement through time producing history as variations on the motif of home departed from and carried within the flower which, if lucky, is ready at its terminus to be part of a new tree, in a new city. And then when those resettlement camps are demolished, either in Shatila or in Calais, the flower is no ordinary remnant or memento; it is what grows anew by force of necessity and will to live. The music that the two brothers play also reminds us of the manner in which the stringed (sic) flowing composition of these motifs nurtures, through its messy, recursive, and lost melodies, the flower that contains home. The flower will grow again, through many variations, into a completely different house, and give a rhythm to the new city. Might this be the fugue of the unrequited, in which home as motif is held, with a resignation to the irretrievability of its lost form, but with some promise nevertheless, perhaps even of an attempt at companionship through the journey? Might this provide an account of a movement that is not only the consequence of colonialism, travels that are caused by the abduction from or destruction of homes, but still try to stay true to their source but not simply to their cause qua origin. They do so by traversing different logics, showing both how the travel that bears the marks of its originary violence remembers and departs from it, holding close, keeping warm, and singing to, an idea of home whose only salvation is in its constant, conscious, awake departure from the colonialist confabulations of the uninvited, or the guests who took our hospitality to mean whatever they wanted to.

The words refugee and fugitive share a root in *fugere*, meaning "to flee," that is present also in the fugue which, both in music and psychiatry, captures some sense of a tethered, burgeoning motion. The movement and stasis of those outside the polis, whether those evacuated from or inimical to it—not the founder, not the national, not the citizen, not the soldier, not the settler—evinces a political imagination, fantasy, and practice. Their movements do not reassure the dominant ideas of home and sovereignty that build towers above graves and ruins, and inform maps of the world as drawn today. These variations on the theme of home—from the fugitive slave, to the homeless refugee, to the pariah, to the partisan, to the freedom fighter and more—run counter to the colonial heimlich maneuver. Unifying these outsider subjects in their fugue states is their remarkably "abnormal" disinterest in and disregard of that particular trap of monopoly, violence, and legitimacy that keeps so many in thrall of the modern nation-state, which has colonized so many of our imaginations of institutions that can be our home. It is really important to show how dangerous that triangulation of legitimacy, monopoly, and violence is, and how it infects our current relation to each of these words. The political imagination of homes that disaffirm these relations cannot come from within those that stand affirmed or protected by the triangular structure that assumes and sits atop someone who has been culled, evacuated, settled, and finished in order to produce the limits and bounds (sic) that make each of these possible, and none of them possible without the other.

This is a crucial lesson for all those who find themselves caught within that other maneuver to match the colonial odyssey's: that violence and voice within a liberal state rely on the monopoly produced by expunging or eliminating that which is deemed illegitimate. Even if that wasn't what Weber intended. His description, in "Politics as a Vocation,"[36] is actually remarkably honest about its terms, covering up the real relations of interdependence, intimacy, and mutuality that exist between them to produce monopoly, legitimacy, and violence as the autonomous categories they appear to be. Their apparent autonomy obscures nothing less than a history of necropolitics, and nothing more than the habitual production of a crisis as an impetus to a return to order. In the context of this economy, violence and its opposites are fundamentally different from what precedes and exceeds the modern state form. From the state form ensues a longing for institutions that understand *both* how the monopoly, the legitimacy, and the violence need each other, and how these desires and attachments must be reconfigured to maintain an equilibrium. These triangular relations can be interrupted; by force of that which remains unsettled, or survives its murder, or dabbles in abundance that violates the belief in scarcity, or chooses death over life promised instead of love, or picks precarious life over the betrayals of a home that could never protect, or asks for a world that is not yet here. In any such interruption, each term stands to change its meaning and signal a shift in political desire. This shift inaugurates "crisis" for those on the inside, and an impetus to those whose deluded fragilities will have them restoring order in the ways they know. They begin, obviously, by returning us, against our wishes, to these terms and their old relations as the only befitting home within which any meaning, and politics, can be made.

The home-turned-flower in *Ayny* resembles the unrequited in its very structure, just because there is nothing unloved or unloving about those who are forced out of their homes. In the case of the unrequited as a figure of politics, the loves and labors that are exploited, abused, appropriated, stolen, humiliated by their ill-fitting recipients, do not cease to be because their form was trampled over or went unrecognized. While unrecognized hurt can grind down the hurt subject, it can still materialize in other forms and other spaces. The acknowledgment of unrequitedness can produce a politics of a different order and be otherwise (tropic toward different institutions of cohabitation and existence) than the reliance or desire of recognition or reciprocation of the initial love itself (rather than even the reassurance that there will be home for the love). The bloom in *Ayny*, in that sense, is not just the love emptied out of the destroyed home; its unrequitedness is a unique formation of that love. And, when planted, it will not simply produce what a love unmarked by its history of abrogations, did or could. It will produce something else. For better and for worse.

Such is the case of the Man with the Tree in Amir Nizar Zuabi's *I Am Yusuf and This is My Brother*.[37] The play, set in 1948 in one of the Palestinian villages destroyed in the Nakba, gives us a view on why people leave, what it means to decide to leave, and what mutually affirming relation might there be between love and haunting, war and exits, fights and flights. Two brothers, Ali and Yusuf, run into a man who is going north travelling with an enormous tree on his back. We find out that the Man, "planted this tree seven years ago. For four years it was too young to bear fruit. A cold winter came, it almost died and took a full year to recover. Then: fruit." He adds:

> What happens to me will happen to it. That became clear as I walked out of my house, so I went back in and dug it up. [. . .]
> I left my house, I left my land, I left my Hills, I left my well in the Ibn Amer valley. Where am I going? I've no idea. I'm fifty and I've never once left my Valley. Why would I? But now, now I'm going to the planes and the dust, I won't leave my tree. I won't become a small ring in a big trunk.

With his fate connected to the tree's, he tells Ali and Yusuf that if he makes it, he will "replant it. It'll recover and bear fruit." "When it's time to go home, I'll pull it up and plant it back where it belongs."[38]

The tree carries both the love and the unrequitedness. With just the forceful clarity with which he tended to the tree, the Man pronounces a relation of his love to someone else's undeserved requitals rather than to some pitiful or polite narrative of being unloved by those (the colonizers or the humanitarians) who stand to be needlessly dignified by the power of the declamation that makes our love beside the point, and us only the successful or failed objects of someone's love. The difference between these narratives matters, even if just for the sake of one's own honor. The unrequitedness is a relation of belief and love that sustains—whereas the frame of unlovedness frustrates, marginalizes, often erases—all those other relations: to the trees we tended, to the memory of what's to come, to the repulsive loves asking to be defied, that sprout through a love held by and in us. The Man with the Tree says,

> To imagine them under its shade. I don't want to . . . Eating chicken, drinking wine! A young couple in love. God, it's beautiful . . . His blond hair and pale skin, her big breast and perfect white smile under my tree, kissing.
> And me in a tent in a place I never heard of . . .
> His hand on her back, lifting her into the air, laughing . . . They grow old, she'll make jam for my fruit, he comes home from work, lies under my tree, reads the paper . . .

In its shade a birthday party for their eldest son. He'll hang a swing on the branch—it's a good branch, it's a good tree!
Their son is sixteen, he carves his initials in the bark and a heart and a girl's name . . .
That would have made the tree happy, I know.
And slowly my tree forgets me, the smell of my breath, the sound of my tongue . . .
I'm a vague memory, that's all, in the rings at the heart of the trunk . . .
That's too much . . . I won't be a thin ring . . .[39]

NOTES

1. E. M. Forster, *A Room with a View* (Penguin Books, 2011); James Ivory, *A Room with a View* (Criterion Collection (Direct), 2015).
2. Edward Morgan Forster, *Where Angels Fear to Tread* (Vintage Books, 1959).
3. Gaston Bachelard, M. Jolas, and John R. Stilgoe, *The Poetics of Space: The Classic Look at How We Experience Intimate Places* (Beacon Press, 1994). p. 8.
4. Hortense J. Spillers, "Mama's Baby, Papa's Maybe: An American Grammar Book," *Diacritics* 17, no. 2 (1987): 65–81, https://doi.org/10.2307/464747. p. 76-77.
5. E.M. Forster, *A Passage to India* (Penguin Classics, 2005).
6. E. M. Forster, *Howards End* (Mineola, N.Y: Dover Publications, 2002).
7. Forster, *A Passage to India*. p. 234.
8. Bringing into conversation "The Souls of White Folk" and "The Coming of John." W. E. B. Du Bois, *Darkwater: Voices from Within the Veil* (Mineola, N.Y: Dover Publications, 1999); Du Bois, *The Souls of Black Folk*.
9. Forster, *A Passage to India*. p. 362
10. David Adams, *Colonial Odysseys: Empire and Epic in the Modernist Novel* (Cornell University Press, 2003).
11. Georg Lukacs, *The Theory of the Novel*, 1st edition (Cambridge, Mass.: The MIT Press, 1974).
12. The idea of secular time has everything to do with the spatialization of time; the world construed as a whole, given to us, which only god can supposedly know, leaving us to spatialize time for the illusion that the world will be known to us in bits progressively, nevertheless completely and always in relation to a totality. Secular time displaces this on to human beings, and the form this takes is "worldliness." Travel is the mode of accessing this worldliness, and thus the core of the modern secular project, invested in the demarcation of space and spaces and the fixing of their ontic character.
13. Lukacs, *The Theory of the Novel*. p. 61.
14. Forster, *A Passage to India*. p. 150.
15. E. M. Forster, *The Hill of Devi* (San Diego: Harvest Books, 1971). p. 288–89.
16. See further my discussion of the end of *Passage* in Chapter 9.
17. Frantz Fanon, Jean-Paul Sartre, and Homi K. Bhabha, *The Wretched of the Earth*, trans. Richard Philcox, Reprint edition (New York: Grove Press, 2005). p. 8.
18. See Sabyasachi Bhattacharya, *Mahatma and the Poet: Letters and Debates Between Gandhi and Tagore 1915–1941* (National Book Trust, 1997); Saranindranath Tagore, "Tagore's Conception of Cosmopolitanism: A Reconstruction," *University of Toronto Quarterly* 77, no. 4 (December 31, 2008): 1070–84, https://doi.org/10.1353/utq.0.0305; Edward W. Said, *Orientalism*, 1st Vintage Books edition (New York: Vintage, 1979).
19. Rabindranath Tagore, *The Home and the World* (Penguin Classics, 2005).
20. Rabindranath Tagore, *Chokher Bali*, trans. Sukhendu Ray (New Delhi: Rupa Publications, 2005); Rituparno Ghosh, *Chokher Bali*, 2003.
21. Sigmund Freud and Hugh Haughton, *The Uncanny*. Translated by David McLintock (New York: Penguin Classics, 2003).

22. Karl Marx and Fredrick Engels, "Estranged labor," in *The Economic and Philosophic Manuscripts of 1844 and the Communist Manifesto*, trans. Martin Milligan, 1st edition (Amherst, N.Y: Prometheus Books, 1988), 69–84.
23. Freud and Haughton, *The Uncanny*. p. 148.
24. Freud and Haughton. p. 148.
25. Hannah Arendt, *Rahel Varnhagen: The Life of a Jewess* (The Johns Hopkins University Press, 2000). p. 248.
26. Arendt, *Rahel Varnhagen*.
27. Arendt. p. 85.
28. Arendt. 1956 Preface. p. 83.
29. Arendt. p. 251.
30. Hannah Arendt, *Love and Saint Augustine*, ed. Joanna Vecchiarelli Scott and Judith Chelius Stark, 1st edition (Chicago: University Of Chicago Press, 1998). p. 67.
31. Out come the contradictions that expose the self-defeating nature of the untwining of space and time (as we know them), so common to the redemptive efforts of the postmodern historian and geographer who both set out to fix things without quite interrogating their own genetics of spatialized time. Thus do we need to historicize the dimensions and concepts of political time and space, and not settle for a predetermined phenomenology that flattens human experience into some discernible contours—just an old desire of philosophy to be science. Certainly, I cannot find a way to teach or think politics without turning to the place and space in which things happen and we happen, but neither can I find a way to simply regard the spaces we trying to be at home in as being just subservient to our actions and desires, and this is not because the mixed messages are all mine!
32. Joshua M. Price, "The Apotheosis of Home and the Maintenance of Spaces of Violence," *Hypatia* 17, no. 4 (2002): 39–70.
33. "The shawl and four walls"—a slogan for 1980s campaigns in Pakistan for enforcement of Shariah Law pertaining to women.
34. Ahmad Saleh, *Ayny: My Second Eye*. 2016. I am extremely grateful for a chance to see this film at the Boston Palestine Film Festival in 2017, and to Saleh's immense generosity in sharing his film with me and trusting me to think with it—and providing the full script for the section epigraph.
35. This image is also reminiscent of the verticality of power that Eyal Weizman speaks of, as he discusses his Forensic Architecture in a short film *The Architecture of Violence* that also tells us of the three legal humanitarian war minutes between a warning missile and the one that demolishes a building that IDF gives residents in the occupied territories to leave their homes and find shelter under shawls "while everything [...] fall[...s]," and *Ayny* begins. See Al Jazeera English, *Rebel Architecture - The Architecture of Violence*, accessed December 3, 2017, https://www.youtube.com/watch?v=ybwJaCeeA9o. See also Eyal Weizman, *Forensic Architecture: Violence at the Threshold of Detectability*, 1st edition (Brooklyn: Zone Books, 2017).
36. Max Weber, *The Vocation Lectures*, ed. David Owen and Tracy B. Strong, trans. Rodney Livingstone (Indianapolis: Hackett Publishing Company, Inc., 2004).
37. Amir Nizar Zuabi, *I Am Yusuf and This Is My Brother* (London: Methuen Drama, 2011).
38. Zuabi. p. 44-45.
39. Zuabi. p. 45.

Chapter Four

Anticolonial Maps for Lost Lovers

Of home become dream become home, a special curse of the homeland, Intizar Husain writes,

> I do believe that things reveal their true self only in dreams. Walls and niches, streets and alleys, plants and trees, the earth and the sky—it is only after we stop seeing them with our eyes that we truly begin to see them when they start appearing in our dreams and calling out to us. First in the first dream, then in the second, the third and so on. It is after so many dreams that my town has come fully alive before my eyes and I am now able to see it fully,[1]

As the writer revisits a novel fifty years after he first wrote it, the same fifty years since the independence and partition of India, he reaches for a story that somehow got away, seeking the person who used to frequent Qayyuma's shop that he wrote about. The compulsion to correct and rewrite the story is fueled by the fact that his dreams have given him more information since then, but have not brought him any closer to that missing person. Despite so many new details and intimacies that have been bred in fifty years of dreams since leaving a town that fell in the wrong country, all the writer has confirmed is that person's elusive appearance, much like the spires atop the receding grounds of Karbala which he can also never quite arrive at. (Not the real Karbala, of course, but one that recalls it, and within the boundaries of which the story of Karbala gets a new life and sensibility year after year.) The writer, also the narrator of the story excerpted above, has perfected the maps and moments, the dizzying crisscross of alleys and people, streets plied by those who would soon not be able to live together anymore. One wonders if maps for lost lovers exist only in dreams.[2] And between the memory of that departure—that one last view of the "sooty, moss-ridden, half-broken parapet of our old house"[3] —and his dreams of the fifty years since having left it, dwell all these dreams that give him bounties in his retreat from the land of the awake, and then always stop just before he can reach those things about which he wishes to write but cannot. The final gift is withheld, and deferred to another sleep cycle. He worries about where he is, if he is anywhere at all, but is grateful for what the dreams do, encircling time, circles of time themselves, that allow for a different view of thinking about who is at the center, if the circle that begins wherever it feels like every night, if the constant motion between streets is centripetal or centrifugal. Some of us have eyes that cannot stop spinning even in daytime. Time continues to be, unfolding in sleeping and waking dreams, the dreams while asleep, the tales to make it through the day, the details that one hopes will not be missed lest they fall through the crevice of time.

Where the time in a body—sensuousness—shifts and asks to be shifted and dis-placed, and seeks new bodies to become other and even new, it often courts intimacies that would not be available on the planes, surfaces, and the flat loveless scapes, and seeks a way out of the ontologies we find ourselves locked within. Often even our own ontic story is at stake—where we seek becoming human to oneself in the interaction with a different time and space, by leaving those spaces where we have been placed, identified, and affixed (think, for instance, the "rehumanizing" as Du Bois or Baldwin leave America, or even Forster when he travels to India, North Africa, and Italy, though different kinds of harvests indeed!). Who finds this home and where is also very telling of what kind of love they set out with. (And, I do not count every luxurious self-imposed exile that thrives among globalization's promised mobilities among these other journeys.) If colonialism and slavery involved bringing entire peoples into history, it also brought them into a configuration of love. The particular modalities of love globalized, popularized, and pathologized in the nineteenth century in the heyday of cultural and economic imperialism were perhaps the impetus behind these spatio-temporal escapes and mobilizations. Or, perhaps, the proliferation of these modalities is made possible by the escapes, fugitivities, and mobilizations, though I would like to think that the imperative to bring the colonized into a certain space of submission and action proceeds much more missionarily as an obliteration and rewriting of their modes of loving.

Hussain's account of waking up just before reaching Karbala or seeing up-close the figure at the shop that would allow him to rewrite his first novel recalls Said's insistence on wakefulness and sleeplessness which has always sounded a little counter-intuitive to me. He writes,

> Sleeplessness for me is a cherished state to be desired at almost any cost; there is nothing for me as invigorating as immediately shedding the shadowy half-consciousness of a night's loss, than the early morning, reacquiring myself with or resuming what I might have lost completely a few hours earlier. I

occasionally experience myself as a cluster of flowing currents. I prefer this to the idea of a solid self, the identity to which so many attach so much significance. These currents, like the themes of one's life, flow along during the waking hours, and at their best, they require no reconciling, no harmonizing. They are "off" and may be out of place, but at least they are always in motion, in time, in place, in the form of all kinds of strange combinations moving about, not necessarily forward, sometimes against each other, contrapuntally yet without one central theme. A form of freedom, I'd like to think, even if I am far from being totally convinced that it is. That skepticism too is one of the themes I particularly want to hold on to. With so many dissonances in my life I have learned actually to prefer being not quite right and out of place.[4]

Said associates a state of sleeplessness with an out-of-placeness and not-quite-rightness that he suspects is more of a freedom over and above a solid self since it keeps things in motion in time; for Hussain, sleep is the occasion to dream and to be in Roopnagar, remarkably emplaced even if constantly in motion through streets trying to get somewhere, but outside of time, the motion brought to rest by waking. For both Said and Hussain, something is at stake that connects being to being in and out of place. Hussain further illuminates why being in the time of the dreamscape is necessary even for a sense of being elsewhere in wakefulness, and he seems to have made his own peace with not being emplaced anywhere but the dream, something Said has not, thus the insistence on the virtues of sleeplessness. (If this is something that reflects the disparity in the poetics of a storyteller and a philosopher, so be it.) The kind of watchfulness, which Said values, required to be alive to the presence and passing of others, can often bring about another kind of wakeful dream state, perhaps closer to Hussain's. Said's sleeplessness allows for the commingling of dream and reality in a different way, but perhaps in the service of something other than getting to know closely what one lost. As it becomes decreasingly possible for some of us to be in the same room with those who shroud their anxieties with their virile calls to order, and refuse any conversation about what we are doing there, in whose name, and summoning which presences, Hussain's and Said's seemingly opposed "methods" both seem furthest from the task of diagnosis in a cold philosophical relation to history and critique, and surprisingly close to each other in their regard of the unrequited. The demarcation of sleep from dream relates to those who can never be found again but are calling on us; the removal of the boundary between sleep and dream accounts for those who can always be lost again. Both are forms of unrequitedness to which this chapter is dedicated.

In this chapter, I develop my earlier claim that love is that which makes present, even and especially in conditions of absence. The word present brings together the temporal and the proximal, both involving a sensory commitment to the production of a certain kind of givenness, and I intend something very different from the work of memory or memorializing. Not a recollection of something that was, but a commitment to imagining it as it could or would be if still around. In this mode of aesthetic production, love plays an important role in organizing the work of the senses within and outside the body, setting the imperatives to temporality and to presence. The figuration of time, and that which is present and given to the available sensuous configurations of time and space, in turn compels love in certain forms. These come braided together, especially when regimes of life and death, and forms of inclusion and exclusion in society, shape relations to time, hope, and the future.

I turn next to discuss the triangular relations between love, time, and sense, drawing out the experience of time in love as well as the many inflections of presence that are enabled in it. This discussion of time and sense makes its way through an examination of tense and presence, to the relation between unrequitedness and out-of-joint time. Critiquing the presumptive narrative of irreconcilability, I characterize the longing that connects the unrequited to the time out-of-joint, in a way that both parses and challenges the aesthetic accumulations—in and of knowledge, presence, identity, fidelity, political desire, violence, etc.—on which repressive sovereign orders in and beyond colonialism are built. In soft tones under all of this is a gentle narrative of the mutuality, yet irreducibility to each other, of cultural and aesthetic production, that might allow us a different angle on the practice of encountering and reading literary and filmic texts. A grasp on our implication in the topography of their meaning, and in the cartography of making meaning with them, might help us puncture, counter, and supplant colonial and liberal settlements of the same.

THE LOVE LIFE OF TIME AND SENSE

> *L'amour c'est l'espace et le temps rendus sensibles au coeur* (Love is space and time made perceptible to the heart). —Marcel Proust, *In Search of Lost Time*[5]

> What if space-time, the transcendental aesthetic, and the coherence/sovereignty it affords/imposes, is an effect rather than a condition of experience? —Fred Moten, *Notes on Passage (The New International of Sovereign Feelings)*[6]

> Human sensuousness is therefore embodied time. —Karl Marx, *The Difference Between the Democritean and the Epicurean Philosophy of Nature*[7]

Exceptions to homogenized times and spaces, which constitute and populate the margins as a relation of love, might hold the key to saving us yet from the embarrassment and, worse, fascism of the kinds of idealist political philosophy that keeps insisting on a kind of proximity and a kind of understanding that disappears when actually asked for an account of itself, and in whose name it is performed. The living labor of these subjects is what holds any promise of a response to the regimes of codified proximity, intimacy, sentimentality, and fervor. If we continue to see the intersecting dimensions of time and space act in submission to the ideology of time and space in colonial and capitalist modernity, as if they had no motion or politics of their own, we would be no closer to disturbing the liberal politics that, with one hand, cloyingly puts its preferred love and sentimentality on superfluous display and, with the other, keeps drawing boundaries and lines to engineer cold withholdings wherever it pleases.

Observing how institutional and political topographies shift within and across societies and histories—such as when boundaries are drawn or removed, when diversity plans get written and followed, when cities and countries disappear while their citizens remain—barely scratches the surface of the existential, temporal, and affective dis/locations of subjects within and from the spaces they inhabit. Thus, when liberalism identifies and includes in the ways it knows to, when neighborhoods get gentrified, or ruins papered over, the changing topography does not say much about the time of those presumed reconciliations, the intimacies desired by the outsider, or the detritus from the dialectic busy thinking and making revolution. When spaces keep purging us or spitting us out, or if our lives and stories spill over outside of the spaces they are supposed to be kept within, time becomes the place to be. Time spent to make sense of our lives far exceeds in form and content the quanta of time that result from an abstraction of the body's capacity to expend (of) itself (such as in Marx's discussion of labor time in capitalism). Here, one rolls out time like a carpet all the time, makes it spacious enough to contain oneself, and to give a chance to the life that might not be accommodated by the spatial, topographic, and topological dimensions. The corporeal poiesis of such subjects in time is ongoing and never done, quite like love. But it is not merely a playful and nimble becoming, even when it is tropic toward the beautiful and the beloved; it knows heavy limbs that just cannot be fast enough, energized by spurts of love, but violating all rules of timeliness and telic gratification. The dominant order shows up once in a while to take a freeze-frame of these becomings to fuel the extortionist enterprise of liberal identity politics that keeps all acknowledgments and consummations of political desire squarely on the terms of those whose own frozen identities—that will be defended until everyone else dies—become the benchmark of what it means to be human and to be at home in the world.

As liberalism requites itself, the organizing and policing of the topography of life through disciplinary power, multiculturalism, and the distribution of rights to consume and be recognized, actually coopts and placates. It precludes any kind of disruption or even adoption of (new) ontological premises, living under the sign of homogeneous space-times and thus creating a totality premised on (the fantasy and practicality of) everyone having a place and being in it. But these located harmonizations, the insistence on knowing and the premium on desiring to know where one is in the order of things, from the perspective of those in power, do exhale their disruptions and dissensus elsewhere. The time that seeks new bodies and new sensuousness is the repose of these disruptions. This process is an aesthetic one: making present, and releasing oneself from presence at the same time, knowing well that the presence will and can never be complete and just. Both the aesthetic task of making appear what had been there, and the process of subjectification as an impression on the scene via a sensuous experience that evades the (grasp of the) liberal order, foreground issues of temporality in the domain of political aesthetics, poetics, and ethics.

The political character of human existence is, thus, not merely an idealist metaphysical given (even and especially when we believe it to be "nature"), but something that is claimed, shaped, admitted, thrust, and rejected, in our sensuousness. These processes are not perceptible to the political order that arbitrarily determines, most importantly and literally, where politics begins and ends. This determination involves two elements: an adjudication of times to be deemed past, present, and future, then contained and arranged to produce history as an object of attachment once it is framed as the story of the consummation of certain desires; and, a judgment that sets the terms for our presence and absence in this political sensorium. The degree to which our senses contest the ordering of the times of our existence as persons and peoples, and the imposed modes of our presence and absence (especially that of our suffering and love), regardless of the ends they script for us—such as the demand that we be present to our own disappearance—is the degree to which we are political. And, still, mounting this contestation and a claim to the political is not equally a need for everyone (just as the need to assert one's humanity, or one's "right" to be human, is not universal, or equally a need across spaces and times).

Sensing Time in Love

Following Julia Kristeva into Marcel Proust's invocation of love as that which makes space and time perceptible to the heart, it could be said that different loves, and different modes of loving, make different spaces and different times perceptible to the heart, and also that they make space and time differently perceptible to the heart.[8] The reverse is conceivable too: different experiences of and approaches to time and space nourish loves various in form and content. Just as relations of love impact the experience of time, the reimagining and reconstructing of the experience and the nature of time, and our selves in it, has the promise of effecting some change in the ways bodies relate to each other. Changes across different times in history corroborate variations in the instituted and embodied temporalities internal to the lives and spaces that were allowed to be and those that were made extinct. Thus the story of where time lives in forms of life and of how life happens in different times is no less important than the (hi)story of how lives are lived over and across time in the stories we are taught and asked to tell.

In attempts to convey a sense of time bound by love—not quite past, gesturally present, not-even-gesturally future—linguistic notions of aspect and tense come up, indexing the texture of time as well as its location (embodied, or spatialized, or neither). And, where relevance by way of continuity (and not consequence) is suggested (a la the perfect tense), it proffers a kind of presence without having to insist that any of it is past. Interestingly, love is not what is put together or made present—it is what occasions the present and presence. The "aspect"—the texture of time—is more important than the tense (its spatialized parsings), but it is also crucial to acknowledge that location can be signalled via the body moving through time as History—time as locus of body—or as the body in love being a locus for time that also gets displaced and de-placed, un-placed, and replaced, for new relations to time and space, and new sensuous containments, to emerge. Time, in love, is not to be collected, saved, and consumed but something to be freed, released, and parted with. We follow it wherever it takes us, the binds of the body undone to be put together over again, to make different perceptions of time, space, beauty, happiness, sorrow, possible. The gesture to solidarity across dissonant temporalities, to the disappeared and the present, to the requited and the unrequited at once, is quiet and undramatic. A longing for the beloved, without the promise of an end, or an impulse to part with the loneliness, enables the continuing courtship and sharing of the world with others at home in another's love.

Prying open the phrase "in your love" to look at love as a space, where time passes differently for those who love, is almost cliché. But on the arrangement of time and space in this interior, further thoughts can be offered. The character of love as a space is such that it is shaped and rendered by what happens to time in that experience, and this space becomes even more interesting if we see voids, portals, hideouts, caves, hills, oceans, and crevices being bored and carved into time itself. Rather than a substance that fills up a hollow cavity and reacts to spatial limits, time can be seen to be more like sound and smell which set bounds of spaces at the limits of their force and perceptibility. This character of time allows us to think beyond political subjectivity as requital of a courtship of the evolutionary unfolding of revelation, access, and immediacy. The making and constituting, not to mention recognition, of subjects as subjects in this scheme asks for a certain submission to temporality as History and as provider of epistemic comfort, to time as, in the words of Lee Edelman "the medium of [the] advent" of meaning, "defer[ring] while affirming its constant approach." (It's a fragile meaning, one might say, if it falls apart at the mere encounter with "the queer who figures its refusal.")[9] In contrast, a sense of expanded sensuality, layered spaces, and overlapping times allows for mediations and connectivities in and of space as well as time, deeming time an actor and agent in its own right, not mere context or backdrop. The materiality and intension of this expanded and elusive character draws on the imaginations, cognitions, experiences, and sensations of those who traverse entire worlds at the same time, those worlds often irregular, shifting, simultaneous, asymptotic. Different inflections of presence come up here, each differently related to the now, to the given, to the available, and to the sensible—each also with very little regard to the consequentiality of the present or its seeming readiness to submit to the past and the future. Not least of this is the second-person possessive (in your love) which cites the lover's presence in that love without needing an "I," as the perfect act (in an Aristotelian sense) of invoking the beloved without implicating a "you" in anything besides a love that is "yours."

At the same time, this does not mean there is no consciousness of time spent, but that is just what it is: texture, element, inextensive yet material, not History—a yielding of sensuousness, a release, a commission, a submission, a pledge, by the senses—necessary to the illusion and the artifice of love and the beloved. It might help to remember here Marx's early definition of sensuousness as embodied time; time could be construed as the constitutive element of sensuousness, as the senses without a body, extended into and reposed in the body's ability to make, feel, produce, compose, love, remember, in this case, the beloved itself. In this artifice of a presence, time also leaves the body as it has known it, and the act of embodiment that follows is a coming together of the senses and time anew, a displacement that de-places and configures time and space again and again in this love. Thus, I have never quite understood how love is so easily equated with comfort, at-homeness, or homecoming, if that is not contradictory to the onto-epistemic recasting—the displacement and de-placement that constitutes and reconstitutes our very relations to space, place, and time—and their relations to each other—that is part of being in *your* love.

Love and the Tenses of Presence

Love is a force that does not just instrumentalize—but constitutes and is constituted by—presence and absence along the multiple spatiotemporal axes of the personal and the political, the interior and the exterior, of lives within and beyond dominant structures. It thus plays a role in interrupting the homogeneous time and space of a liberal capitalist politics and metaphysics, already brought up in Chapter 2's discussion of the margins. Our experience of time and space can be seen as shaped by what our love—in the spaces we occupy or are kept from occupying—is able to produce and not produce, and also by which times nourish our ability to remain in the presence of the failure of our loves (and hence in love itself). The staying-in-love that is, ironically, sponsored by unrequitedness, weaves together the out-of-jointnesses—understood as the impasse of irreconcilability or unfulfilled longing—to give us a version of love as an act complete without consummation in any conventional sense, stretching the unrequited to span unreturned, ill-fated, prevented love. Binding these together are the margins of privileged spaces and times, as the ports of departure and arrival of love; not only the marginal times and spaces in which love happens to dwell, but also those that love makes present and necessary.

I am thinking of the kinds of spaces of shared temporalities, the dreams, memory, and spectralities, in which we are able to be with each other and with non-being, where even Benjamin's constellation is a far cry from the stardust some of us are left collecting and relishing in. Resonant with Hussain's agentic dreamscapes, and Said's vigilant confusions, Tim Edensor's dissident planes, perspectives, and textures of industrial ruins can carry over into thinking about love and time, as he seeks to problematize social memory against the ruling ideas of concrete memorials which never actually allow us to confront absence so we can make appear, in any meaningful way, "disappeared potentialities."[10] Minimally, meaning involves an embrace of the accidental, contingent, and distant, but not merely in the name of imposed possessive, colonialist, administrated asynchrony that keeps the epistemic demands intact (whether in romanticism, postmodernism, or fascism).

Aesthetics making appear what had been there thus bears an uncanny resemblance to the tasks of love. And where this is in or out of sync with making oneself appear, "impress[ing] oneself on the scene, in order to become a subject,"[11] we can appreciate the way in which aesthetics and political subjectification might converge and where temporalities of impressing oneself and constituting another presence (other to oneself, and other to the experience of the now) might invoke interdependent but not identical poetics and ethics. These overlaps and residues might point us to the kinds of becoming necessitated by kinds of love, and to the subjects that "appear," and on imagined or actual scenes and scapes.

The Time of the Unrequited

Drawing out some of the determinations between time, sense, and the body as location and dislocation of time and sense, facilitates an instinctive, even inevitable, gesture to the unrequited. Those who always desire to but can never be of a place; those who, laboriously and lovingly, build spaces that might love them back but cannot help becoming the question that can only be answered by some psychopathic final solution; those who are not in the business of making pie-charts of their DNA; those who never claim to pass as someone they desire (to be) or hate less than they do themselves; those who are still never claimed by a people as their own; those who got included but were never allowed to forget who included them and on what terms; those who feel most at home when at their most animal and least human, like Marx said about the worker. In different ways, time resides in these bodies to produce sensible subjects that are misfits in spaces, or the bodies of time cannot bear the burden of the time they are asked to host and which refuses to move, so they convulse and must start over.

Elissa Marder's *Dead Time* conceptualizes the "temporal disorders" (more dis-order than pathology depending on who is reading) that ensue when liberal, colonial, and capitalist modernities command bodies to house them, and subjects to fill spaces.[12] Marder's (rather, Baudelaire's and Flaubert's) are subjects in the metropole who, because of some abjection to their own internal oppressions, are still never completely able to consume, or be consumed by, time. Either way, the issue is consumption, since theirs is the bourgeois, extractive, body in estranged, often obscured, relations of (aesthetic and other) production with the laboring and eroticized body in the colony that even the flâneur will likely miss. But to match these temporal disorders, the unrequited in (the wake of) the colony have bodies that are meant to produce and disappear, to be objects of desire and absent. Distant from problems of consumption and distribution, these bodies in the colony are the producers of time and sense in many forms (many of which we will turn to in Part II in the discussion of necropolitical subjects). The manner of subjection (as subject and subjected) that is desired in the colony accents the intoxicated or addicted, anorexic or bulimic, relations to time which Marder narrates, with a consideration of production and presencing. The body of the colonial subject is one that is effectively displaced, pushed to find a new home, a new body, a placeless place for the time without a body, in the transcendent realms of nationalism, fascism, and all manner of romanticist, ethical, or spiritual idealisms. The body of the worker or the slave is the body whose sensuousness is similarly unhinged and then reappropriated into a narrative of time as productive or redemptive, developmental and telic.

These disorderings of time and sense beg a key question, and then some. Is the ill-fittingness and the tension between the times and spaces of inhabitation an accident or a necessity? Is the discord between the spaces of time inside us and the times of the spaces that hold us, between the presences of time and the times of presence, inevitable? In what ways does lost or unrequited love shovel and chisel its way to disjoin time and temporal experiences of spaces that produces multiple timescapes of our existence? The gesture here is to where the unrequited live and set up homes in a way that does not get reflected at all in liberal and colonial understandings of spatiality and the spatialization of time that enable the queuing (and cuing) of these spaces into History and onto the train tracks of "progress"—as preferred passengers, as cargo to the gas chamber, as fuel for the engines, as cut up breasts in gunny sacks, as traumatized soldiers coming back for revolution, as bodies on the tracks themselves, and sometimes as the gangs that raid these trains.

THE LOVE THAT REMAINS AND TIME OUT OF JOINT: THE UNRECONCILED, OR THE UNREQUITED?

Vishal Bhardwaj's *Haider* rereads, and rewrites, Shakespeare's *Hamlet* in the context of Indian-occupied Kashmir and the Kashmiri freedom struggle. A doctor, Hilal Mir, confesses to his disapproving and distant wife that he is on the "side of life" as he tries to save the life of a militant freedom fighter. The next day, he is handed over to the Indian security forces in a raid masterminded by his brother Khurram, a lawyer and politician, aided by information shared by his own wife, Ghazala, in a fit of passion that seems to be more a betrayal than a conspiracy. The son, Haider, a poet studying in Delhi (sent far away at the first sign of sympathies for the armed freedom struggle), returns to Kashmir to find his father gone, his home burnt to the ground, and his mother living in his father's ancestral home in close quarters with his uncle.

Haider begins searching for his father in various detention and interrogation facilities, some old hotels, some former cinemas. Then appears, in full view of everyone and not just Haider's, Roohdaar (literally, one possessing a spirit or soul), Hilal's companion from prison and one who miraculously escaped death being preserved by the very icy waters of the river in which Hilal's body was dumped after torture and execution. Introducing himself as "the soul of a doctor," Roohdaar stages out the news he gives Haider, punctuated by trust-winning details from Mir's most personal anguish and memories, beginning with the betrayal and the complicity of his mother and uncle, then an account of the execution, to lay the ground and then instructions on how Haider must set right the state of affairs—that curse that has left time out of joint. The bodies that are preserved through death, and time that ossifies in order to live, recall Elizabeth Freeman on queer temporalities, "When Shakespeare's Hamlet says 'the time is out of joint,' he describes time as if its heterogeneity can be felt in the bones, as a kind of skeletal dislocation. In this metaphor, time has, indeed *is*, a body."[13]

Interior Decorators in the Time of Occupation

The waiting period during which Haider looks for his father, is also the "half-widow"[14] period for Ghazala before her union with Khurram is legalized. Away from the personifications of betrayal surrounding him, Haider finds a community in the crowds of families who do not know if their loved ones are alive or dead. While the uncertainty is anathema to those who cannot wait to overlay a new life on to the one past, Haider does not begrudge the wait at all. The difference between his relation to this time, and the time after the gravediggers confirm the unnamed but numbered grave of his father, has nothing to do with an epistemic relief or closure the confirmation of death provides, or with the redirection into revenge it morally endorses (just for the sake of argument). The commingling of betrayal and knowledge throughout the film allows there to be no one who knows all or completely; even the ghost as seeming emissary from outside history bearing history's truth seems fundamentally unreliable. Roohdaar's loyalties are dubious—we do not know whose side he is on—we hear that he is a separatist, and then we hear that he is a Pakistani intelligence agent. But we know that he is interested in Haider's revenge, presumptuous about what that means to Haider. The "meanwhile" of the non-knowledge of disappearance forestalls Hamlet's madness qua indecisiveness as we are often asked to regard it as, in favor of a field of ghosts and presences within which Haider emerges relationally as a political actor, of interest and value to the separatists who can harness his anticipated revenge for their own causes.

The occupation of time is an occupation of space. In assessing the psychic and corporeal costs of the occupation of Palestine, the lines of waiting at checkpoints are primarily not about the partitioning and occupation of space, but of the time, the very being, the life, the presence, the appearance, of those who need to cross over, and often, in a fugue state.[15] For those on the other side, there is no coordinate on any cartography—physical or emotional—that is equal to or opposite to this ontic reality. So, what could reconciliation even mean? Simona Sharoni has written about how this chasm of time at the checkpoint, whether for the guards or for the Palestinians, becomes a strange occasion for the playing of certain kinds of roles of love, affection, and negation—especially reifying patriarchal gender relations among the border guards and indulging politics and mannerisms that would not fit in their lives and ideologies away from the checkpoints—and also for solidarities that this space with its own logic away from other spaces, existing in a time suspended above time, can contain.[16] The absolute depletion and sickness that the checkpoint stands for is of interest to me in how it disables or simplifies the loves on offer at the end of the day. Omar Robert Hamilton's "Refugee Stasis" brilliantly discusses an entire sensorium of neoliberal statelessness built on waiting that at least brings us one rung of some dialectic away from one built on isolation.[17]

> The camp spreads high up the hillside, tents, barbed wire, containers, rubble, trash, people, waiting. Moria. Every day people come and people go, but he stays. Moria. The camp of listening. Every day they read names out and hand

papers back through the metal fence at the center of the camp. But whose names? Whose papers? TZEZHS4XS01082016 has been here so long. Sometimes people pass through within a week. And some, it is true, have been here even longer. If they would just give him a sign, an appointment, a look at a list, anything. If he knew they weren't going to call his name he would walk into the city, he could maybe buy some shoes, he'd spend the day keeping warm inside his tent. But there is no list, no sign, no answers, there is only waiting.[18]

The period of suspended presence in Haider is the period of mourning those who "are" and "are not." *"Hum hain, ke hum nahin?"* (Are we, or are we not?), Haider asks in his riposte to Hamlet,[19] and continues thus, "Do we exist or do we not?/If we do . . . then who are we?/If not . . . then where are we?/ Did we exist at all?" These are the disappeared whose life and death remain unevidenced except in the photos their families carry, or in the extortionist legal practice of people like Khurram who strike deals with forlorn families that end up supplying the Indian government its victims. It is also the period in which, with the love and friendship of Arshia, a character that conjoins Shakespeare's Ophelia and Horatio, Haider finds himself time and again at the site of his burnt home. This is the location where all key departures and unions seem to happen in the film—a site of betrayal that is also a site of knowledge. This betrayal as knowledge enclosed in the uncanny is matched by Roohdaar's recollection of Hilal's memories with his son, songs he would sing, poetry he loved. (Not to mention the friendly ghost of Shakespeare allowing the film to speak through citation what it could not show or tell without.)

The time that follows the knowledge of the murder finds Haider in the throes of grief but also manifesting a kind of political subjectivity whose witnesses are many, as he takes Hamlet's soliloquies to the town square, pushing at the literal and poetic partition of the sensible in more ways than one. He never really follows the script of revenge written by anyone who regards him (and valuable) only as a subject whose actions can be anticipated and judged on the basis of a relation to time, waiting, anticipation, and longing that is infrastructural to the epistemology of colonial and liberal modernity and its matching moral rational subjects in search of the "homes" we discussed in Chapter 3. Haider attempts to displace the logic of revenge with a kind of interim justice which, minimally, entails being present to these presences: allowing them to be by continuing to be.

Haider's analogue of Hamlet's travel into madness is not a journey across a divide of knowledge or reason; if it is a journey at all, it is a transformation into a subject not in linear time across a boundary of appearance or on a map. It is more like an interior redecoration of the space of his love and longing, of his own interiority in tandem with the haunted ruins of his home, and with the collectivities that are coalescing outside in the world. This brings him into presence as other beings and histories heretofore unknown, unrecognized, absent, or unimportant come into their own presence. These contemporaneous presencings—whether or not they originated in each other's name or not, and whether or not they were based in that epistemic parity or exacting experiential commensurability of injury or unlovedness that is often called identity—tempt each other into appearing and relating. These presencings seduce into being a community of confluent lost times within this space of captivity or detention—detention in disappearance unto death itself a kind of détente that allows Roohdaar and Hilal to "meet" even as imaginary dimensions of each other. In this community, these presencings find succor in each other and are given a chance at a relation that might bring about something new. Relations between these presencings in time, like mothers who find themselves in refugee camps after the partition of India bemoaning daughters lost to the depths of wells, and write-in new filiations, even new names for those they want to save often from their *own kind*, fill out a timescape that resembles the fugue brought up at the end of the last chapter that unsettles the colonial home. It shows, for the sake of a politics at stake for me, that unrequitedness organizes the history of accumulated withholdings, betrayals, and stolen and lost loves in a way that produces a world which indexes and cites the oppressor in a different way, to suit *not* the sensuousness that precedes or transcends all loss. That sensuousness is figured in the fragilities of whiteness and the vulnerabilities of the settler, never having lost anything that was not calculated, compensated, and consoled for by an imperialist, liberal, racial, capitalist, juridicality whose favors are limited to, and repeated for, some. In contrast, the unrequited produce a realm of the sensible that constellates presencings that adduce the oppression and hurt in a manner more becoming of a sensuousness marked by and constituted in grief, which has lost, and which does not constantly pin all imagination on a self more whole, more in control, and more in possession. It stays away from such suppositions because it knows what they, along with the entitlements and the favors that follow from them, have done to others and their souls. At the least, this means that the oppressor is not at the helm of a narrative of linear dispossession and displacement that keeps never naming what was lost and left, or what we did with and despite it, ironically circling us back to our victimhoods and identities as curses. The only comeuppance here can be an attainment of perfect victimhood which unwrites and overwrites any other claim to relatedness besides the fantasy of being present at the beginning of time—the first occupants of time itself, if you will—that can only result in a courtship of revenge, return, and redemption to the tune of Odysseus or his fascist friends and descendants.

A Convocation of the Homeless

If all longing for home erupted in nationalism and fascism, then it would be a sad state of affairs indeed. If all desire were sentimental affection and a wishful relation to the past, then we would be in even more trouble. Are there forms of nostalgia to counter Odysseus, or kinds of wishing and desiring, that are bred in (between) those who might inhabit spaces with us but live in different windings and unwindings of time? If homes are what contained these times or placated them, and secret attics hid those with yet more dissonant relations to time barely held together, then their destruction means those times have been released and are homeless. If it is time, then, that escapes and encircles the remains and ruins, then it must be searched for and visited with, to court an appearance to match or counter Roohdaar's. Any reductive understanding of homesickness as a painful (as in hurt *and* hurtful) wish for a home that was left behind fails to capture the plurality of the desired or the attachments that fill up these ruins inside and outside us. Because often there is no past that was home in any way besides the fact that we are no longer there. Except, sometimes, in the sense that what is past, lost, never had, or never desired, comes to sound and look a lot like home in a commingling of sense and tense.

A noteworthy moment in *Haider* happens when the play within the play in ancient ruins also shows that there is a history before the time at which stories are often begun, and betrayals before we are cast as Kashmiri or Muslim or Hindu. These new distensions and joints expose new possibilities of entwined poetic and political subjectifications by shifting which times we answer to, whom we ask for an account, and in whose accounting of themselves we no longer have interest. This is also what allows *Haider*, and its conversation with *Hamlet*, to etch a sample timescape of the politics of unrequitedness.

Unrequitedness is, then, the sum of inherited betrayals; we try to recover what is lost in the presence of that loss, crafting and confronting (in Elia Suleiman's words) "the chronicle of a present absentee,"[20] always still investing in every moment just in case something could shift, some wrong righted, some self redeemed. The narratives of self-protecting boundaries and coping through denial just do not stand a chance next to the sensorium of those taught that love's abundance comes with a responsibility. They do not mark historical time by seeing who we were and who we then became, but by marking who we are by the time that we cannot bear to leave behind, which we perhaps carry with us as flowers in our hands or as a pendants around our necks. Just like *Ayny*, with prayer and memory coming full circle since it the essence of what is lost and, like a *ta'wiz*, the prayers and symbols that might ward off the evil, lest it is not done or still to come!

Longing, Remaining, and the Hospitality of Hauntings

The question of revenge in *Haider* is far from settled—since Haider himself constantly resists his mother casting his desire as revenge. Just as she sat in judgment on Hilal's support of what she sees as the freedom fighters' thirst for revenge, Ghazala proceeds to tell Haider that revenge only begets revenge, never freedom, and that no freedom can set him free until he frees himself from the revenge. In both these misprisions, as well as in the brash inability to read, and disinterest in meaning, that Ghazala's idealist conflation of freedom reveals, Haider's love and longing go unnamed. Obsessively unpacking the event as an overwrought psych(ot)ic break across the line of confirmed betrayal and death only implicates Haider in a declensionist eschatology (the next step in which would "requite" him as a fanatic terrorist). Instead, that divide can be read as marking a shift of the love and longing into something that will never be requited—either because the subject of the love has given himself over to it, or it has irretrievably detached from its irretrievable object (two sides of the same coin that enable the love to stay and someone to stay in it). It is not the hackneyed realization of justice's impossibility that allows Haider to rewrite the law from his own state of exception, or a kind of formulaic psychopathic unleashing of revenge on anyone in his way. Both of these would require a dramatic act of dismissal or abdication of the longing; in my reading, Haider is culpable of neither. Both these options would saddle us with an evolutionary bildungsroman of Haider's politicization away from being a poet, whereas I do not see him suddenly turn into something he was not (either across the period of the film, or from Shakespeare to Bhardwaj). Haider's work as a poet is continuant in his hospitality of hauntings. His desire is for something that is not just waiting to be comprehended, understood, and absorbed into the order of the police (qua Rancière but also the security forces), and he finds in the unfulfilled desires for politics (as a reconfiguration of meaning and sensuousness), democracy, and justice, a home to share with others because he can never be in any other home anymore.

A longing for that which remains absent can only be ascertained if one is attuned to what remains of what we have lost, in our fathers' ghosts, for instance. Time out of joint, time of the remains, the remains of those who have left, the remains of someone else's desire to which we are beholden. Could this be seen as a signal of solidarity, and not just whether we are who they are, or that we want what they want? The latter is an epistemic fantasy that can only be had by those who were never displaced, and who always loved only what they could have (or quickly changed the meanings of having and not having so they could have never have not, only *more*).

Within Haider's fugue, it is his love for Arshia that gives him any stillness of home, but whose entrusting of her villainous father with details of

Haider's murderous desire activated by Roohdaar also betrays him. Arshia's guilt and anger at her father's role in weaponizing that innocent betrayal drives her to take her own life. (More on that in a moment.) It is telling that there is almost no literal refuge for Haider except the flat suspended above the video rental store (run also by versions of Rosencrantz and Guildenstern who will betray him). With the local cinema turned into a torture center, what should not be lost on us is this "interim" role—please recall Hamlet's "the interim is mine / and a man's life's no more than to say 'one'"[21] —of Indian film in this vagrant context across all sorts of grids of sovereign power.

Here, it seems that the ghosts of particular readings of Hamlet lurk in the thematization of revenge, a depoliticizing pathology to match psychoanalytic readings of the play, common to both an extraction of meaning that is possible only if, instead of heeding the implications of Hamlet's insistence on out-of-jointness, we relate to the play in linear time, and reduce its relation to time to historicism at best, as a kind of advent of meaning at hand on which those in power count. Add to that the new trend of seeing Haider's madness as a descent into militancy, even "terrorism," as if its meaning is clear to us. This is also a suffocating closure which, upon close consideration, Haider can defy on his and Hamlet's behalf.[22]

The kind of reading Bhardwaj and Peer signal is one that allows the durations and aspect of longing first as search and then as mourning, first as prayer and then as memory, to be cast together across and beyond different modes of disappearance, in life and in death. We realize that the question of madness in *Hamlet* and *Haider* is fundamentally misread, and betrayed, if we give Hamlet no credit for a relation to time that is not going to be resolved by verifying narratives, reconciling the known with the unknown, or recalibrating the shock of betrayal. But the question of love, for meaning or freedom or those lost, coexists with betrayal as a specific kind of unrequitedness. This shifts the onus from knowledge and behavior to something else that shapes Haider's relation to time. Time's out-of-jointness implicates desire and longing for something other than knowledge, reconciliation, or redemption. In abdicating these objects, the object as cobbled together in the epistemology of colonial modernity is also given up. And that is a good thing; it allows love to exist as an objection.

Often this loss is considered a crisis, with the suggestion that preempting this crisis or returning to order automatically involve (re)attaching the love to nation, state, ethnos, or other extant institutions as love objects. Such thinking remains attached to the need to validate our love by reference to the desires we, supposedly, cannot bear to not have. In reading Haider's relation to time as arriving at a narrative of unrequitedness rather than irreconcilability, at stake is a relationship of continuance, concert, concomitance, confusion, and concatenation, not consequence, concord, consistence, consensus, or congruity. Another kind of accounting of discord and disagreement sprouts alongside the determinative subjectivities and political performances of the moment. For instance, the trendy forced reconciliations of and with free speech as the holder of all promise of co-existence—which see speech as an occasion for us to be or not be beings instead of our beings as the occasion for speech—can then be rejected. Additionally, what can be set aside is the purist, anti-miscegenist, and provincial politics of the irreducible ontologies variety that sanctions against the possibility of making new meaning by condescending to those of us who might want to decide who we want to love and be with, and what the relation between our and others' irreducibly different ontologies ought to be. This is why unrequitedness does not imagine a home to return to, and it also does not interpret being on the "side of life" (in Hilal's words) as being on the side of merely one's own life or the life of one's own. And this is a hard pill to swallow for many who are eager to see love as anti-political, fanatic, and automatically fascist, when they are the ones always insisting that its unrequitedness be displaced and quickly subverted. The trusted saboteur can be the object, in nationalist and fascist fantasy, or the subject, in romanticism, where the lover is the site and container of love rather than the love for the beloved an occasion for the lover to appear. In the latter case, the lover, as pure and exclusive subject, eclipses the love itself as well as the beloved. Those benign traitors act very much like the malignant friends of today who get worried if we do not love in the same way as they do; in fear, their imaginations shrivel while ours go insurgent. The fear of the indeterminate nature of the presences that staying in love might generate drives these and other conversions and infiltrations. Those who cannot love fear those who ask for it. Ironically but not shockingly, the unrequited, and not the loveless, are pathologized.

Lost Love Objects

Love involves imagining and the sensual draw to actuate a presence, and at the same time this kind of production is one that does not automatically entail any reliance on a notion of the future, or with any future productions of this love—and it is important to note that the lack of an anchoring in a redemptive or telic future does not mean a lack of the past in the scape of being, unless one actually thinks of time only as duration. There is also the fact that the lack of future is too frightening to most and, more importantly, use-less—so this love is harnessed into what Edelman terms a "reproductive futurism" as the only solace and place to go for society at large.[23] I take this in a broad sense—in terms of the reproduction and maintenance of current systems of thought and practice, the actual mode of reproduction based in forms of planned and now accidental or unconscious obsolescence, the reproductive uses of sex and inheritance for the reproduction of power in society, the preferred modes of liberal representation with which comes the great conceit of subjects recreating themselves in acts of triumph rather than as tragic repetitions. In such conscription and conversion of love, and the disfiguring (or less cynically, the normativized transmogrification) of its temporalities, lies one of the most potent mechanisms of power and the tragic lack of intimacy and attachment in a society with proliferating linkages, dependencies, networks, and addictions. Is that what Haider/Hamlet long for? Not a shock at what people are capable of, but a lament over what they are incapable of, having invested in the capacities of a humanity that has gone bankrupt or succumbed to planned obsolescence.

In another way, everyone's attempts to save Haider proceed by appropriating his desire, and denying him any authorship—and Haider (also Hamlet) counters this by a mode of authoring that only a poet can manage: like pitching a tent on ruins where you are invited to read, the hospitality of hauntings to which I referred earlier. And no one seems to accept that offer. It is within the order of the police, and the technical state of exception in which the freedom fighter dwells with the disappeared—a point I would like to remember—to see affronts to state sovereignty as *naturally* violence, exposing the complicity of the revenge reading with a kind of secular worship of the state that dramatizes violence only when the poor and the miscounted begin to somewhat will it amid all their unwilled and unwilling ends.

I remain uninterested in the pathology of Haider's loss of hope, and crossing over to some dark side, becoming a separatist, even a militant, because it arbitrarily begins with an at once overconfident and anxious mismatching of love and its object and never owns up to it! His and his father's archives remain quite consistent (and reliable) throughout the film: the poetry, the songs, the memories. While the amplitude and attachments shift when Haider has to handle absence as presence, and presence as absence, his constant fidelity flouts everyone else's recognition and projection. This is where it is not Haider's madness, but the incapacity of those who have proven incapable of withstanding their own attachments and are busy drawing lines between presence and absence, between past and present, between freedom and revenge, and between love and violence, deciding what, where, when, and who love can be.

It is also the case that Hamlet is far from unloved. This throws a wrench in the story of unlovedness when it becomes the trope through which to understand oppression and injustice, to counter unrequitedness as a trope for understanding resistance to oppression and the desire for justice. Haider is just not in the business of having to reconcile absence and presence as if on a ledger or a ray diagram. But he confronts its popular appeal wherever he finds those who are always drawing the lines, maintaining the existing order of the police, and circumscribing their accountability by quickly invalidating any claim on their sensuousness by those who are lost or soon will be lost. Whether or not Haider kills Khurram in the end has everything to do with the fact that the lines everyone else is drawing between the living and the dead are just not his weapons. Haider still manages to avoid the subsumptive collapse of distinctions and remains diametrically opposed to Roohdaar's mystical fantasy of himself as everything evinced in the monologue Roohdaar delivers in captivity when he becomes one with the doctor, the soul to the body:

> *Dariya bhi mein, darakht bhi mein/ Jhelum bhi mein, Chanar bhi mein/ Mein dair hoon, haram bhi hoon/ Shia bhi hoon, Sunni bhi hoon/ Mein hoon Pandit/ Mein tha, mein hoon, aur mein rahoonga /Varna kaun sunai ga yeh sachchi kahaaniyan waqt ko?* (I am the river and the tree. I am the Jhelum and the poplar. I am sacred, I am also forbidden. I am a Shia and a Sunni. I am a Pandit. I always was, I am, and I will always be. Who else will tell these true stories for all of eternity?).[24]

Haider's is hospitality; Roohdaar's is occupation (even if in the name of freedom).

Maybe it is *my* desire to perform a distinterest in sovereignty via my disinterest in the question of violence conventionally posed (i.e., is it good or bad, justified or not), because both sovereignty and violence are propositions non-consensually introjected by the ruling political order. This is enough to compel me as a reader to make room for Haider's own longing and unrequitedness by disentangling them from sovereignty and its pretend impasses that accumulate more time for killing the longer their drama is allowed to continue. It is a desire that, unlike sovereignty, cannot be fulfilled. And that is why it is best if it stays that way. What it must instead be, I don't know. But, for now, being relieved of a presumed attachment is not nothing.

While Haider walks away from a scene of carnage at the graveyard—having forestalled the shootout long enough to spend some time with Arshia's corpse following her suicide—it is Ghazala who, bedecked in a suicide jacket from Roohdar in order to save her son from Khurram, blows herself up and leaves Khurram's body mutilated but not dead. Haider does not stop to grant him the serenity of death either. The oldest and freshest corpses or pieces thereof are women, perfecting the pact of the foundational mutuality between violence, the state, and stilled bodies of women, enclosed either in a home or in a coffin, in a shroud of cloth or palm leaves, left for carrion at the edge of the city, or sunk in the Tigris.

The fine point of murder versus suicide matters only if we fall for the drama of will and consent that casts templates of subjectivity at once prior to the body, outside of history, and within the polis—rather than those whose internal and external marginalizations from the polis always means that their ends are willed by the very history that has needed them to be first and foremost bodies and bodied. Whereas Roohdaar exemplifies the (admittedly beleaguered) sovereign that relies on the bodiedness of others, the woman's is the body over which the sovereign writes and rewrites, affirms and reaffirms, itself. The moment in Roohdar's last conversation with Hilal where he recites his everythingness (in the epigraph to this section) can be recalled here, just for its ambiguous potentialities: of the lover as well as the believer, of the mystic as well as the fascist, of the host as well as the settler. If that recitation (as prayer or memory) gets reified into Roohdaar's fantasy of the sovereign in the final instance of the film, then Haider bears the burden of the unheard, restless, but reverberating, remains of that prayer, not to mention the only one who would mourn Arshia and Ghazala. In the throes of the patriarchy and misogyny that is so committed to the constantly fungible and tentative value of certain bodies conditional on their constant use and function, the betrayals by Ghazala and Arshia have some relation to them being such bodies. Their betrayals of Hilal and Haider, and their own betrayals by men they trusted (even if to another's ultimate detriment), and the subsequent unrequitedness, have no room in this world because they cannot be reconciled any more with the use to which their bodies can be put by the state and patriarchy, especially once they have crossed the boundary of the home into the polis. (After all, how could they not be made to pay for sacrificing their domestication to their love, and being complicit in the destruction of their own homes?) No fugue state—between appearance and disappearance, madness and reason, revenge and freedom, home and ruin, India and Pakistan — is available to them like it is to Hilal and Haider. Their claim to match Roohdar's wishful transcendence of history takes the form of their bodies pushing the boundaries of history and then being expunged or exploded out from it. This is not to glorify Hilal and Haider as some blithe postmodern border-crossers; but depending on which margins they fall into, their queered bodies—queer for being marked by contesting biopolitical regimes of identification, security, law, violence, reason, and perception—move between the poles of sovereign embodiment suggested above, unable to rest in either. The women specifically cannot fugue in the same way Haider can, and that has something to do with the polis' reliance on women's usefulness in producing and mourning the killed and the killable, and not being the ones mourned. I am reminded here of Assia Djebar's discussion of the Sultan Haroun Al-Rachid whose mourning of an anonymous woman found in an olivewood casket at the bottom of the Tigris was easily consoled by the affairs of the state, and only an excuse to strengthen and re-bind the sovereign social contract anew.[25] Haider outliving and mourning Arshia and Ghazala at least allows him to court their presencings and host their hauntings in their death, not build a city on their graves.[26]

CODA: IN THE PRESENCE OF THE BELOVED

The unrequited might get us out of a spatialized, diachronic, and linear understanding of the transactional relations between time and desire, having and losing, prayer and memory, conflict and coexistence, and consensus and dissent. Bringing their internal relations into view, one hopes, might bring them closer to each other. While I am not making a strictly normative or prescriptive argument about this, I am saying that an inevitable result of the temporal antics of colonial modernity is History as an order itself, which castigates as reaction, or covers over, or both, those kinds of flagrant, non-compliant, or recalcitrant times that swirl around in a centrifugal motion to resist the physics of this historical ordering. If the naming of the "problem" of disorderly times is not ceded to the control of the spaces that posit themselves as answers, we might have a chance at treating the pathology of this form of solution-making and problem-solving in which liberal multiculturalism and fascism are both complicit. Or else, we can commit to the reproduction of supremacies in response to supremacies, and victimhoods in response to victimhoods, just because we are still attached to and reacting to an ever-shrinking realm of discourse about experience, desire, and attachment, that has taken for its starting points things that were painstakingly and systematically produced and enforced as norms. Failing to see that which was distorted and left aside, and left unrequited when the last dreams were fulfilled—and that a relation to unfulfilled, ill-fated desires of eras past might give us an idea of how and what to desire in the moment—will find us continuing to prefer to converse with what was gratified and embodied in the time and sense of the oppressor.

So, here's to the unrequited internationalism before nationalism, to an overwritten mode of existing as nations before nations as we know them, to a kind of failed project of counter-modernities that were not nationalist, to women abolitionists before women's suffragists, to class before functionalist sociology, to the color line before liberal identity politics, to culture before anthropology, to Muslims before Islam in the vision of the West, to imaginations and realities of being-with that were at different points in conversation with each other, to that which was frustrated, to that which still speaks to us and wants to hear back. Thus expands the world of the unrequited to include those that were lost, and those that were never found—those that were ill-fated loves even when they were reciprocated. This is a kind of materialist and anticolonial love of the unrequited that I am in, alongside relations that never were realized or materialized, and the pathways between which we are only finding now. Like the dreams of a lost city called Roopnagar. That city with a beautiful visage.

NOTES

1. Intizar Hussain, "Daira" ("The Circle," in *The Death of Sheherzad* (Noida: HarperCollins India, 2014). pp. 1–24.
2. The title of this chapter is owed to Nadeem Aslam's *Maps for Lost Lovers,* the book as well as the writer's other works being formidable companions in thinking, feeling, and writing our way through these times.
3. Hussain, *The Death of Sheherzad.* p. 21.
4. Edward Said, *Out of Place,* New edition edition (Granta Books, 2000). p. 295.
5. Marcel Proust, *The Captive & The Fugitive: In Search of Lost Time, Vol. V,* ed. D. J. Enright, trans. C. K. Scott Moncrieff and Terence Kilmartin, New edition edition (New York: Modern Library, 1999). p. 519.
6. Fred Moten, "Notes on Passage The New International of Sovereign Feelings," *Palimpsest* 3, no. 1 (2014): 51–74. p. 68.
7. Karl Marx, "The Difference Between the Democritean and the Epicurean Philosophy of Nature," Chapter 4. https://www.marxistsfr.org/archive/marx/works/1841/dr-theses/ch07.htm Accessed 26 June 2018.
8. Julia Kristeva, *Time and Sense,* trans. Ross Guberman (New York: Columbia University Press, 1998).
9. Carolyn Dinshaw et al., "Theorizing Queer Temporalities: A Roundtable Discussion," *GLQ: A Journal of Lesbian and Gay Studies* 13, no. 2 (May 14, 2007): 177–95. p. 181.
10. Tim Edensor's *Industrial Ruins* provides an account of the provinces of time and memory in the design of modern urban public space and how they interact with abandonment, dilapidation, and other onslaughts. Edensor writes: "…[T]oo much urban space is impoverished through prescriptions about which social activities may take place, and it is tainted by the homogeneity of aesthetic encodings which endow space with pre-ordained meaning. Idiosyncrasies and contingencies are an affront to such schemes. The intensity of regulation impedes the occurrence of accidents and things which do not fit in. Ultimately, then, there needs to be a radical overhaul of the urban design process so as to allow difference, oddness and incongruous juxtapositions . A host of alternative forms of public space—in which people may play, mingle, linger, and mix with non-humans—are called for, spaces full of objects that are not commodities, spaces whose function is open to interpretation and inarticulate spaces which contain a range of dissident planes, perspectives, and textures." And also:

"As far as ruins are concerned, there is a case for a politics which allows them to remain, to crumble at their own pace, to ultimately form a gap which reveals where something was in contradistinction to spaces of memorialization, perhaps somewhat akin to the remnants of spaces retained as wounds which radiate loss in the architecture of Daniel Libeskind. Such a politics would problematize social memory from the start for it is only through confronting absence, identifying change and acknowledging disappeared potentialities that the rigidities of official forms of commemoration and heritage can be recognized and critiqued. In this fashion, 'the city itself becomes an archival form constituted from the fragments and shards of memory traces' rather than a stage for fixing preferred memories." Tim Edensor, *Industrial Ruins: Space, Aesthetics and Materiality* (Oxford U.K.; New York: Bloomsbury Academic, 2005). p. 172.
11. Todd May, *Political Thought of Jacques Rancière: Creating Equality: Creating Equality* (Edinburgh University Press, 2008). p. 70.
12. Elissa Marder, *Dead Time: Temporal Disorders in the Wake of Modernity,* 1st ed. (Stanford University Press, 2002).
13. Elizabeth Freeman, "Introduction," *GLQ: A Journal of Lesbian and Gay Studies* 13, no. 2 (May 14, 2007): 159–76.
14. See Baba Umar, "The Dilemma of Kashmir's Half-Widows," accessed December 4, 2017, http://www.aljazeera.com/news/asia/2013/09/dilemma-kashmir-half-widows-201392715575877378.html. Also, "The Other Half: For Many Kashmir 'Half-Widows', Remarriage Ruling Means Little | The Indian Express," accessed December 4, 2017, http://indianexpress.com/article/india/india-others/the-other-half/.
15. Please see discussion of this concept in the previous chapter.

16. Simona Sharoni, "Compassionate Resistance: A Personal/Political Journey to Israel/Palestine," *International Feminist Journal of Politics* 8, no. 2 (June 1, 2006): 288–99, https://doi.org/10.1080/14616740600612962. See also Hagar Kotef and Merav Amir, "(En)Gendering Checkpoints: Checkpoint Watch and the Repercussions of Intervention," *Signs* 32, no. 4 (2007): 973–96, https://doi.org/10.1086/512623.

17. Omar Robert Hamilton, "Refugee Stasis," *N+1*, May 18, 2017, https://nplusonemag.com/online-only/online-only/refugee-stasis/. On isolation, see Hannah Arendt, "We Refugees (1943)," in *Altogether Elsewhere: Writers on Exile*, ed. Marc Robinson, 1st edition (Winchester, MA: Faber & Faber, 1994), 110–19.

18. Hamilton, "Refugee Stasis."

19. With a nod to "To be, or not to be: that is the question:/ Whether 'tis nobler in the mind to suffer/ The slings and arrows of outrageous fortune,/ Or to take arms against a sea of troubles,/ And by opposing end them?" (Hamlet, Act III, Scene 1). In another translation of the script, "Do we exist, or do we not?" Vishal Bhardwaj and Basharat Peer, *Haider*, 2014.

20. The subtitle of Elia Suleiman's *The Time that Remains*, 2009.

21. William Shakespeare, *The Oxford Shakespeare: Hamlet*, ed. G. R. Hibbard, Reissue edition (Oxford England ; New York: Oxford University Press, 2008). Act V, Scene 2. Also, thank you, Ian Bickford, for co-reading this moment.

22. Sulayman Al Bassam, *The Arab Shakespeare Trilogy: The Al-Hamlet Summit; Richard III, an Arab Tragedy; The Speaker's Progress* (Bloomsbury Publishing, 2014). For instance, p. 45.

23. Lee Edelman, *No Future: Queer Theory and the Death Drive* (Duke University Press, 2004). p. 4.

24. Vishal Bhardwaj and Basharat Peer, *Haider*, 2014.

25. Assia Djebar, *The Tongue's Blood Does Not Run Dry: Algerian Stories* (Seven Stories Press, 2006). p. 98–99. I will return to this in detail in Chapter 8.

26. Ranjana Khanna begins *Algeria Cuts* with the story of Kheira, *la louve* , who had been systematically gang-raped over many months by dozens of French soldiers in an internment camp, and brutalized in several ways after that, and lived "like a ghost, in a cemetery […]. In a small space between two graves, she had constructed a place to live with a tarpaulin and a door." Ranjana Khanna, *Algeria Cuts: Women and Representation, 1830 to the Present*, 1st edition (Stanford, Calif: Stanford University Press, 2007). p. 2.

Interlude

From Cosmopolitan Modernity to Necropolitical Austerity: Episodes in the Life of Capital and Colony

Kisi aur aadmi se	We ought to have met
Humein chaahiye tha milna	Another Human
Kisi ahd-e-mehrbaan mein	In a kinder era
Kisi khwaab ke yaqeen mein	In the reality of a dream
Kisi aur aasmaan par	On another sky
Kisi aur sarzameen mein	In another land
Humein chaahiye tha milna	We ought to have met

—Parveen Shakir, "Yeh Haseen Shaam Apni"

The story of sovereignty and citizenship witnessed a shift during the Algerian war of independence that exposed the systematic disposability of bodies in struggles for sovereignty. Restoring any kind of voice attempting to apologize, to reinstate order, to rectify, or to trace a story of the exceptionality of violence is an alibi when the circumstances show that it had become the norm. And if the revolutionary desire for national sovereignty ends with exceptional violence as the norm, how is it possible to think of the postcolonial project as anything other than a lost cause in which a military-backed state of exception can be declared at any time and without much need for rationalization? How is it possible to conceive of hope when those categories of democracy and sovereignty that have become in enlightenment thought the framework within which justice has been conceived seem adulterated at their foundation? How to maintain hope when state politics seems to have been reduced to war, with the total war of nuclear power threatening absolute annihilation and a strong economy being the rationalization for a form of constant war through which states can maintain their imperial power? How also to maintain hope when, as

> Mbembe would put it, the attempt at sovereignty in, for example, the Palestinian situation has been reduced to an overt mechanism of death in the figure of the suicide bomber? —Ranjana Khanna, *Algeria Cuts: Women and Representation, 1830 to the Present*[1]

We meet a century after what Walter Benjamin saw as cosmopolitan modernity set the stage for the fascist imperial project. Despite the century that separates us, the conditions of necropolitical austerity in the wide-reaching postcolony of the twenty-first century leave one to often question if they are harbingers of what is to come, or an extended play of what never left us. I take the term "necropolitics" from Achille Mbembe to refer to the "contemporary forms of subjugation of life to the power of death" that "profoundly reconfigure the relations among resistance, sacrifice, and terror."[2] Marina Gržinić observes that this "regime of the regulation of death" extends beyond the ex-colonies on which Mbembe focuses, "as a result of discrimination, regulation, flexible labor, and a parallel process of institutional normalization and control over which discourses have the right to be presented." She adds to this the preponderance of "the 'war-state' that has as its outcome the decline of the dream that the nation-state can decide its own affairs," since "issues from the economy to the legal system to international affairs are controlled by transnational capital."[3] Understanding necropolitical austerity in all its force requires understanding the economic and affective resources it corrals not merely because it is new, or never happened before, or will happen never again. Its reach, sources, and resources are impossible to miss when we see exactly who it targets and where the logics of what the state performs elsewhere complete their odyssey to return home. Either it has already happened here, or we have not noticed what is around, or it will be here soon.

It is clear that something sets contemporary austerity apart from the classic capitalist or liberal narratives of scarcity. It is as if austerity equals scarcity plus a kind of attachment to the scarcity, as if scarcity is not just a condition but the object of love, where its subjects not only "interiorize scarcity" (to use Sartre's words),[4] but enflesh and incorporate it. Far from a fetish object, it becomes an intimate ascetic ideal, carefully preening the subject's harsh, unadorned, puritanical reliance on (one's own and others') abstention and sacrifice, presumably as a way to survive, interpreting "needs" and "abilities" from the "from each according to ability to each according to needs"[5] dictum via an imperialist and customized biopolitics that still has us cradling the wealthy and the powerful through their anxieties, lacks, and night panics with rocks or bombs tied around our children's waists.

Just as the first and second world wars together with the interwar period can be seen as a thirty-years war redux, it might be possible to see the extended century since World War II, the United Nations, decolonization, and neoliberalism, to be one of a very long war within which European fascism and colonialism seem like episodes always available on demand, to be refreshed, replayed, and re-entered at different moments, with varying ease, on a spectrum of sensorial and interpretive immediacy, depending on our geopolitical location. Or, perhaps, it is technically the *post*colonial age understood as a political project not ensuing outward from the ex-colony, but more broadly of life after (and hence with) fascism and colonialism, to different levels of incorporation in the idea of normal life in state and society, over the course of the last seventy-five or so years. Drawing on the previous chapter's discussion of discrepant and marginal temporalities, the *after*math that figures in formation of the *post*, does not map on to a linear sequence of events, but to modes of uncoloniality that exist within coloniality, attesting to different communities and enclosures of time that shape each other, but not always consciously or in a "self-possessed" way or always in relation to colony. It is post*colonial* because it has learnt from colonization, and sustained an attachment to the colonial project despite appearing to be just capitalism, or something new altogether. My gesture to the *postcolony* is, thus, a broad one—referring to the character of spaces in the aftermath of colonization—absent which it would be hard to understand how the colony is brought home to the metropole or is always already present in its laws and logics, especially when we see the homecoming of what we once subjected others to, from Structural Adjustment Programs to the Greek debt deal to stay in Europe, from the police state that sends drones to Afghanistan to the imperialist and white supremacist state that shoots its own, in schools, churches, and theaters. The post/colony and its necropolitics can be invoked anywhere as a tense of existence.

Instead of imbibing the crucial lesson that all states are settler states that have internalized a mode of colonial organization, the "provincializing" or parochializing of the colony in discourses that have helped us understand what has happened in the world after World War II, serve to either render colonization as a project of capitalism that was subservient to it rather than sponsoring its survivals, or see it as only a secondary condition with some traces left behind. When capitalism and communism become *the* two forces in the century past, the story of the colonial lessons informing those state forms and the constitutive relation between colonialism and fascism can be easily forgotten, something that, in this moment of potentially thinking politics anew, we need to take into account. Why, if the whole world is falling apart, must we stick to conventional ideas of politics or geopolitics, even confess to them, except in some vestigial blackmail of order that makes us fear that this will cost us something?

Trying to understand fascism (and its contemporary versions) without a connection back to the colony (and its affinities and comforts in the contemporary postcolony), we miss an acute lesson from history. The lesson: while our relationship to historical injury and suffering might be best understood through what liberalism in conjunction with capitalism does to our labors, it is also crucial to understand that the claims to this world are perfected through a history of colonialism flaunting a conscription of love incomprehensible in terms of labor alone. Perhaps the proverbial "end of communism" allows this to become clearer, in the sense that there is a grand unification of the capitalist project but also an exposure of what happens when the questions germane to colonization—body politics, identity, language, affect—become not rendered irrelevant but are cruelly set aside or managed. The language of labor alone that requires a flattening out of the body and its conversion into units of time often forgets both the body whose outline is still found on the factory floor, and the affective economies that abound when the body flattened out flexes itself in acts often of its own destruction and disposal, but also sometimes to love, dance, sing, and play truant. Also, we would be amiss in thinking that the question of abundance is one primarily that of exceeding the boundaries set by the other. The real question, for me, is of the demands that come as unrequited love, and their ethics and politics.

UNDER THE SIGN OF NECROPOLITICS

In "Necropolitics," Achille Mbembe asks,

> Is the notion of biopower sufficient to account for the contemporary ways in which the political, under the guise of war, of resistance, or of the fight against terror, makes the murder of the enemy its primary and absolute objective? War, after all, is as much a means of achieving sovereignty as a way of exercising the right to kill. Imagining politics as a form of war, we must ask: What place is given to life, death, and the human body (in particular the wounded or slain body)? How are they inscribed in the order of power?[6]

Mbembe offers a way of thinking about how ideas of biopower and sovereignty can be updated to synopsize better the nature of politics in our contemporary moment. This historicization involves (1) showing how death is involved in this enterprise in a different way than it was in the thanatopolitics that historically preceded biopolitics in Foucault's narrative of state power, and (2) impressing that sovereignty as we know it is accreted through lessons and practices from imperial conquest and its management of populations through killing and destruction, and these are neither things of the past nor exceptional encounters in the present. The end result is a more colony-conscious Carl Schmitt,[7] updating and editing Frantz Fanon to yield a concept of politics understood to be the regime of sovereignty that entails the work of death,[8] irrupting in a subject in the present moment, the "figure[s] of sovereignty whose central project is not the struggle for autonomy but the generalized instrumentalization of human existence and the material destruction of human bodies and populations."[9]

In Mbembe's reading, the ideas of politics, sovereignty, and the subject are shown to be substantiated not by enlightenment ideas of truth, reason, and communicative action, but the "less abstract" stakes of life and death. The politics conjugated in necropolitics relates directly to sovereignty, equated with war. Rejecting, like Schmitt, liberal ploys of communicative action and a community of individuals as the lynchpin of sovereignty, Mbembe also, interestingly, buys into all the myths Schmitt renders for us in his critique of liberalism, in order to counter them with a "truth"—solidifying and reifying the compact between liberalism and fascism by pretending they were ever not mutually constitutive. Schmitt's aspirations in exposing the flaccidity of the liberal state is a kind of therapeutic attempt, conferring it a chance to accept and become what it truly is (quite contrary to Weber for whom the exposé becomes an attempt to forestall or redirect the unfolding). Despite his protest, Schmitt emerges as liberalism's loyal narrator and cheerleader, pushing it to its logical, even natural, conclusion. In a more than important departure from Schmitt, though, Mbembe, despite deeming life and death to be extra-linguistic, extra-hermeneutic, or pre-political absolutes, gestures at least to the possibility that it is necropower itself that gets coded as reason and truth, respiring, conspiring, learning, and muscling up in the realm of the colony, and now the post/colony.

The move from biopolitics to necropolitics signals that it may not be quite enough to say that war is politics by other means, since those other means have not quite given up relying on the death and the killing to have what it takes to be politics. While biopolitics already did address life, death, and the body, necropolitics could gesture (even in its seeming clarity about the immediacy of death and hence life) to the fact that life and death can no longer be seen as cleansed of each other. Contra thanatopolitics, death is no longer regulated only by the power to kill or to regulate acts of individual annihilation, but by letting those decisions be made obliquely and consistently at the level of juridical necessity, population management, and through governmental reasoning about life itself. The act of making live is no longer only attached to letting die, but to making die as well. Not the compulsion to kill, but the pathology that insists on the production of life surrounded by death.[10]

Marina Gržinić and Šefik Tatlić, in *Necropolitics, Racialization, and Global Capitalism*, further problematize the move from biopolitics to necropolitics. Following thinkers like Talal Asad, Gržinić sees the biopolitical realm, in which life could have ever been presumed to be produced and maintained, to have always only existed in the advanced capitalist west (the First World), a world which hides away death and makes life its project. She writes:

> ...[W]ith the predominance of biopolitics, death would be gradually banned. Foucault warned that death is "something to be hidden away." Foucault asserted in the mid-70s that "power no longer recognizes death." What Foucault meant was that First World Capitalism's biopolitical power was not prepared to recognize death, as death was exported outside the West and let to "live" there, also on the other side of the Iron Curtain.[11]

Entering this picture, Giorgio Agamben names life which is set aside and not "worked" over as part of this project a form-of-life, a bare life—a differentiation internal to the biopolitical regime, not an all-out contest of life and death. "[L]ife that was in the past seen as the antagonism of death has been divided now into two."[12] The contentless form of life that is presented as a mode of managing life also sets the tone for an emptying out of historical specificity that allows politics to be displaced by anthropology. The object has not been done away with—it tempts, and it is filled by, a new mode of colonization invited by political theological mystifications and declarations. Bare life as the new limit. Anthropology as settler colonialism.

For Gržinić, the logic of capital in late liberalism and neoliberalism, and the war machine as the motive force in the cartography of necropolitics, together necessitate bringing death back into the conversation. The fact that the literal postcolony becomes the exemplary (but by no means only) location for this death follows Fanon's predictions, and invites us to think of the *post/colony* as not a geographic location but one that is through and through historical—in that all states are settler states and the forms in which they exist are all derived from colonization, of spaces but also time.[13] Gržinić connects this to "necrocapitalism," which organizes its forms of capital accumulation around dispossession and the subjugation of life to the power of death. The pure abandonment of structures of care, austerity politics (even in the first world), the letting live without means, is necropolitics—life always in the presence of death. This is not limited today to the postcolony as conventionally understood. Postcoloniality is a condition that requires us to treat colonialism and empire not as exceptions to the paradigm of political inquiry and analysis, requiring special or "exceptional" terms. Rather, this condition inflects all "normal" concepts reserved for the rest of the world—to wit, the continuities of affective lives perfected in neoliberalism and late liberalism on lines other than the boundaries of nation and state. Gržinić gives examples of private indirect government, security firms, and general corporatization of life, the logics of which affect the metropole and the colony alike and bind them in a postcolonial con*sensus*. Sherene Razack speaks of these "death-worlds"[14] in addition to the empire of camps, as projects underwritten by the idea that some have to be killed so others can live. They occur in Palestine as they do in Western Europe, creating abandoned populations marked as outside the racial kin group that is the nation.[15]

The effect is the social, political and economic incapacitation of citizens—but also the nourishment, harvest, and harnessing of affect and political fervor for the production and reproduction of contemporary fascisms. This bespeaks the consensus between the affectivity of violence and the comfort with war, an unaccepted consequence of wars elsewhere that then return home. The "event" of necropolitics reaches far, and manifests not only in grand wars fought but also in the very ordinary acts and mentalities that fill everyday life. Not just incapacities, but very particular capacities.

OUR ACCURSED SHARE

Consanguinity with terror comes easy in a time when the destruction of state and society like the one that happens in states declared "failed," states always at some war or the other, is inseparable from the increasing xenophobia, everyday brutality, and boundary-drawings that refuse to be masked over in the United States and Europe. There are increasingly evident continuities of both sense and structure, even if the empirical phenomena seem different. With these societies built on war, it is hardly a surprise that signs of social wear and tear, nay exhaustion and destruction, manifest themselves ubiquitously for those who discern. The wars have produced, and are producing, parched, scarce, loveless, societies and subjects to match them in the name of some kind of plentitude, fervor, and love. I say loveless not to foist any nostalgically positivist conception of love, but to recall a deep anti-politics of the modes of love that are the gifts of our shared colonial pasts and of our shared neoliberal present. There is no way to distance oneself from the loves and their possibilities destroyed by this moment. It is no easier to neglect the tithe that the abstract love—for nation, self, property, market, the future, etc.—takes from other loves. I am interested, beyond and away from the narrative of the death of morals or ethics, in how these realities manifest and are worked through to forge political subjectivities in the present. That might be, in this moment, the only place to turn to, in order to acknowledge and release the life that is being harnessed into courting and fostering death.

As this reality intensifies, the sites of the politics of unrequited subjects multiply, taking cover in and drawing sustenance from the ordinary negotiations that constitute sensorial life within and across times and spaces. The narrative of the colonial subject cast as the subject of death no longer needs to remain sequestered from the more common and generalized subject of terror (wherever it may be found). Neither must be invoked without also referencing the margins where a counter-politics and counter-subjectivity are being negotiated and forged, unfortunately often through death. As the form of this subject standardizes across familiar boundaries, exceptions to this exception need to be invoked and provoked. A particular form of political subjectivity germinates in the contemporary discourses and dislocations of terror. I am interested in identifying those capacities and harnessings that might enable a departure from this stifling consensus over politics and subjectivity, and the mode of aesthetic production of the sensible that maintains it.

In order to do this work, a conception of political subjectivity is needed that can incorporate and illuminate the impact of a history of colonialism on the sensorial makeup of the "post/colony" not as a cartographic fact but as political experience. Here, with the help of Bataille and Mbembe, I bring forward the previous section's extraction of the Malabou/Žižek diagnosis of our current trauma, and its contact with a Rancièrian notion of political subjectification, into the post/colony. Bataille's idea of "the accursed share" offers a way of understanding notions of sacrifice, war, and destruction that may hold some relevance to the sensual economies of the neoliberal capitalist post/colony. In his book with that title,[16] Bataille speaks of a general economy of human energies by way of which societies channel the excess of their productions into modes of consumption that negate a utilitarian calculus, and "succeed" in making true subjects (in acts of sacrifice) out of those who would otherwise become things of use harnessed into the functioning of the normative social order (the restrictive economy). This is certainly a complicated claim with several normatively dubious implications. Here, I am only interested in seeing how this opposition between a general and restrictive economy plays out not in the realm of labor or even productive activity per se, but at the level of sensuous capacities. Suspicious of the reactionary sanguinity of excess, I want to propose focusing on the forms of these capacities and their productions instead of on the discharge of an already-known energy. This would raise some crucial questions. Is the excess in a relation of active negation of the restrictive economy? Is scarcity still internalized in the mode of excess so that the negation does not quite subvert the scarcity? If yes, then we are trapped in a scenario where the state and the market as we know them know this general economy well and exploit it. If, on the other hand, we find that the excess channels different capacities in different forms, we may have a possible revolutionary politics, most apposite to the poiesis that Rancière attributes to political subjectivity.

Thus, both fanatic destruction and an equally destructive lack of pathos can be understood via the excess that Bataille theorizes, the colonizer and the colonized now trapped in this general economy. Mbembe's discussion of Fanon and Bataille in relation to the sensorial makeup of the postcolony (a geographical, historically precise, ex-colonial marker for him) helps with the next step in our methodological journey. He channels Bataille into thinking about how the postcolony is a debased "mirror" of the colony, and saturated with terror. He reminds us of the necropolitics of the postcolony: excess manifested as death harnessed either by the state in wars that make no sense, or by nationalisms and other abstractions, giving over life and its energies to them, offering sacrifices to the nation-state, if not gods, in confusing erasures and reclamations of body and subjectivity. The nation-state knows this well, dependent as it is on the form of violence as a container of this excess economy; it could not exist without it. In order to foreground the fluxes of economic, political, and sensual realities that connect the "center" of the colony to the "center" of the metropole, and the "margins" to the "margins," one illuminating the other, Mbembe's invocation of Fanon and Bataille can be extended to the post/colony as a global condition.

Bataille's "base materialism" can be inflected with this post/colony by considering the fact that the colonizer and their colonized have their own (pathological) modes of escaping the restrictive economy. What seems to be a love that has been indentured beforehand is energy in the service of a principle of death. The abundance that is needed to counter the brutal scarcities and mortifications of love, then, has to be taken into account. For the tired and the exhausted, it is not abundant *action* that is a rebellious departure from a logic, but acts of (and in) *abundance* that defy the potent scarcity of those in power, not serve its purposes. These acts of abundance are acts of love and acts of suffering that defy the imposed logics of the kinds of intimacy, knowledge, and premises the structure wants from us; they are exceptions to the prescribed modes and unfoldings of love and suffering that do not fit liberal utilitarian calculus and governmentality.

When Mbembe speaks of the accursed share in regimes built around death, of a kind of necropolitics that is lived by the postcolony, one can feel one's way in this deathfulness by being sensitive to the ways available for negotiating the inheritance of such a curse; the ability to suffer these deaths follows an articulate historical relation to them. The relation between these various ventings of the excess brings to light the disposable body and its draw toward death. Who exactly "deserves" to live off (or primitively accumulate) our cultivated terrors? Might this question spur an exit from the spate of self-loathing and self-destruction in which we find ourselves? Those who have never loathed or destroyed themselves (or never been aware of doing so) can stick to their rich, affluent, partialities to moderation, and to the language of freedom, newness, and compromise. This is because they have other non-negotiably destructible and disposable bodies on which to premise their own negotiable fears. Here, though, even they might need some more love in place of their tyrannical narratives of hope that are as bloated as their fears, and no less parasitic or predatory on those "other" bodies.

If the general economy is taken to be an economy of form and not merely of content, we may have to be more agnostic about, and yet more willing to observe and acknowledge, the modes in which the accursed share manifests. This is to say that in apprehending terror, destruction, and wretchedness, not merely the abundance or lack of love and suffering would become evident.

Rather, we would find a particular configuration of love and suffering that we may not already know of. In the same way, when faced with the relentless desire to amass wealth and raise fences, we would find a different configuration of love and suffering, not just different quanta of each. That violence, art, sex, joy, happen in excess of some limit is certainly noteworthy. But, it is the relations between those productions that substantiate a framework of political subjectivity in a manner that indexes the trajectory of the form and capacities of the subject in question. It also, importantly, augments Rancière's understanding of this process by emphasizing that the nature of political subjectification *as if the colony happened* requires factoring in the destruction and re/production of the aesthetic field beyond politics qua *le partage du sensible* (a distribution of the sensible).[17] Only then we might be able to attend to the history of imperial, colonial, and neoliberal policing of the very modes of love and suffering that erupt into a subject.

WHOSE DEATH? WHOSE POLITICS?

What does it mean for any notion, such as necropolitics, to account for the prevalence of death and destruction predicating the longevity of the political as we know it today? In asking for an account merely in the sense of corroborate, record, or explain, one might also ask to whom is a concept, such as necropolitics, accountable, on whose behalf, and to give an account of what? In other words, what and where is the politics of necropolitics—what does it articulate and what does it disarticulate?

Gržinić, for one, sees Mbembe as intervening with not just a new, improved term appropriate to the present reality, but to show that no discussion of any kind of politics with normative democratic conceits, can happen by disregarding the vantage point of this condition of a kind of deathfulness. She writes,

> Mbembe firmly believes that democracy as a form of government and as a culture of public life does not have a future in Africa—or, for that matter, elsewhere in the world—unless it is rethought precisely from the condition of "necropower,"—a sovereign power that is set up for the maximum destruction of persons and the creation of deathscapes, unique forms of social existence in which vast populations are subjected to conditions of life which confers upon them the status of the living dead.[18]

Lines between life and death, drawn by the political theologian or the historical materialist, are all arbitrations over materiality, and have their own history—and subsequently effect what work the concepts of death (or life) will do in discourses of politics. Like other arbitrary points on lines and surfaces, the demarcation of the exception is also to determine what is contained (and the other way around). With the arbitrary conferrals and suffocations of materiality, the annihilation of history is palpable, an annihilation to correct other annihilations, if you will: the never-forget that makes sure a lot else is forgotten.

Such zones of containment are created, for example, by political theology of recent eras that cartographs life and the polis from up above, also stamping political subjectivity with an incontrovertible stigma, answerable to certain tendencies, needing resolution in an outside, demanding an exception, or waiting for redemption. This "theology" is itself never accountable for where its own tent is pitched, which bodies normalized, and what desires, labors, and sufferings acknowledged in need of reconciling and redeeming. That frame of redemption too frequently imagines self-involved political subjects fixed in their locations, waiting for either the sky or the ground to open. Time collapses with the same mixture of confidence and anxiety in the transcendental empiricist's body as it does in liberal humanist universals, ethical absolutes, and the very policing exceptions of political theology.

This collapse of time validated by the focus on death fences and polices the sensible, to return to Rancière for a moment. Dissensual politics happens in contesting these closures. Far from arguing that death or the dead are irrelevant to the task of political theorizing or action, a case can be made for actually allowing the dead to matter in some other way than markers of time and space or as surfaces to be written on or walked over. This requires entertaining the idea of death as something other than the opposite of life, and of life as something other than the trumping of death. This also involves looking at the two not on a linear or quantitative continuum, but to each as discrete labors of the living that are imbricated with each other and deserve more attention than as proofs of a priori logics. I am arguing that we find in the assignment of these limits of life in death, or of death in life, something more/other than a naïve, benign, or condescending love for the human. I am making a plea to allow us to displace philosophy in so far as it is interested in death as a place that serves as a premise of consensus, and we might be able to look at the life caught, wasted, tormented, reclaimed, assuaged, cradled, relieved, within the consensus, especially the rampant necropolitical one that Mbembe diagnoses for us, leaving a lot more work to be done. Those on whose ostensible behalf death is brought up as the limit, as the equalizer par excellence, as beyond argument, are those who will also prove, if given a chance, that much of these limits are agonized over in the everyday, and any absolute only discredits by domesticating our negotiations with subjection through life and death.

An honest historicization of necropolitics would have to go far behind modern colonialism, to see how the body does not originate, but is assigned, the meaning of life and death in relation to each other, along with an assessment of who needs how much life and who can withstand what kind of death.

This is something that a turn to contemporary "necrocapitalism,"[19] and the wariness of seeing labor as always already violence, forestalls. The shortsightedness of our critique of contemporary life, tying it to capitalism or, the anthropocene, often leaves undisclosed where and how the body itself becomes an object, and how the incidence of modern slavery and colonialism enables a turn to the body in some way, perfecting the acts of extraction and accumulation in ways that do not follow but anticipate dicta about humanity and life. They are anteceded by eras that adjudicated the differential body and soul of the slave and native, in turn foreshadowed by the medieval demarcation of the limits of corporeality and substance in the bodies of Jews, Christians, and Muslims. It is because we do not see how the body itself is posited as an object that when it comes to understanding what is done to it, and how it fares under the sign of what is done to it, there is either a silence or a resort to one-sided accounts that assume their object instead of explaining the conditions of its possibility.

Let us suppose that definitions of life and death are not pre- or extrapolitical. For those deemed excepted or damned to bare life, one might ask if Mbembe finds the possibilities of politics to themselves be necropolitical, or whether an argument over living and dying, and their meanings and coexistence, might still count toward a politics. The claim to death as signifier par excellence affirms a shared world despite the state of exception—a world shared that is based on our finitude. If life is defined only as fragility, then we are off the hook; no need to separate out what and whose life is produced how, under what conditions, and by whose labor. If death is the ultimate equalizer, we can give up on arguing about suffering and its causes, and how to experience it—nay to even experience death. This is the way of holding on that is a way of letting go, a laissez-faireness that might actually never hold us accountable to or for anyone's lives or deaths. Or, keep us from understanding how life and death are themselves produced and for whom.

So, when Mbembe asks necropolitics to give an account, then the accounts of what exactly is included, and what is kept beyond them, produce these limits. Necropolitics might pry open how death is experienced by the living, and how death is produced, how and what people produce with death. Often, in the mad rush to make sense of a crumbling world, philosophers-turned-ethicists create new categories of the "living dead" or "socially dead" to explain them as departures from real death. At other times, these variants are not variations on death, but variations away from it, not quite death, so that philosophy (including social science, or any expert discourse) can keep inquiring into them as its new pastime and produce new frontiers, new thresholds, new marginalizations, and a new beyond. Such serial appropriateness or propriety is a kind of "sovereign" closure.

With Rancière, it is worth imagining who gets to talk about life and death, who takes necropolitics as what kind of narrative (expertise, story, philosophy, politics)? While the language of what is proper to something is certainly valuable and is abundantly prolific within the ethical turn, politics calls for the lexicon of the impolitical, the improper, and the out of place.[20] My concern is not with the entailments, reach, scope, accuracy, or "truth" of necropolitics as a concept in and of itself, as much as the work it does, and for whom. What other notions does it cohabitate and constellate with, and whose are they? Necropolitics diagnoses a condition that stretches from death outward, from an idea of destruction and disposability with few and only internal variations, adding a degree of unifying non-negotiability to it, such that everything remains in the right place. Certain criticisms of the discourse on biopolitics might apply to necropolitics as well. These include: insufficient historical and cultural contextualization; "monolithic, reductive, and homogenizing claims";[21] vestiges of a theological lexicon such as that of sovereignty; and a kind of secular humanism that is arbitrarily attached both to a hegemonic and ahistorical meaning of politics even in ostensibly rejecting it, and to some ontological truth of the meaning and value of life and death. However, it is impossible to reject the need to think in response to how every new political crisis is at its core that of the arbitrary dispensability, pulverizability, and immaterializing of certain bodies who bear that mark in the presence of death done or foretold. Thus, there are some further questions on this road.

My questions come from the encounter of two methodological necessities. First, the ontological premises of any inquiry into the condition of contemporary destructibility, such as the very subject presupposed in any inquiry into this being, the plasticity of this subject, ways of being, forms of life, sensoria of existence, and so on. Second, the implications, for possibility of the positing of a different political subject, amid the tempting ontological turns that carry with them the histories of epistemological crises that have been solved by finding solace in various purities and supremacies, arbitrary starting points, the given, the present (rather than dismantling the very structure of knowledge that drives the "crisis"). The two are not as opposed as they might seem. On a good day, a turn to political ontology finds a friend in someone like Rancière, just as long as we are able to expand the domain of what counts as being and negotiate what burdens the subject carries (and is not allowed to shed) in the ontological account, corralling the gestural and the figural, and the capacity to withhold and resist becoming the object of truth. Both still impel a way to actually think about how and on what terms the inquiry into the relation between contemporary life and claims of politics should proceed, what about the post/colony should factor into every conversation, what goes assumed in any ontological claim, and how political ontology can be kept political and away from the temptations to anti-politics that often engird the ontological turn parading as materialism.

This encounter becomes an impasse when one is confronted with the figure of sovereignty on the one hand, and the anonym who has no location or history on the other. The former is a character in the drama of sovereignty already written, and the latter is bestowed a politics (and possibility) only if it forgets its lines or starts speaking in tongues, and sets up a new scene even if no one comes to see it. In the company of sovereignty and a vestigial political theology that picks its historical battles with much care (and in great omission of the history of the West before modern colonialism), necropolitics sets aside any idea of politics that is not normatively or descriptively beholden to the state or to the project of becoming-subject that proceeds through a mode of grand gestures (of either the embrace or rejection of autonomy, for instance). The company that aesthetics in the Rancièrian sense keeps leaves the door open for the dissensual subject. This subject also seeks freedom, but everything else it does may actually unsettle, reject, or attenuate the desire for sovereignty. Other relations emerge in which the subject lives. It is not that these are irreducibly different kinds of subjects in essence, or merely that people are doing wholly different things, or that the same act can matter differently. There is much that the necropolitical accounts for but its scripted desires and positings fail to grasp the work of death in the efforts of people to stay alive, to keep others alive, or to make life and death have different meaning at different moments of one's becoming. What does the concept itself do as it moves in between us subjects contemplating what it means to be in this world now? Why should asking those questions ever bring autonomy or sovereignty to mind as answers? Why have we been fooled into thinking that those terms could be generalized as desires or problems to solve, rather than the fact that their framing as problems was the solution to other problems, deflection from other threats, and the palliation of other anxieties?

Mbembe's concern is, ultimately, on the order of what inscribes people, what is done to them, and to what they are subject. The inscription within the order of power suffocates me. When confronted by the imposition of a world (an order) I must share with others—not tentatively, not seeking verification—the only hope I have, of writing out of love for things without hope, is taken from me. What can be said of stories that hold us in their death-grip, populated by those quasi-bodies given over to this order, confident about life, world, and possibility, or alternately confident about death, world, and impossibility—for whom little love is possible, because with whom no world is sought or possible to be shared? Whose abandonment do the figures of this order—consensual to this order either in the sense of accepting it or in being reducible to it, but in both cases being of it—bespeak? To be able to write with love of the terrorist, or of some other accursed figure of sovereignty, I have to see in that figure not a politician waging war; in order to be able to write with love about those who kill themselves as a way of killing others, I have to see something different in them than those who kill and find safe haven, regardless of whether the former also found a heaven for themselves. Seeing which loves are rejected in the name of which others, what flesh was given to which words, and which words given to which flesh, requires broaching the dissensus that confronts the necropolitical and is born of it, as well as the life that coexists with it. I do not seek to call it resistance, and I do not seek to reconcile what I find.

NOTES

1. Khanna. pp. 26-27.
2. Mbembe, "Necropolitics." p. 39.
3. Marina Gržinić, "From Biopolitics to Necropolitics: Marina Gržinić in Conversation with Maja and Reuben Fowkes," *ARTMargins*, October 9, 2012, http://www.artmargins.com/index.php/5-interviews/692-from-biopolitics-to-necropolitics-marina-grini-in-conversation-with-maja-and-reuben-fowkes.
4. Jean-Paul Sartre and Arlette Elkaïm-Sartre, *Critique of Dialectical Reason* (Verso, 2006). p. 423.
5. Karl Marx, *Critique of the Gotha Program*, ed. Bi Classics, trans. Friedrich Engels (CreateSpace Independent Publishing Platform, 2017). p. 11.
6. Mbembe, "Necropolitics." p. 12.
7. Carl Schmitt, Tracy B. Strong, and Leo Strauss, *The Concept of the Political*, trans. George Schwab, Enlarged edition (Chicago: The University of Chicago Press, 2007).
8. Frantz Fanon and Adolfo Gilly, *A Dying Colonialism*, trans. Haakon Chevalier (New York, NY: Grove Press, 1994); Fanon, Sartre, and Bhabha, *The Wretched of the Earth*.
9. Mbembe, "Necropolitics." p. 14.
10. See further on these questions, Kathleen Biddick, *Make and Let Die: Untimely Sovereignties by Kathleen Biddick* (Punctum Books, 2016).
11. Marina Gržinić and Šefik Tatlić, *Necropolitics, Racialization, and Global Capitalism: Historicization of Biopolitics and Forensics of Politics, Art, and Life*, Reprint edition (Lexington Books, 2016). p. 23.
12. Gržinić and Tatlić. p. 23.
13. I am trying to distinguish the postcolony as a specific space of former colonization and the post/colony as that which signals a global affective and political order that purveys racial and colonial logics even without an overt history of colonization or a "successful" independence struggle to speak of. It is my attempt at deprovincialized the postcolony, but perhaps I can do without it?
14. Mbembe, "Necropolitics." p. 40.
15. Sherene Razack, *Casting Out: The Eviction of Muslims from Western Law and Politics* (University of Toronto Press, 2008). p. 85.
16. Bataille, *The Accursed Share*.
17. Jacques Rancière and Slavoj Žižek, *The Politics Of Aesthetics: The Distribution of the Sensible* (London; New York: Continuum, 2004).
18. Gržinić and Tatlić, *Necropolitics, Racialization, and Global Capitalism*. p. 25.
19. Gržinić and Tatlić. p. 28.
20. See Roberto Esposito, *Categories of the Impolitical*, trans. Connal Parsley, Translation edition (New York: Fordham University Press, 2015). Also Jacques Rancière, "The Thinking of Dissensus: Politics and Aesthetics," in *Reading Rancière* (London ; New York: Continuum, 2011), 1–17.
21. Timothy Campbell and Adam Sitze, "Biopolitics: An Encounter," in *Biopolitics: A Reader*, ed. Timothy Campbell and Adam Sitze (Durham: Duke University Press Books, 2013), 1–40. p. 5.

Chapter Five

The Sanguine Subjects of Love and Terror

When terror is pronounced a part of our current global human condition, I take it to mean that it has come to live with and in us, and we are subjects being wrought in and through this conjugation. How one is attached, and how one desires, says much more about how one suffers to become a subject of terror beyond a superficial, generalized, relation to the commission of violence and deliverance from it. Thus, how terror lives with and in us in this moment in history testifies to our inheritances and genealogies not only of terror and scarcity, but also of love and abundance.

The nature of the subject of terror in this moment cannot be separated from the eros and the attachment that produce, foster, validate, necessitate, and mourn it. One possible history of the political subject, the contemporary subject of terror being no exception, can be gleaned from the ways in which the capacities to love and suffer are produced, operationalized, and experienced in different ways across regimes of time and space, including in the production of the experience and act of terror. These capacities are materially interdependent and historically produced, and together make creation, destruction, and absence present, sensible, and apprehensible. Such a characterization is incompatible with a manner of theorizing affect that places love and terror in a binary or dialectical relation of positing and negation, lack and excess, within a finite and naturalized economy of externalized action and sentiment.

The experience or embodiment of terror cannot be disentangled from the question of love itself. This is because it is through loving, desiring, and being attached, that one suffers with and for another, becomes available to another as an ethical-political subject, and musters the energy to sustain or interrupt reality. Setting aside the hackneyed characterization of love as inherently violent or violence as another form of love, it is worth asking about the intimacies sought in our relation to terror and the loves which permit or compel this seeking. In order to unsettle the unilateral orientalism observed by Edward Said in the discourses of terrorism,[1] it is important to probe where the orientalism and the terrorism abide together, and where terror, like violence, needs to be apprehended as a historical form containing, precisely, significations to things other than itself, such as love.

This turn is in service of bringing closer the subject of terror that is both famed and erased in focusing on terror as object, which keeps us from apprehending the forms in which the loves of the subject of terror are cast. The othering and distancing of terror implicit in that focus keeps us from seeing ourselves partaking in those forms of love. Much damage is done when the subject of terror is disavowed and isolated in thought; this move affirms, even reproduces, its constitutive destruction by allowing it ambient and oblique intimacies and dwellings, regardless of our conscious will or conscientious objection. In contrast, in this chapter, I set out to explore where terror has settled in each of us, and to inquire into the ways we are intimate with terror.

Even when the axiomatic regurgitation of colonial violence is our primary way of grasping the very instance of terror, it would be a mistake to forget that colonialism, our history with it, and our overcoming of it, all operate through practices of love and desire that sustain our lifeworlds. Just as we find in colonialism the roots for the modes of terror that inhabit us today, the collusions of colonialism and liberalism are formative of our abilities to desire, produce, and attach—our abilities and possibilities of love—that are as much part of the same story. Thus, if politics is to address propensities to want and to destroy, the question of murder must be accessed via love rather than the other way around. Even when seeking causal explanations for terror that vary with the chosen points of origin and destination, it behooves us to be honest about what it really is (about terror, about ourselves) that we are trying to explain, why, and to whom. In that very question, we might see our complicity with or rejection of the modes of love that are on offer.

IN TERROR, WITH LOVE:
INTIMACIES OF THE NECROPOLITICAL

The modern and postcolonial state system built on a real or wishful monopoly over violence requires a relation of love to the terror that instantiates sovereignty, whether on the part of the state or of the partisan (in Carl Schmitt)[2] who enters the picture to challenge it. Thus, sovereignty, a temporal claim on space that serves as its limits, already entwines love and terror. The empirical cartographies of the distribution and appearance of terror necessarily address only one side of a complex political and sensual economy that foremost relies on the production of and the ability to make in/sensible these realities. It is hardly surprising that one's distance from, or proximity to, terror seems to follow the conceits of the same spatial cartographies that were set in place by colonialism, and are now being upheld, even reified, in the frenzied erasure of certain boundaries (only to erect new ones). Experiencing this distance and proximity brings home, time and again, the arbitrary nature of the claims to the sublimity or the newness of terror; both are essentially temporal issues converted into spatial ones. For instance, far before the 9–11 "inaugural" of terror and its aftermath, I used to have nightmares about Karachi around the time of Ashura every year, the tense relation I always had to the really intimate fear mixed in with devotion to the martyrs, sympathy, the revulsion I felt toward a procession of mourners, and a warmth toward the fact that tragedy was actually in the air, palpable, hot, repulsive, seductive, all at the same time. Never before coming to the United States had I known a "bystander," for the ontological assumptions that allow casting out any constituent of an experience into categories of victim, perpetrator, and bystander, did not seem to be natural givens, and could only arise from a particular constructed, historical relation to loving and suffering.

Then the film *Caché*[3] left me with the inescapable feeling of guilt and embarrassment at having missed the degree to which the knife, wielding it, and slashing something with it, came so "naturally" to my people—that consanguinity to which I referred earlier. After all, who could not connect the public slaughter of animals, the release that psychopathologists read into women who "cut" themselves, the video of the Daniel Pearl murder, or the christening with blood (in name and act) of town roundabouts in Northern Pakistan? Think also of the wives of the same butchers who went around a neighborhood taking care of the sacrificial animals on Eid, or the wives or mothers or sisters of those who found new ways of flagellating themselves with a bunch of small knives at Ashura; how they could possibly love them and sleep with them, feed them and wash their clothes? How could I possibly place these "savageries" on the same plane as the savageries of the "civilized," where we could still shamelessly be invited to conversations about civility in public discourse?

Of course, I know better, and am allergic to any discourse that pathologizes and normalizes at will, damns and redeems in some mimicry of science, or religion, or theatre, and pitches the abstract table for conversation with non-negotiable moralities about violence and non-violence. I am allergic to the preemptive evacuations of politics, arbitrary demarcations of times and spaces, and the recolonization of the sphere of human thought and action where meanings and limits, indeed entire modes of life, are supposed to be negotiated. All this defiance does not change the fact that I am continually haunted by how my fantasies for love are shaped entirely by my fantasies of terror, not in a formulaic sadomasochism, but because the closeness to the abjection of the martyr and the butcher is what inspires protecting another out of love and being a witness to someone's disappearance, where things still have the ability to haunt because they are more material in many ways and sown into all the abstractions courtesy of which one lives to see another day. Yes, these are *my* issues, and perhaps it is not accidental that my turn to love in order to address terror is not an act of grace, charity, or transsubstantiation, but a thoroughly historical materialist one, out of the necessity of not abandoning what is made distant and expunged at will. Love is both my motive and my access to the subject of terror.

WITH THE PUZZLING SUBJECT WHO HAS SURVIVED ITS OWN DEATH: METHOD AND POLITICS

By terror, I mean a condition wherein the doing and the experiencing of violence meld together inside us, and it is tough to distinguish the fear of what might happen to oneself from the fear of what that self can do. I understand terror to be an emotional state, impacting the aesthetic constitution of political subjectivity in a particular way. When we turn it into "the ultimate fear," or "the unsaid that can only be condemned, never condoned...,"[4] terror resembles a sublime that we cannot understand: we give it a sense of otherness that keeps it distant, and us uninvolved and uncomplicit. Then we rely on it to gather us into a collective moment of recognition of the ungodly injustice and incomprehensible insanity of it all. I am concerned here not with terrorism as a tactic, but in terror as an emotional state and experience shared by both doer and the recipient. Terror's specific form in the present moment aligns with the body's increasing pulverizability and dislocation that also makes it more scattered, and with its utility to production and destruction that also makes it most disposable.

Beyond the consensus on this condition by radicals and reactionaries alike, opinions diverge on, among other things: its provenance, its uses, consequences, the original terrorist, the political utility of violence, the very existence of anything like (merely) political violence, its novelty for most of the world beyond its the most recent and most valuable victims in the West, its remedy. Far from any real disruption, though, these differences enable deflections and prejudgments that buttress the core consensus and obstruct politics. The consensus on terror and terrorism as object, and on the terrorist as protagonist and subject of interest, amounts to an avoidance of the urgent political problem: the form of the meaning-making sensuous political subject that is generalized, affirmed, and cultivated in order to maintain this consensus. What emerge are shared sensoria like never before, cutting across usual lines. Displaced is the form, mode, and capacity of the sensuous subject as the true and effective site of political contention. More deleterious than the wrenching disregard of potentiality ensuing from this rejection of politics and this colonization of embodied spaces of contention, however, is the defacing blindness to the actuality of how different relations to suffering, love, and life itself configure these subjects of terror, as well as those subjects that are continually being massaged into being in order to serve the consensus human condition and its categorical (sic) imperatives.

Here is an opportunity to turn to these subjects in a different way, setting aside the fascination with history as consolation, with provenance as a solution to riddles, with the event of terror as climax or catastrophe beyond paltry meaning, and with the blameworthy or pathologized agency of the terrorist as yet another kind of closure. In trying to understand the contemporary political subjects of terror, it is necessary to acknowledge the spatial and temporal, epistemological and ontological, permutations that are made manifest in them, and how they churn out life despite its impossibilities, perhaps life that is illegible or dissensual to the normalized understanding of love, terror, and located-ness.

In confronting a new contemporary subject who is "autistic, indifferent, without affective engagement,"[5] Slavoj Žižek converses with Catherine Malabou's idea of "destructive plasticity" in an era where trauma is no longer an interruption, but a way, of life, so that we have a "new wounded" subject who survives its own destruction, experiences all violence as catastrophe, and is molded through this trauma rather than merely navigating it.[6] Žižek speaks of destruction today itself as a "form of life." "More precisely," he writes, "the new form is not a form of life, but, rather, a form of death."[7] (Nothing about this is new to anyone who works on the intersections of postcolonialism and feminism: where the issue of our affective encounters with what destroys us is always center-stage.) For Žižek, today's trauma is that loss itself takes an affirmative form, especially when trauma is said to make the victim into something other than it was before, and that we can no longer expect them to be human in the same way. Thus, he writes, "the true traumatic heart of the matter [is] not the subject's desperate effort to recompense his loss, but the subject of this loss itself, the subject which is the positive form this loss assumes (the disengaged impassive subject)."[8] The mode in which destruction happens is now so total, so reminiscent of naturalized and normalized catastrophe that political violence—which I would define as violence one is compelled to make sense and meaning out of (whether or not one succeeds), or which is connected in any way with the making of meaning (and thus one's own subjectivity) in relation to others—has all but exited the scene. One can retain the force of the new wounded without indulging the anti-political gesture of placing this new trauma into catastrophe beyond politics (which is to say, catastrophe as beyond politics). Resisting the incipient idealism of Malabou's psychoanalytic epistemology, two key insights can still inform a materialist political method: plasticity as a way to think of a subject's history, and the shift in the temporality of trauma and violence.

Rancière defines political subjectivity as "an enunciative and demonstrative capacity to reconfigure the relation between the visible and the sayable, the relation between words and bodies: namely 'the partition of the sensible.'"[9] Extending this, political subjectivity need not be limited to the sayable qua logos, but include other forms of enunciation and demonstration as well. Also, instead of being tethered to a determinate aesthetic or perceptual field, the repartitioning of the sensible can be seen as involving a production and destruction of the sensible. Thus, a concern with political subjectivity in a time of terror (one populated by the post-traumatic subject of terror signaled above) must turn to the capacities in which this manifests, which are, in turn, historical forms with which the present moment's "sovereign acts" negotiate (in practices not only of terror). And, it must embrace its formative relation of political subjectivity (even in its supposedly "healthiest" forms) to violence, terror, and destruction—in order to acknowledge its debt to the violence on which state and capital have historically depended for their own existence, and the terror on which state and capital now desperately depend for their sustenance.

Contemporary framings of terror and of the fraying of the subject and the social fabric in which it is suspended often rely, on the one hand, on the narrative of people being desensitized to bad things happening and, on the other hand, on a declared consensus that we have nothing to do with it, being logically, empirically, and practically opposed to it as civilized moral beings. These framings leave unquestioned, normalized, and static, the morality and the structures of sensibility and affect that enable and sustain the subject at the helm of, and served, by this condition. The conundrum we face is not emblematic of too much suffering, but of an inability to suffer, a saturation with terror that ends up installing itself as a discontinuous emotional form, a reality separate from other pathos, sealed from sentiments that were once perhaps known to us or available to us. There is no way out of this form unless the sensible, in Rancièrian terms, is pushed to incur a re-partition or reproduction that reclaims the ability to sense presences and absences and to see that we have been suffering, defeated, or grieving. Or, perhaps, where a new relation to this reality supplants or (in Malabou's terms) stretches, disfigures, and refigures the old one—an acknowledgment of plasticity that is fundamentally materialist if it has to have any meaning, and must of necessity imbibe the lessons of the postcolony, the space and time thus far reserved, not quite far away, for the production and suffering of death and its subjects.

To sum up, approaching the question of terror politically requires attention to the forms of sensuous life that constitute the mode of political subjectivities that erupt as the form called terror colludes with the forms of love (and suffering, though the latter is not my focus here) in contemporary culture. This requires going beyond the empirical cartographies of terror's distribution and appearance, and contending with the question of its production and of one's relation to it as a particular manifestation of the capacities to love and suffer. This question of production must, in turn, be placed in relation with the production of the worlds that suffer, sustain, and make sensible or insensible these destructions, and withstand the production and maintenance of—eruption into and eruption of—the subject of terror. Considering these subjects is inseparable from considering the subject who continues to defer the love on offer, forms and deforms regimes of times and spaces to which it is forcibly betrothed, and asks for something different.

THE FIGURES OF SOVEREIGNTY AND THE NECROPOLITICAL CONSENSUS

On the sixth page of "Necropolitics," Mbembe announces, "Having presented a reading of politics as the work of death, I turn now to sovereignty, expressed predominantly as the right to kill."[10]

It is now almost a ritual for me to turn back those six pages and find out exactly what this work is and who is doing it, and where, with Rancière, must I tell the story that is being told here. How might I find the subjects that I look for? I feverishly insert different things on those pages at different times. It is not that I do not understand the postcolony as the space of death, as a space marked for death, or as a place where certain things conflate and conjoin and produce death. But I have also seen that space as one that has been abandoned by everyone but capital, and still wonder exactly what kind of life or death is imbricated in that not-abandonment. Even I thought I had abandoned that postcolony but I didn't really, it is in and with me—capital knows it and enjoys that. So, I look and try to find the subjects I know. Yes, I feel I can put in those who kill and those who are afraid of being in the wrong (right?) place at the wrong (right?) time, Rancière's "fundamentalists," the Christians burnt in a bricklayer's oven for blasphemy and those who saw them burn, the two bearded Muslim men lynched and burnt to death in response to a church's destruction and those who saw them burn. ISIS, Daesh, and everything else.

I am not in search of a taxonomy for the good or bad necropolitical subject, those who kill and those who do not, but something that might gesture to both and also not enclose either, to see the structure as needing reproduction (so, not quite post- or anti-economy qua Bataille), and also filled with ordinary people trying to do what they can to be able to reproduce a life worth living, often through death. Beyond these spaces that I know is the solidifying consensus on the supervalence of violence and of physical cruelty, on imminent vulnerability and the bodies which can bear it, on the reification, objectification, and commodification of suffering, and what follows.

Maybe I have been spoilt by Rancière, and have become a formalist traitor to good causes, so much so that in telling this story, I do not know what or whose politics Mbembe is writing about. I believe that more than any other location of and from which one writes, the postcolony as a site to which to be accountable plagues the critic with a complicity in what is being written of. Very differently from an ethnographer or participant-observer anthropologist, though that bears a semblance. A different part-melancholic, part-mournful sense of being involved in whatever it is one is describing, a kind of absent subject that is always and forever present in its absence. Questions. Who claims sovereignty? Politicians? People on the streets? People who never come out on the streets? Suicide bombers? Or, is the desire for that sovereignty so total and universal that there is no way to read people's acts as truly otherwise? Mbembe pulls out Bataille to write of how death circulates in an "anti-economy," which is to say death beyond "reason": production that has no need (Marx), or a distribution that has no resource (political economists that Marx thought could do better).

Death is therefore the point at which destruction, suppression, and sacrifice constitute so irreversible and radical an expenditure—an expenditure without reserve—that they can no longer be determined as negativity. Death is therefore the very principle of excess—an anti-economy. Hence the metaphor of luxury and of the luxurious character of death.[11]

Subjects are formed through a work of the negative, which Mbembe extends into a struggle with death unto more death. He accepts, with Hegel, how one's becoming historical, or becoming part of history, requires living with death in a certain way. But, with Bataille, these subjects that Mbembe normativizes—makes normal and proper—to necropolitics are those that are not to be rendered insane or exceptional, since he sees them defining the nomos of our existence, harvesting the accursed share accumulating from times past so that killing is only of the last prohibitions in a series of those that must be flouted. Then there are those subjects who live alongside these figures of sovereignty, but no less with and through death. Often the transcendental empiricist (biopolitical or necropolitical) move abstracts from the subject in the name of the subject, where what is subjected is eclipsed by the how of the subjection. Might we find subjects that do not merely exemplify or evince necropolitics, but engage with it, appropriate it, instead of becoming appropriate to it? What does working with death actually entail, and where is its politics?

The specialness of necropolitics in relation to the old right to kill lies, in Foucault's and Mbembe's (insufficiently historicized) views, in the division of populations enabled by the biopolitical logic of state racism that leads to making live, letting live, letting die, and making die, entire portions of these populations. As discussed earlier, one might say that prior to the modern state, the logic of the right to kill is also racialized in medieval political theology, for one, and informs the manner in which the very idea of the body that deserves to live or die is instituted.[12] This is not an argument against the special relevance of necropolitics to our times, but a gesture to what might be lost in *not* historicizing the idea of sovereignty that is brought along wholesale in all of these formulations, as the alpha and omega, the undisputed hermeneutic, of politics.

For Mbembe, the necropolitical consensus finds one of its most advanced manifestations in apartheid, which brings together "biopower, the state of exception, and the state of siege."[13] The importance of race in this formation is no accident or coincidence—one of the crucial lessons of Mbembe's work—since many of these things are first practiced, learnt, and perfected in the work of death qua colonial administration. Bureaucracy and massacre happen together, in the incarnation and verification of Western rationality. The joint project of capital and colony shows the absolute inefficiency with which it was wrought and fraught, and that colonial violence finds its pinnacle in moments of the failure of empire.

IN TERROR, IN POLITICS, OUTSIDE OF SOVEREIGN TIME

In understanding "terrorism as political violence" to be "the ground upon which sovereignty is in many cases defined in the colonial present,"[14] both *colonial* and *present* are noteworthy. The essential link here is of sovereignty to time, not least because sovereignty is iterated in declaring the time of the now, a declaration that already signals (the threat of) its effective (actual or potential) undoing. Spaces which seem outside of time whether they lie inside or outside the colony, the increasingly merging times of the colony and the metropole (not least through movements of bodies, labor, war), and the enclaves of different temporalities in the standard sovereign grounds, all threaten this. Similarly, (unsettling) exceptions to the colonial present (in terms of experience rather than physical location) can be found in professed and manifest counter-temporalities.

The definition also suggests that the sovereign is sovereign over a moment of time, and not merely in the bounded space of the colony conventionally considered. If terrorism institutes sovereignty over time in the colony, we would be well-advised to not make the familiar move of seeing the colony as the exception that produces terror, but to see continuities with colonial time as the grounds for all political violence, whether in "healthy" or in "failed" states. This invokes a more nuanced criterion for separating forms of violence than just who is deploying it (such as the state vs. the partisan or the terrorist) or whose sovereignty is asserted in them, a rote anarchist and theological fallacy, each relying on simplistic notions of location, source, and agency. One might even be able to cite the very emphasis on sovereignty as already a conceit toward a particular temporal relation to spaces that serves to unify authority (a temporal principle) and community (a spatial one), subsuming the latter into the former. A better approach finds the form and the relations manifested in a given subject of terror to be more meaningful indicators of the politics of these acts. In the best-case scenario, this allows politics. This happens when the temporality of authoring prevails over its congelation in authority or its temptation to submit to an imagined, ahistorical, community, and when a premature, complete, and/or authoritarian subsumption of community into institution is prevented.

When the state of terror and of emergency is seen as an exception from time, it is tempting to bring other exceptions to the table. Perhaps, then, seeking exceptions to and ruptures in the sovereign probably should also involve seeking exceptions to and ruptures in the political principle of sovereignty as wielded by subjects. The colony and the margins then appear inhabited and haunted by the repeated acts of excepting and excluding, not least in the realms of being, sensing, and meaning. When political theology, for instance, goes in search of the outside of time, for the moment of emergency where law is suspended and can be re-invoked as justice by those who have nothing, this state of *emergency* carries no surprise for those spaces that are defined as *states* of emergency, margins which are always outside of time of the sovereign state and whose existence is premised on that exclusion.

These claims to outcast time—time that is, oddly enough, the effluent at once of sovereignty and the state of emergency—are essential to understanding and making more proximate the terror and the love produced in these spaces. Thinking of the post/colony, in its various connotations, as defined by alternate temporalities rather than geopolitical spatial boundaries, we are forced to accost the problem of time in the subject's destruction, destructibility, and attachment to terror. The destruction of the known subject of politics thus rings in a very differently "emergent" register in places where time has always been an effluent to time, life an effluent to life, and lives are cast into emergencies to which only violence is the response, whether physical, linguistic, material, or ideal. Here, political subjects are constituted by logics different from those that reassure the reputable, healthy, subjects of politics whose waywardness or destruction is today being lamented. The manner in which we do approach and evoke a politics has everything to do with how the question of, in this case, terror, must be cast in a light of its production and its sustenance in the contemporary global subject of terror, beyond the question of its distribution and of the how and who of lives valued or dispensable. Thus, in arguing for approaching terror politically via love and time, I cannot help argue against an idealized, utilitarian, mystical, or romantic relation to violence as redemptive or remaking (associations that pervade both liberalism and its supposed terrorizing enemies).

Those spaces that have stood for the "failure" of the post-WWII project of liberal capitalism need to be looked at not as horror stories but as lenses into the process that has led to the current spate of "crises." Entire worlds, albeit not always pretty ones, erupt on margins with a new vocabulary of love, devotion, and redemption, or with a different material relation to existing vocabularies. Their spatial dis/continuities are much less meaningful here than their temporalities coalescing as signals to a new politics (or at least a different one). The heartless and loveless economies of fear and brutality apparent in the globalized sensorium of terror can only be challenged and subverted from spaces where the consensus over the body, over anger, over murder, over love, and over politics and its promises, is still fluid, and occasionally even explodes.

Violence relies on intimacy, regardless of empirical or physical proximity, to have any meaning. No wonder, then, that all too often, understanding postcolonial violence begins with a consensus on one or the other materially borne and infectious pathology. This is itself an intimacy. There is Bataille's accursed share, there is Mbembe's necropolitics, there is Fanon's misogynist object of the *fidai* woman in a veil. There is enough in these frames, and in the idea of a lifeworld pitched at the threshold of necessity and desire, that suggests that even a decrepit and necrophiliac system is not held together only by mechanistic desire, pleasure, and pain, but needs emotional upkeep and adhesion, through the labors of love and suffering it exacts and manages over time. The forms of inherited and imposed love might be the modes that enable terror, spurred by moralistic invocations of feelings turned into idealized empirical absolutes in discussions of intolerance, violence, terror, and terrorism. In each of these formulations of affect, morality, and experience—utilitarian calculus, ahistorical morality, idealist empiricism, neoliberal securitization—time is corralled and conscripted in comparable ways, consistent with the temporalities of the colonizer, nation, nation-state, religion, and the market. Terror has a politics if (and because) it invokes a counter-temporality in the face of these guardians of a frozen past and a congealed futurity. Thus, when terror mimics the same temporalities as what it claims to oppose, and affirms the forms of destruction and death that produced it, it has exited politics. If it challenges given regimes of time and sense, it is political. This determination is squarely a matter of political judgment, of an intimate kind, and might bring some politics back to Malabou's new wounded.

Despite, but also because of, all this, speaking of love was and remains necessary. We have to turn to where we learn and are inscribed into and onto attachments. This lesson proceeds from the history of anticolonial struggles and also from the history of what they were trying to counter: colonization and fascism as claims to one's being, rather than to one's non-being or non-claims to being (like capitalism's, and sardonically "compensating" for that).[15] It also goes beyond the discovery of objectified desire and fetishism to that which attaches to the fetish object. It reaches for the labor not simply expended but maintained, kept, held, upheld, in our relations. It attends to time as neither the unit of labor alone, nor what is spent as the body gets spent, but that which ensues from the residual body moving through this world.

In desiring a politics that counters these productions, the forging of forward-looking solidarities cannot be separated from the attachments and capacities to love that have been shaped and conscripted so far, which are connected to suffering and death produced in the colony. As for being out of time, we can no longer hide behind the urgencies of any supposedly progressive or materialist politics that is shamelessly inattentive to a history of colonized spaces, times, and subjectivities that have produced societies and subjects who have survived their own deaths and annihilation. We confront a moment that can ill-afford to disavow or ignore the entanglements of colonialism, liberalism, capitalism, and fascism, whether in assessing our current "crises," or in articulating an intervention to the famed "end times" in which we live, or in addressing the convergent experiences of destruction and grieving on the proliferating margins of the colony and metropole alike. There is no way any of these interventions can proceed on the ontological or epistemological terms that have been in play so far. Otherwise, all I see in these anxious urgencies, and these problems of terror, austerity, and other precipitous horrors, are late and unschooled arrivals to the consistent experience of destruction and grieving in societies that have already been sacrificed as a precursor to this crisis. If at all one can, in this moment in history, have the gall to make a furtive gesture to reading and thought, in the name of either the seemingly inviolable and irreversible consensus on the lives of Palestinians, or the agentic suicides of farmers and protesters wherein the human body becomes a weapon of a different sort,[16] we might be able to see where the non-negotiability of this begins in history, with which requitals of which loves. It might challenge our understandings of how desire and attachment collate in the many kinds of love for freedom. It might yet be able to caution us about the sheer confidence of our own desires for sovereignty, habitation, recognition and whose sacrifice they will next demand. Who knows where it might put a dent in our hubris about and whose presence automatically means our absence, who we are to ask for another's sacrifice, whose history allows which theft, and who adjudicates to whom and where we must return.

NOTES

1. Edward W. Said, "The Essential Terrorist," *The Nation*, August 15, 2006, https://www.thenation.com/article/essential-terrorist/.
2. Carl Schmitt, *Theory of the Partisan: Intermediate Commentary on the Concept of the Political*, trans. G. L. Ulmen (New York: Telos Press Publishing, 2007).
3. "Caché (2005) - IMDb," accessed December 6, 2017, http://www.imdb.com/title/tt0387898/.
4. Elleke Boehmer and Stephen Morton, "Introduction: Terror and the Postcolonial," in *Terror and the Postcolonial: A Concise Companion* (John Wiley & Sons, 2009). p. 6.
5. Slavoj Žižek, *Living in the End Times* (Verso, 2011). p. 296.
6. Catherine Malabou, *The New Wounded: From Neurosis to Brain Damage*, trans. Steven Miller, 1st edition (New York: Fordham University Press, 2012). p. xv.
7. Žižek, *Living in the End Times*. p. 296.
8. Žižek. p. 308.
9. Jacques Ranciere and Davide Panagia, "Dissenting Words: A Conversation with Jacques Ranciere," *Diacritics* 30, no. 2 (Summer 2000): 113–26. p. 115.
10. Mbembe, "Necropolitics." p. 16.
11. Mbembe, p. 15.
12. Biddick, "Unbinding the Flesh in the Time That Remains"; Biddick, *Make and Let Die*.
13. Mbembe, "Necropolitics," p. 22.
14. Boehmer and Morton, "Introduction: Terror and the Postcolonial." p. 6.
15. The reader might turn back to the discussion of Fanon in Chapter Two, and the predicates and consequences of the framing of "existence" in existentialist discourse, even when anticolonial in intent.
16. Please see Banu Bargu, *Starve and Immolate: The Politics of Human Weapons* (Columbia University Press, 2014) for further discussion.

Chapter Six

Love Stories as Dissensus: Aesthetics Out of the Postcolony

> Storytelling then, in and of itself, or recounting— one of the two basic operations of the intelligence according to Jacotot— emerges as one of the concrete acts or practices that verifies equality. (Equality, writes Jacotot, "is neither given nor claimed, it is practiced, it is verified.") The very act of storytelling, an act that presumes in its interlocutor an equality of intelligence rather than an inequality of knowledge, posits equality, just as the act of explication posits inequality.
> —Kristin Ross, Introduction to Jacques Rancière, *The Ignorant Schoolmaster: Five Lessons in Emancipation*[1]

Nadeem Aslam's "Leila in the Wilderness"[2] provides glimpses of the palimpsest of terror as life, mediated by love, in our post/colony. It tells the story of a woman, Leila, married off as a child to a feudal lord who contrives the magical construction of a mosque as a ploy to annex the "hallowed" land that surrounds it: at once the site of profuse sacredness for the unloved poor, of Leila's rape by a band of priests, of her attempted escape by growing wings that are then cut off and her skin sown back to together to prepare her for one man after another. She gives birth to girls whom the husband kills (a few saved by a nanny), and every mishap of the birth of a girl is rewarded by compensatory futuristic impregnating sex. Engirding this story is the story of her lover looking for her with his little music box, and a magnet in his heart like hers.

The story seems ancient, but it is not: there are cellphones around. But that is not the only temporal trick pulled. Time is played with not only at the level of narrative/expressive tectonics, but in the normative aspects of subjective experience—certainly old-fashioned, but welcome. In one of the closing scenes, the two lovers, reunited, and most likely headed to their death at one of the butchers' hands at any moment, return to a room full of dead animals to release them in an act not of scarcity that comes with conventional notions of (bare) survival. What is driven home here is that love and the sensuous experience of time are tied to each other. Another retrieval is that, pace the modes of interiorized scarcity that shape life today, acts of abundance (what Nietzsche might call acts that are life-affirming) are not always dizzyingly plentiful acts (i.e., always in excess out of resentment and reaction). Their abundance is not to be understood merely in a limited currency of the act itself, but in the manner in which it comports this scarcity and abundance. In the first case, we prioritize the quantitative economy of action and sentiment, and consider it to be exclusively based on distinct actions relating to each other, counting, countering, and compensating in turn. In the second case, scarcity and abundance are qualities of and orientations to action and experience.

In *Leila in the Wilderness*, temporal schemes of reigning orders are defied. Life and death matter differently. There is much life among death, and so many moments of turning back to save the dead animals, those caught in and by time, as an offering of love, when every second counts for the escape. Far from indulging in a narrative of hope or a finality about optimism or its absence, the story is silent on it. The lovers do not give us hope cast in the temporal mold to which religion and its professed secular undoings in capital and nation are beholden.

At moments, this still might resemble a devotion to an ideology, a god, or a nation, for which one's life or death does not matter; it is very different. That is because this love is neither traumatized by the departure of god, nor asks for something else to fill the hole. Leila and Qes's experience of unrequitedness is not a *lack* of love that lashes out; it is *another* love. Their love's material negotiation with time and space allows for it to be a more material principle of action than hope in a conventional sense. The latter assumes a particular relation to time, and holds tight to a trench of time that will swallow whole any sacrifice we can give to it. In the former, the question of ends and beginnings, of necessity, gets transposed onto that of presence and absence, appearance and disappearance, in time instead of space. De-emphasizing beginnings and ends allows worlds to co-exist and not eliminate each other in the name of History, and as long as the lovers are hospitable to hauntings, they will preserve more life than what is harnessed to destroy them. There is much life among death, and it is not always in submission to the laws of life and nature that we know.

THE NECROPOLITICAL MODE OF AESTHETIC PRODUCTION

"You cannot tell the story of Kashmir except as fiction. Only fiction is truth in Kashmir. You can't write an evidentiary essay telling anyone the truth of how bizarre it is there."[3] So says Arundhati Roy speaking about her book *The Ministry of Utmost Happiness*. I would like to place this next to Ross reading Rancière on storytelling, in the epigraph to this chapter. My drawing this connection—placing explication and evidence—next to each other, reveals a bit of the conflation that often happens in the descriptive modalities of social sciences that uphold a positivist monogamous relation between "knowledge" and "reality" and their immanent mutual availability qua access, always sharpening the knives of triumphant knowing on the object to be supposedly saved by them—even if that becomes, on the part of the marginalized and oppressed, the constant necropolitical production of their own selves as object.

To be honest, Rancière himself does not tell many stories about violence, death, and disposability. There is an unabridged vitality in his discourse of politics as democracy (or democracy as politics) that gives many of us, if nothing else, some sense of dignity and self-respect walking out of a situation in which no relation one posits to those in power could ever be intelligible or verified. Rancière (hopefully) makes one a non-condescending teacher and writer and gives a way to make sense of and dispense with the exhaustion of the endless war of positions in a conventional view of politics. So, perhaps the equality via storytelling promised in Rancière via Jacotot is not about raising oneself to the level of the other, but a temporary or tentative, tentative as in awaiting verification, claim of sharing a world, a relation that usually turns out to be false and misguided.

The closest Rancière comes to speaking of, for instance, the suicide bomber is in differentiating sacrifice as verification of the word from sacrifice as obedience (the camp in which he places suicide bombers). He says, in an interview titled "Aesthetics Against Incarnation,"

> Don Quixote gives his life, not to obey the books of chivalry, but to make them true, just as the Christians have to give their bodies because, if they didn't, the book would not be true. The great reference here is Saint Paul; I verify in my flesh the sufferings of Jesus Christ, who himself verifies the book, the truth of the book. I think it is different from what happens in fundamentalism, where it is not a question of verification but just a question of obedience. Making a crusade in order that your religion be victorious is one thing. Taking upon yourself the responsibility of the truth of the book is another. In the case of suicide bombers, it is not a matter of enfleshment in the sense of Saint Paul. It is a matter of sacrifice, indeed, but sacrifice in the form of obedience. My life is nothing; I give my life as a sacrifice. But it is not the idea that your body has to become the body of verification of the book.[4]

Is there a way in which Rancière, despite his commitments, forecloses the meaning and reach of the act of enfleshment, and in this particular situation allows the relation of flesh and word to be closely configured and not open to reconfiguration, to politics? Are the patriotic militarism of the soldier and the insurgent terrorism of the wretched both policings of the relation of flesh and word that forestall hope for a politics, in either flesh or word? Rancière, in *The Flesh of Words*, looks at a particular pre-novel moment where modernity presents to us a radical choice between the relation to the book as one of testifying to it with one's body, and the production of "quasi-bodies," "fictional devices that construct [their] truth as the truth of [their] abandonment,"—"their" referring to those who by virtue of "being subject to suffering and derision are no longer able to verify the truth of the book."[5] Here, Rancière is making a claim that, to match Foucault's discussion of state racism (or modern slavery or empire), there might have been a historical moment where the proliferation of those who have no part allows for the proliferation of art and literature that are sites of the reconfiguration of the sensible, and of the relation between flesh and words—the coming of the aesthetic regime of art.

How must we, then, tell the *story* of Mbembe's "Necropolitics"? It is a story of spaces where a consensus over death and violence structures life, where politics is understood as sovereignty understood in turn as the production of death, installing as the new figures of sovereignty those who will remain bound to the sovereign promise of autonomy but via the heterogeneous and dizzying logic of violating prohibitions, especially killing. Importantly, not limited to the state. The old Hobbesian fiction come alive of the body imitating the body politic, the subject imitating the political order, an inversion that verifies the other fiction that the state mimics the soul. If Rancière is right, that the bourgeois "anti-epic" epic qua the novel can no longer support (and actually comes about in response to) those who, by virtue of being subject to suffering and derision, cannot verify the truth of any book. It is then odd that the *Leviathan* can still continue to tell not the tale, as in a novel, of a world that has abandoned us or cannot rely on us to testify to it (as in the novel), but of a world of the book which, perhaps only apparently, still needs our bodies to verify it.

The disposability of body or life is not an issue of being abandoned as in unvalued, as much as relegated to the mercy of a particular kind of valuation—something that likely separates biopolitics from necropolitics. Rather than being left to die for reasons of indifference, a purported non-relation, one is made to die because there is something counting on that death, it is valuable, indexed to something else, hence within the realm of relations. Killing has, thus, become a (value) relation in and of itself. Indeed, the (vulgar) materialists are home. Going some way with Mbembe, I agree that sovereignty was never clean of this logic of death, even when it said so, or focused on the moment of decision about decisions. Perversely, decisionism is often (but not solely) associated with Schmitt (and interestingly with the kinds of agonistic politics that find something to work with in the friend-enemy distinction) seems only relevant in the case of dying or killing, or letting live (but not, interestingly, "giving" life). So, the mutuality of decision and death is historically—and literally—secure.

But, why accept this fiction and its claim on our flesh, and sign us up for it wholesale? Lives only *appear* to be lived as a drama of decisions, and it is often the task of politics to produce a relation, to make a decision appear where it was not. To expose death where it was not being sensed or seen. That, to me, is a different project than keeping death in its place, in some way, and not seeing what counts as death. Within the capital-colony matrix, was there ever any moment where the body as labor had no index of a kind of value, or "mattering" in some realm? It is hard to imagine how, in the confluence of slavery, state racism, and capitalism, any death could ever be deemed death of the disposable, of the disposable as if the unconsidered or of no value. The issue for me is not that of the denial of but the active annihilation of materiality. So, "black lives," have always "mattered," have always figured in extremely neatly and meticulously, going back to the Zong case, in the calculus of life lived anywhere, life trained to live amidst and off death. The disposability of life is actually the value of death itself, so it may behoove us to think in other terms besides life and death as inverses of each other or found at each other's limits. And it may, too, become imperative for a dissensual politics to think more broadly about what it means to ask things to matter and be valued in a system already does so, just in its own way.

A NECROPOLITICAL MODE OF AESTHETIC PRODUCTION?

Rancière sees political subjectification as the act of the self-creation of subjects with recognizable voice, and whose crossing of that threshold of familiarity fundamentally shifts the sensible, aesthetic, realm. However, it is needful to go beyond the focus on voice and expression that seems to sometimes trip the aesthetic turn (for instance, in Rancière's work) in a mimicry of the fate of the linguistic turn: the radical claims of the assertion of those uncounted or miscounted still happens in conflicts over comprehensibility, cognizance/cognition, and externalization. Despite the express desire to redeem the aesthetic, the politics of reconfiguring the sensible seems to proceed through objects and objectifications of various sorts, either in the production of works of art or the proliferation of language. The normalization of the sensible via voice is already a circumscription of the domain of the political. The reduction of aesthetic resistance—metapolitical, corporeal—to a demand for sensual redistribution of the political realm already assumes a regime of the body in a transhistorical mode of production. Or, perhaps Rancière never claims more than the fact that this redistribution forces new productions which force new redistributions, and so on.

While Rancière acknowledges the fundamental dissensus that marks politics, I am interested in examining the moments in which he procures and arbitrates the consensus on part of the demos. I wonder whether there are dissensions underneath that are being overlooked in the agreed-upon modern democratic and egalitarian presuppositions. While he is cognizant of and sympathetic to the "interval between identities, whether these identities are determined by social relations or juridical categories,"[6] I am interested in the nature of this interval and the continuity and interruptions, locations and timings, that constitute, dissemble, and overcome it. Together with Foucault, Rancière seems a worthy ally in the realm of thinking about a history of sense experience. But they both falter when they become (or are made into) sociological pragmatists or quasi-pragmatist sociologists. Consensuality could then refer to the unspoken, unclaimed, consensus on the "equality" of the senses (and I would say their embodiment in time, which is a presupposition I cannot go along with) that grounds modern aesthetics, and also Rancière's egalitarian political aesthetics, even as he tries to disrupt other kinds of consensus and to save politics from obliteration by the ethical turn and by governmentality.

Rancière's view fails to capture the full scope of poiesis, presence, sensibility, and relations therein, that the aesthetic can and must accommodate if politics as the contestation over the sensible is the manifestation of a presupposition of equality and democracy in the manner that the uncounted and the unsensed seek to redefine and reassess those terms. Or else, this is just one other form of bourgeois patronage of the poor, something Rancière probably picks up from the bourgeois artworld. Even though the demos, in its "metapolitics" demands a reconfiguration of the sensible, the intelligible, and the possible, Rancière accepts that it cyclically submits itself to the count of the police order. So, while they are now supposedly heard or recognized, we are not given much in terms of what the new imperatives, for everyone, of the reconfigured sensuous realm look like. In what way is the body (and body politic) formed, deformed, transformed, and where do the unrequited within it reside?

So, while the demos does metapolitics (as a level of politics and critique) in a bid to conserve politics and to allow it to engage—in dissensus and tension—with the realm of the police (the order of epistemic comfort and ontic indifference/dismissal in my view), there are two other levels within Rancière's architecture: the parapolitical, and the archipolitical.[7] In some way, these levels are three different framings of the relation between the human and the political, not mutually exclusive over the course of a political existence. The demos dwells in the metapolitical, immanently demanding (often just by their presence) the repartitioning of the sensible; the "wronging," loving, feeling, dreaming, demanding, desiring to be counted. The police activate the parapolitical, keeping the disciplinary machine going, where the demos enter as formed and intelligible, a party in litigation, appropriated into a sense of ongoing time and laws that give life (history) to the institutions and the calculable subjects they need. The archipolitical deals with structuring, constituting, incorporating, and organizing the community from which the demos begs or declares exception in order to do its metapolitics. Žižek, in "The Lesson of Rancière,"[8] suggests a category of ultrapolitics to identify this begging of exception, this dis-corporation and the movement to not remain caught within the fascist straitjacket of the community as police. The architectural bent of this political "cosmology" might be enriched by a temporal infusion, so that we can go beyond time as either the history of these various incorporations and disembodiments, or as a succession of various identities and intervals between them, in order to look at time as itself being embodied, re-embodied, and disembodied.

While Rancière radically shifts the locale of politics to define it as the space occupied by those who are unnamed, excluded, and invisible, he still ends up replicating the topographical unity of modern liberal cosmology. This resemblance is, in my view, rooted in the way liberal democracy's flimsy claim to equality is radicalized by Rancière, but maintains a connection to the kind of bourgeois humanism of the American or French revolutions. I am certainly not taking away the empirical and sociological commitment to the "poor" in Rancière, nor dismissing the bounties of the revolutions. However, I am intrigued by how the claim to equality as a fundamental element of a democratic instantiation of, say, the sphere of aesthetics stands the test of time to be invoked as the formula for understanding and scripting political resistance and subjectification of those miscounted and uncounted. The aesthetic has a congenital correspondence to this in the modern world, as a historical example of the claim to the equality of the senses in the presupposition of equality between subjects that seems sometimes to be only a voyeuristic version of Kantian autonomy.

For Rancière, the demos' asserted claim to equality becomes the condition of the declaration of a wrong to which the reigning order he calls the "police" does or does not respond, by acknowledging the demos as an arrived political subject, ushering located harmonization and appropriations of the wrong into a new subject. This would be the death of politics, for Rancière, but it is not. Politics survives this interface with the police because these subjectifications are never complete and the dissonant excess, the unrequited reserve, which does not cross the threshold over into the realm of the police, continues to proliferate words and sensations.

THE RELATIONS OF AESTHETIC PRODUCTION

What understanding of aesthetics can be brought to spaces where politics as dissensus is framed by the necropolitical consensus over death and violence? How might the dissensus in these spaces inform ways we already think of aesthetics as politics, so that necropolitics does not name an exceptional space elsewhere, but what life anywhere today lives under the sign of, consciously or unconsciously? If, as I have argued, politics is seen as the power not only of making real, but of making material, it is the task foremost of those who are immaterialized by, or who are immaterial to, or whose frames of materiality do not quite fit within, the necropolitical consensus of neoliberalism and neofascism in the global postcolony. Thus, in keeping with (and extending) Rancière's idea of politics as the repartitioning of the sensible, a politics that encounters necropolitics in the post/colony would have to do two things. First, it would emphasize the work of poetics and aesthetics in the realm of the production of the sensible (in order to give due credit to the body's history in racial capitalism as the repose of time then harvested in the plantation, factory, or war). Second, it would find the repartitioning and rearrangement of the sensible insufficient given the history of cultural and knowledge production in colonialism. In other terms, if capital and colony have to remain (or be brought back) in this narrative, then modes of aesthetic and poetic production of the sensible must displace our focus on repartitioning of the sensible, and our fascination with cultural production.

If Mbembe finds autonomy to be a premise of acts of sovereignty, Rancière turns to equality as a premise of politics. (Emancipation, for Rancière, happens as a result of the claim to equality, in a more derivative way.) Equality turns out to be Rancière's own vestige of sovereignty. The idea of the part that has no part, and the idea of the partition of the sensible, both potentially set aside Marx's lesson of the issue of production that underpins and precedes distribution. If Mbembe can be taken to show how death is produced, we might be able to bring Rancière to address the production of the sensible, the insensible, the material, and the immaterial, that underpins any claim of the part that has no part. Otherwise, we are left with a plane of appearance on which one's claim to equality (a relation being elaborated with whom exactly?) can be made without asking to whom it is addressed, and what happens when we are not standing on that plane. This brings up at least three sets of relations that Rancière invokes: (1) the body with its irritable attachment and tactility that, in his later work, gets rethought more widely as the sensible, (2) the topos of politics, and (3) the axiom of equality as a (premature) claim to a we.

The Body and the Sensible

On the issue of what is distributed, whence it is produced, and what needs to be left open in any attempt at invoking the aesthetic in necropolitical spaces, Alexander Weheliye is resonant. He turns to Hortense J. Spillers's separation of body and flesh,[9] and conjures *Habeas Viscus*[10] as an ante-body potentiality capable of mobilities and vibrancies inaudible and insensible to the political order (or the diagnosticians thereof) that immobilizes them and relegates them to a realm of non-being and non-life. He is attuned to forces that would never be registered by the modes of materialism or transcendental empiricsm, let alone liberal idealism, that frame the search for a kind of redemptive voice or agency of the outcast, drawing attention to the "anti-matter" force of the flesh/habeas viscus, to the ways of not-being (human) and not-living (biopolitically) that exceptional populations have practiced for centuries (if not millennia). Weheliye insists that "the genres of the human" he discusses "ought not to be understood within the lexicons of resistance and agency, because, as explanatory tools, these concepts have a tendency to blind us, whether through strenuous denials or exalted celebrations of their existence, to the manifold occurrences of freedom in zones of indistinction." Not wanting to leave behind these concepts as completely irrelevant, he insists that holding off on the kind of theoretical decisionism inherited by a mode of reading "agency," we might be able to come up with "a more layered and improvisatory understanding of extreme subjection if we do not decide in advance what forms its disfigurations should take on."[11]

The Planes of Political Encounter

With the exception of the discussion of the architecture of sovereignty in Palestine via the work of Eyal Weizman,[12] which emphasizes the layering of zones of exception and the control of life and death by way of a vertical occupation, Mbembe sees the "topos of sovereignty" structured around reason in late modern normative democratic theory. In doing so, he effectively removes a number of other elements that have played a role in the emergence and codification of sovereignty as we know it. "From this perspective," he writes, "[T]he ultimate expression of sovereignty is the production of general norms by a body (the demos) made up of free and equal men and women. These men and women are posited as full subjects capable of self-understanding, self-consciousness, and self-representation. Politics, therefore, is deemed as twofold: a project of autonomy and the achieving of agreement among a collectivity through communication and recognition. This, we are told, differentiates it from war."[13]

In Rancière equality replaces autonomy, and dissensus is valued over the idea and reality of consensus. He writes:

In sum, the logic of political subjectivization, of emancipation, is a heterology, a logic of the other, for three main reasons. First, it is never the simple assertion of an identity; it is always, at the same time, the denial of an identity given by an other, given by the ruling order of policy. Policy is about "right" names, names that pin people down to their place and work. Politics is about "wrong" names—misnomers that articulate a gap and connect with a wrong. Second, it is a demonstration, and a demonstration always supposes an other, even if that other refuses evidence or argument. It is the staging of a common place that is not a place for a dialogue or a search for a consensus in Habermasian fashion. There is no consensus, no undamaged communication, no settlement of a wrong. But there is a polemical commonplace for the handling of a wrong and the demonstration of equality. Third, the logic of subjectivization always entails an impossible identification.[14]

Rancière's favored invocation of the 1968 slogan, "We are all German Jews"[15] is helpful here. He recalls the slogan as an example, even beginning, of the kind of "wrong" identification (not to be read only or at all as misidentification, but as an "an identification in terms of he denial of an absolutely essential wrong"). He finds crucial to 1968 the "ability to draw consequences from a 'being' that is a 'nonbeing,' from an identification with an anybody that has no body." His discussion of the German Jews and this "logic of the other" comes on the heels of how the French had no success in identifying with murdered Algerians, but could dis-identify with the French people in whose name those murders were committed. There he speaks of the gap between two identities, neither of which could be assumed, and he sees politics emerging in this gap. This stays in Rancière's work as the space of politics as that inhabited by those between, held together by a crossing of names and identities.

Equality and the We

Rancière is, admittedly, wary of the we that deems itself to be ontological and extra-linguistic, or extra-political. That also coincides with his adumbration of an aesthetic distance in the poetics of politics, worried that the encounter with what is produced might not leave room for the object to become what it needs, in order that the subject can become what it must. Emancipation for Rancière is deeply connected with letting the object be outside of our demands for it, and to learning to relate to it in a way that disrupts the "efficiency" of political art (or action)—by which he means the expectation that certain acts and works of art are determinative of certain consequences because we have a claim on knowing them well or being close to them. Emancipating the object is the way we (learn to) emancipate ourselves. In this way, there is certainly a healthy suspicion of the we that precedes and outlasts claims to a poetics of knowledge and a poetics of politics. Perhaps, on a generous note, Rancière is not a radical individualist suspicious of whatever binds us to each other, but someone who wants the affective bind to be articulated anew, a we that morphs and is conscious of itself as an aesthetic intervention in politics—an aesthetic intervention as politics. This is also the only way I can understand the axiomatic reliance on equality, but perhaps, I read it as a story that tells me that every political act is an attempt at establishing a premise of a shared world in which we might be equal, but with no guarantee of it. What can be read as a relation withheld, abbreviated, or too skeletal to be meaningful, in both the advocacy of distance and the axiomatic declaration of equality, can also be read as giving more room for this politics to decide what and whom it is actually about.

In the name of countering a scripted, thick order of inequality, this (little to no) role, or at least a negated role, that history must play in Rancière, often drives him to places where his formalism and his desire to unsettle in the name of politics might affirm a kind of unbridled presentism. His deep disregard for a kind of deliberative communicative consensus saves him from becoming a Rawls or Habermas, but he does not seem too far away from the liberal or deliberative democratic model when "we" still need to speak to be heard (though do not expect to be), and still need to be gesturing to a scene of interaction with the oppressor, a scene where equality can be claimed and a common ground for settling the wrong can be invoked.

Speaking of the axiom of equality in Rancière, Bruno Bosteels writes,

> The ultimate goal is to come to an understanding of politics without prefixes, of the real of politics set free from the typical efforts of philosophers to appropriate, displace, cover up and/or unmask its essential scandal, which is none other than the scandal of democracy when properly understood, that is, the staging of equality in the form of an empty liberty, over and against the purported naturalness of the existing order of domination. "This equality is simply the equality of anyone at all with anyone else: in other words, in the final instance, the absence of arkhê, the sheer contingency of any social order," writes Rancière. "Every politics is democratic in this precise sense: not in the sense of a set of institutions, but in the sense of forms of expression that confront the logic of equality with the logic of the police order." (*Disagreement* 15, 101). [16]

This relation to another opens into the possibility of politics, though I wonder if equality is quite the right way to frame it because, as discussed, there is a vestige of sovereign humanism and a kind of bounded plane of sensibility. The arbitrary setting aside of history to claim equality makes Rancière's world looks remarkably Rawlsian, but for the permission to mess with language and to show up refusing to be understood or denying understanding.

This has to be corrected in some way by opening up both the body and the word, and in that way the entire practice of incarnation to which Rancière gestures in *The Flesh of Words* would seem to be in need of serious historicization and update. When we speak of the part who have no part, the idea of exclusion should encompass exclusions from time and history, and the partaking should extend to inhabiting incommensurate times and spaces to produce differently with and in that time. There is also the cost of constantly performing the bad faith of equality, exhaustions that often know no register until someone blows up or disappears in the completion of someone else's project. I am not a fan of the idea that everything is only bound in a relation of non-relation, or incommensurable with any great consequence, but would like more substantiation of what equality is being claimed, and on what ground. Or else, the unconfessed, unexplicated, and unnegotiated produce their own superiorities. A case in point is Rancière's discussion of suicide bombers, where he sets aside the fundamentalist as having no relation to language, but one of belief or faith. Also, to him, the suicide bomber's incarnation of the word is not the same as the incarnation of faith warriors in the crusades, evading that the body is what it is now because of the potentiality that is reserved only for Christianity.

Subjects of Im/possibility

What character does necropolitics write for a political subject? The project of the poiesis and aisthesis of a subject who lives within zones of exception and exclusion can complicate the idea of necropolitics, and also address a compulsion to respond to contemporary political ontology in a political way. The poetics of politics is the work of the outsider, because it is a question of desire and bringing close what is not close, making present what is not yet. The metaphor becomes a way of filling out gestures, so that many things may exist in the space of that imprecision and impropriety. A mixed message from/to Rancière: close, but capacious?

The question returns to the claim to a shared world, and the impossibility of its verification. Not just impossibility, but the costs to life, heart, and mind of the failure of this verification. What if the body that appears on the scene of politics claimed a capacity to be with others rather than a relation of equality to them, or a capacity to love and suffer rather than produce words? One might have to think of dissensus at the level of the capacities on which the necropolitical logic relies. It will not suffice to speak on behalf of life versus death—for many reasons enumerated along the way. How do people queer the logic of "no futurity" when the state appropriates and enforces it? And what of those lives that have "value" only in being cast to death—farmers in India, death fasters in Turkey, soldiers with PTSD, debt-ridden young unemployed Japanese men? What yet of those lives lost under and amid all this death, possibly alternate existences, being sort of absent but vibrating underneath, unregarded?

What form of materiality will be corralled into the politics that actually disrupts the consensus of necropolitics, in a way that augments and edits Rancière's premises of dissensus? Dissensus would have to be staged at the very thresholds of materiality, with a kind of affective closeness that can withstand and support the depth and extension of this order of subjection (and its relief). Something in the love stories from the post/colony suggests this is possible, and may have important implications for the production and partition of the sensible.

SPECKLED SCREENS: LOVE IMAGINARIES PAST COLONIALISM

There were some other, one might say *less English*, keepers of our love imaginaries besides Merchant Ivory and E.M. Forster collaborations. But none of them made to a wall in that many-doored room, their presences and residues always far more sonic and suffusive than could be gathered on a poster. I wonder, though if I have fallen in an old trap when an immigrant, non-resident Indian writer can speak of citizenship in the cosmopolis created by Hindi cinema—"I am a resident father, a non-resident Indian, and a global citizen of the world created by Bollywood"[17]—and a resident Indian film director left to deal with the consequences agrees with his own film's villain in thinking that "Bollywood" is to blame for India's inability to deal with reality. In the words of his villain, "Every fucker is trying to become the hero of his own imaginary film. I swear as long as there are fucking movies in this country, people will continue to be fooled."[18] Then, Rima Mondal tells the following story:

> Bashir Hajam was an auto driver from Saraibal, Lal Chowk. He would park his auto in the premises of Naaz Cinema, which is till date, occupied by the Central Reserve Police Force. In 1994, he went missing. He was 23 then. It is said that he went inside the cinema one day and never came out.
> A week later, boatmen fished his body out from the Jhelum river near the Amira Kadal. Bashir was well known in the locality, and even in the state that he was in, he was identified by them immediately. His eyes had been gouged out and his body bore cigarette burns, as a resident recalls.
> By then, Kashmir had fiercely changed. People had stopped stepping out of their homes after twilight. And cinemas had become detention centres and torture centres.[19]

Thinking about colonial and anticolonial loves continues to be inseparable from the modalities in which they make itself available to us; for every Forsterian colonial/metropolitan love imaginary, there were a dozen Indian films writing their own relation between love and imagination. The aesthetics of cinema after independence, partition, and under ongoing settler-colonialism, is crucial in thinking about not simply cultural production but aesthetic production of the sensorium of the postcolony. After all, how is one to make sense of the centrifugal force that must bear witness to its surreal exhaustion in the cinema turned torture center on the one hand, and the destruction or permanent closure of cinema halls in Gaza around the time of the first Intifada, which has remained irreversible to this date.[20]

Nourished on the sound and image of Hindi film, I find the fabled outrageousness of Indian cinema to be not only an understandable response to colonial ideas of love and home, but also a counter to them. One, at least, wonders if there was something about film as medium and about the set up of the industry in India that was connected with thinking about love as a colonial act. We learn, for one, why there cannot and should not be a seamless validation of image as reality alone. Whether we find that wish fulfillment to be the goal, or its denial some sort of affront in our own acts of pedantry, I want to suggest that we ask for what and in whose name the aesthetic production of the sensible evades realism as a modern and colonial optics, and what kind of recalcitrance does it have to be in order to be both political and anticolonial.

In 1980, the VCR and the Kalashnikov both came to Karachi. Before the war of 1965, Indian films could legally run in Pakistani cinemas only for eight weeks, and after that were forbidden and banned entirely. The cinema might have been a vital institution erstwhile, but not in the time I was growing up. We heard stories of elders going to the cinema in olden days, Indian films offered us citizenship of an oddly provincial, domesticated, kind; we had the VCR. This is way less idyllic than the romance of the celluloid confessed by so many including the confident self-referential subtext on which many Indian films are built to this date.

It is true that routine film theory reference points feel insufficient in describing this citizenship of love, even if its optics had nary the same kinds of thrills to which Kumar confesses, or the thresholds of worldliness that Baldwin narrates.[21] But perhaps we all inherited that past in our bones. The pictures had come to and for us. Given where we encountered them, they became more discursive than visual. They were more like shortwave radio than the lost glory of Reno cinema. Pretty much every experience of the "cinema" was at home, or stealing away to someone else's home because your aunt had a VCR with a routine. This is a kind of phenomenology that forestalls the spectacle, or at least fundamentally transforms it, incarnating the subject through sight and hearing rather than in relation to a larger than life gaze. In a strange way, none of them were larger than life. This is why, perhaps in the absence of cinema proper, there is a different kind of intimacy born of this back and forth with Indian film, not least because different kinds of communities form to challenge the hold of the home as some unilateral and one-dimensional concept. It shows that one's own phenomenology of the experience is not the same as one's imagination and absorption of the film's own phenomenology, as one of the most spectacular feats of human cooperation and collaborative labor, something perhaps also instilled by a particular romance for the worker in the same households where we had to figure out when would be a good time to borrow someone else's VCR. There is something in common between the domesticated experience of the film and its underground quality, an entire world of economic and cultural relations that (on the surface) had nothing to do with the state. This is the protestant reformation in cinema that I quipped about earlier, just to mark the shifts in aesthetic production even when the cultural form is supposedly the same.

When critics and directors find reality and imagination frustratingly opposed, they recall the manner in which political scientists use the term "realism" to speak of nothing but a bizarre imagination that would not have to be forced down our throats so much if it had anything to do with how things truly, and fundamentally, were. The question of reality and imagination might itself be framed by which other binaries, such as mediation and immediacy, map onto that division, and how we factor in access, having, fulfillment, and gratification as the sine qua non of relating to the world, and interacting with other subjects and objects.

Perhaps giving all of Indian film a badge of anticoloniality is characteristically preposterous itself, and/but not my point here, since I am not (yet) speaking to content or even genre. I am intrigued by how so many different types of films have in common a mode of production of the sensible (rather than a mode of sentimental distribution) that proposes and proffers a relation between the senses, a relation across the senses, and relocation and rearrangement of desire. This mode of production highlights the complete reductionism and one-dimensionality of the reason that rules the experience of visual (and other) art from a privileged Western position. Here, I am cautioned by Martin Jay who, in his magisterial *Downcast Eyes,* points to the multiplicities of sensoria that exist within a given moment that might keep us flattening out and castigating entire historical periods for their complicity in a particular mode of knowing.[22] So, for the purposes of this argument, what I take from him is that one has to understand in some basic sense that a way of seeing only gets articulated in relation to other ways of seeing, and hence we already are dealing with relations among and across multiplicities. There are ways of reading with and against Jay's gleaning of gaze, glance, and vision, just to see if there might be something to be said for the modes of seeing that connect to an optics that emerges in, but counters, colonialism—which might suggest both a production of the sensible, and its partition.

Put another way, perhaps the unbelievability and incredibility of Indian film is its own way of thinking about a struggle with the colonial and liberal sensorium. The challenge is serious and begs examining beyond the settled and prevalent optics, or beyond the repartitioning of the given sensible. Perhaps these films as Platonic forms are the counter to the "denigration of vision" that David Levin and Jay both document and lament in their respective works.[23] I am thinking about whether there is a way to examine the mode of aesthetic production in these films—various artistic and sensory inputs held together by diverse relations between text and word, between plot and music, and to emplotment and the sensorial infrastructure—as not merely prescriptive but modeling a different, sensorial, relation to reading the real. In the same mode exist the interrelations of the senses and the synaesthesia of postcolonial film, exemplified in the role of music as more than a soundtrack but as a character in the films that produces a sonic structure for visuality. This adds a dimension to the encounter with love and desire, their requital and consummation, and the characters that always seem to be able to have all those things.

Even a firebrand independent-spirited film director like Anurag Kashyap who makes films that are real, heavy, unresolved, unreconciled, unstoppable and serpentine in time, like "a filthy, great freight train, carried along by relentless narrative momentum, fluid camera work and a throbbing soundtrack" makes common cause with a villain of his gangster epic who thinks that films have destroyed an entire generation (quoted above). He speaks of the retrogressive effect Indian films have had on "exhausted and miserable" Indians who do not want to watch depressing or real films, who prefer to stand outside the movie, and who want the movie to do everything for them like servants, including carry the "the burden of making [them] happy."[24] But this judgment begs complication. At least it requires seeing the shared aesthetic and sensorial infrastructure across the "good" and "bad" films, which make and unmake each other in hidden correspondence over time. For one, the politician's grudge that everyone wants to be a hero, and write one's own story—as if they are the same thing, like they are for the colonizer—cannot possibly be Kashyap's complaint also, because his films explicitly show how *our* hero is never writing his story, as much as he thinks he is, and likely will not be around to tell it. So, thanks to the colonizer, we have taken the hero and the story and are doing what we can with them.

Perhaps under all the fabled (sensible) irrealities of Indian cinema—"obsession with hygienic clean spaces," "[. . .]song-and-dance numbers, [. . .] muscular heroes, [. . .] leering bad guys, [. . .] compliant females, [. . .] luxury brands," "pseudo-Hollywood movies set nowhere, [. . .] with everybody good looking and having great physique," the average film "a shiny yellow Lamborghini"—encapsulated in the moniker "Bollywood" for Bombay cinema,[25] is an invitation to take seriously the manner in which certain kinds of limp recoveries of our senses from the onslaught of the colonizer's "love" point to something else that will remain fundamentally unrequited and a kind of ill-fated union (for instance, the hero and the story).

In turn, these recoveries in the realm of cinema inspire their own new recoveries. The very history of Indian cinema and its (re)productions and examinations of colonial loves and their lifeworlds cue the retooling of aesthetics to counter the settlements in the aesthetic realm. This is not an evolutionary story, but a synchronic one. I believe that for all that is the surface in Indian films, there are signals to ways of sensing and perceiving reality and the not yet real(ized) that are helpful in thinking about loving, desiring, seeing, not-seeing, in an arrangement of times that is film—a colonial gift that also relates critically and (ant)agonistically to that inheritance.

For Love of the (Under)World: A Democracy of the Unrequited in the Postcolony

The aesthetics of love are intimately related to the aesthetics of politics; this is what we owe to a history of having grown up in the 1980s as seers of things, including things made absent. Love stories in Indian films, incidental to and abundant on the banal and seething "criminal" margins of society, are deeply instructive in rethinking the aesthetics of immediacy. This happens by not only countering realism but also by finding a genre that, instead of harboring a seething disregard of the rationalist binary, pushes it to its limit so that the relations between imagination and desire, as well as love and reality, get rearranged. None of this would be possible without the stories of ill-fated love, and the possibilities of poetry and of love as poetry, that reside in the asymptotic, always failed, relation that does not spurn the relation in favor of non-relation, but recasts a new relation of unrequitedness in love. Recall here the sufi poetry that imagines Allah as the beloved, and the beloved as fundamentally beyond our reach but always with us. To read this as austere, self-denying, or abstinent only belies a lack of imagination itself. Not to mention that responding to fascists with empirical reality or "truth" never works; the point is to out-imagine them.

It is no accident that the protestant reformation in cinema of the 1980s coincides with the long Islamic revivalist moment of Zia-ul-Haq's Pakistan. Underground economies in video cassettes with Indian and Hollywood films boom right next door to markets flooded with Kalashnikovs and refugees, both products of the Afghan war. The topographic revisions of the polis and what and whom it contains flail in one direction toward the woman around the outlines of whom first the shawl is wrapped and the home is built, and in another direction toward those which must be kept out, the infidel, or the refugee, the transgender, the blasphemer, the Christian, the Shia, or those declared Ahmedi. Both these moves get to install the home as the proper locus of certain bodies and certain imaginations and fantasies of bodies. This moment is important for me not for the unmistakable sensorium and cultural lifeworld that is specific to these confluences, but because it says something about another confluence: the unrequitedness at the core of democratic politics and projects, the relation of visuality to a kind of distance and not to immediacy, and the synaesthesia requisite of counter-colonial aesthetics within which, among other things, a different reading of visual experience beyond the cinematic as larger-than-life becomes necessary. When the spectacle of the cinema is displaced by the privation of a home filled with presences and hauntings, are fantasies somehow also sullied? Or, can we find some sort of a retooled sensorium, a kind of inversion of the domus that might help understand exactly what fills those spaces of cordoned revival and protestantization? These have something to do with the ability to imagine a relation to self, others, and possibility that is ill-understood by focusing on the technology of the cinema via the society of the spectacle in an aesthetics and politics overpowered by crass representational understandings.

But, when I consider shuttered cinemas in Palestine, or pellet guns blinding hundreds of young Kashmiris,[26] it is not just the theft of the sense of sight, but of the capacity to own experience in a certain way. I find that film from the post/colony, with my discussion mainly focused on South Asia, has the capacity to reflect on the sensory worlds in which, among other things, we do not merely mimic what is happening, but where our suffering and our love have meaning by coming into contact with others'. This is what has often peeved me about representational understandings of art that speak of "learning" violence or masculinity from films, when it is much more interesting to ask what voids they fill, which they preempt, and which spaces inside and in-between various selves, and between selves and others, they open up for relations to live.

Across the marginalized sensoria of a people, the sensorium of the household that is at once the removal from the public rather than the production or source of one, and the capacity for unrequitedness in the form of a more extended relation of non-immediacy that is hidden in the seeming availability of images (rather than a simplistic narrative of mimicry or absorption), sight is the sense that indexes a prospective politics of the sensible. A relation to home that is bred through dream and fantasy, like Intizar Husain's (Chapter 4), by no means needs to be fated as a particular imagined community conjuring a nationalist future; history and love seem to still be deciding where to set up home, since they keep meeting in a different place. Transporting this to film, we can surmise how these fugal temporalities make it a democratic medium not for its availability or accessibility to people but because it counters the state's spatialist politics with a democratic and sometimes even republican idea of feeling and being in times to fills out a space that is not colonial or nationalist (but not by staying silent on it).

Three films in the contemporary Bombay noir genre come to mind to illuminate this: Anurag Basu's *Gangster*,[27] Ram Gopal Varma's *Satya*,[28] and Vishal Bhardwaj's *Omkara* (the second in his Shakespeare trilogy, this one being Othello displaced on the streets of Bombay and the broad political temperament of the state of Maharashtra).[29] Any film I like ends up being a love story to me, but not every film's claim to being a love story works. The former is peculiarly so in these films, where there is a willingness to assert the claim as if to make them citizens of a province "of love" that would ordinarily not accept them as such: they are violent, testosterone-laden, there is often a raucous dance number picturized on a woman who is vampish without being pathetic, dismissable, or heroic. And of course when were high-velocity, compulsive, heterosexual relations among poor people ever a promising fight against patriarchy?

But, something does happen. The relations of love in the film *Gangster* allow an interesting recovery from the novelistic subject-centered unfolding of a human life where every character is just tempting you to probe their history and genealogy, or dying to bare their hearts. There is a certain presence in all the characters that compels taking stock of the love between them, just as it was, a love despite availability. The female protagonist is not a woman abused by the man she loved, or the man who was a criminal otherwise, but by those who did not *need* her, to whom she was dispensable. And she is the one who betrays our improbable hero, another one for the innocent betrayals list from Chapter 4. Then there is *Satya*, the story of warm fraternities on the poor and criminalized margins of society that can come across as hypermasculinist, but it is clear that terror and killing is never a place of great strength for anyone involved. Nor, however, is there ever a plea that "these gangsters are people too," or an apologetic fascination with "reasons they are this way" (not that the self-congratulatory nature/nurture industry in film did not run amok among a rapidly industrializing and reformist India back in the 50s and 60s; even *Law and Order SVU* is unbelievable with the structuralism of the DNA!). *Omkara*, an adaptation of Othello, is an intensification of the logic of each of these other films. Dolly is the object of affection, and of immediate devotion, to someone who is no one because inferior by caste and racialized as such. And then he becomes somebody. While this becoming might not be a dialectical affirmation of her being in love with her, it is true that there is an interesting moral of the story where becoming one who loves, and becoming someone else, are at odds with each other. Perhaps becoming one in love is always already mimicking the undoing of the hero, at the same time as he is the one who kills her because he cannot bear the person he has become in love with her, but she can bear that blame even in her death. Perhaps the undoing that is requisite of a kind of love is necessary? This is where the idea of masculinity gets flipped around. The women in love are certainly already aware of what this undoing even means, and while they wait, it is not for a surprise.

The films impress on us that often there is no way to fully feel the force of corrupt colonial and bourgeois relations unless you see them carried to perfection into a criminal one, and that once that happens, then even the redemptions of those relations can never be too confident of their claims on what spaces—of home and the world, inside and outside—mean to those who are written out of any concept or experience thus bounded, and whose lives expose the utter nonsense of many a dualistic narrative of oppression and liberation that does not address how those spaces and the times they contain are produced and by whom. The worldly criminality of the household is especially highlighted once the woman shifts from one to the other (which is why *Omkara* is so much more brutal and haunting than *Gangster*). The woman in *Gangster* is already out of a traditional family home, lives alone, and most of the affirmation and exchange of love happens at a distance, unsexualized to boot, and seems to be just a pure longing. Without romanticizing prudish purity, there is certainly some lack of brash virility in this, which possibly has to do with the fact that the woman is not *at home*, no repressed waiting to return. When she is domesticated (often when she is an object of love), she is most vulnerable, rather than the other way around. In *Omkara*, it is in the spaces most familiar and most safe that all the evil descends (such as an eagle dropping a snake in the midst of Dolly's bridal ritual). So, to return to Chapter 3, it messes with the moralistic clarity of the home and the world, for those for whom these lines are drawn in a way unimagined by the "west" (see Tagore, or *Gangster*), to show us that domestic spaces can be the only place where the "world" gains its comeuppance, via those who produce domestic time and spaces, and where it isn't the place of clear at-homeness. And the unanswerable question, where does one go?

When love is understood only as affirmation and constitution, in line with these constructions of interiors and homes, it keeps us from comprehending the experience and the relationalities that keep the margins the home they are, and allow them to be the spaces of life and labor that would otherwise be much more dead and controllable than they often seem to be, when someone acts out of love, deviates, terrorizes, or murders. Tied together by their comment on love and marginality, these stories and films unsettle the colonial aesthetic in the same breath. Beyond a representational or epistemological relation to its subject/s, these cultural productions have something to say about the aesthetic in an ontological sense that is often lost in (bad) reading: such as how time gets drawn or framed, and how certain framings of temporality and existence question the ontic dominion of colonial, and now neoliberal, times and spaces. Far beyond redemption and closure, there is an irreducible challenge to the bourgeois romance of spatial conquest, domestication, home, and salvation, and a post-disenchanted irreverence toward (and not merely clever artistic control over) bounded and overdetermined temporalities and the anthropologistical "life history" imperative after colonialism. The close-at-handness of death forces a rethinking of the bourgeois prejudice toward life and time only as we know it. There is no chest-thumping celebration of violence, just as there is no philanthropy of a "humanizing" narrative either, which always proceeds from either suffering, violence, or love first being considered alien from "consensus" humanity.

Coda: The Challenge

Advocating an anticolonial mode of aesthetic production of the sensible commits us to the following. One, to asymptotic desire (of another or of knowledge) that is not immediately transferable into access, possession, or consumption. Two, to time as a structural actor with a range of motion and stillness, activity and passivity, in and across spaces, and not just as a contextual variable whose only meaning is in becoming history. Three, to formations of imaginaries that understand the public and the spectacular in a different way after colonization and counter the imagined community produced by print a la Benedict Anderson. Four, to realism's irrelevance to the poor or the oppressed; the idea that we have been waiting for our truth to be shown on screen just seems preposterous to me. Five, to unsettling, counter-colonial, optics that take into account the history of seeing in modernity in close connection with the relation of desire without psychoanalytic reductionism, and propose other constellations when we displace the sensorial configuration of colonial modernity to find new relations between and across the senses, where each sense and its function shifts in new relations of production of the sensible.

NOTES

1. Kristin Ross, "Translator's Introduction," in *The Ignorant Schoolmaster: Five Lessons in Emancipation*, by Jacques Rancière (Stanford, Calif.: Stanford University Press, 1991). p. xxii. Printed with permission of the publisher.
2. Nadeem Aslam, "Leila in the Wilderness," in *Granta 112: Pakistan*, ed. John Freeman (London: Grove Press, Granta, 2010).
3. Charlotte Sinclair, "Arundhati Roy: Why Happiness Is a Radical Act," *Vogue*, July 27, 2017, http://www.vogue.co.uk/article/arundhati-roy-interview.
4. Jacques Rancière, "Aesthetics against Incarnation: An Interview by Anne Marie Oliver," *Critical Inquiry* 35, no. 1 (2008): 172–90, https://doi.org/10.1086/595633. pp. 179-80.
5. Jacques Rancière, *The Flesh of Words: The Politics of Writing*, trans. Charlotte Mandell, 1st edition (Stanford, Calif: Stanford University Press, 2004), 123.
6. Jacques Ranciere, *Hatred of Democracy*, trans. Steve Corcoran, Reprint edition (London New York: Verso, 2014), 59.
7. Jacques Rancière, *Disagreement: Politics and Philosophy*, trans. Julie Rose (Minneapolis: University of Minnesota Press, 1998). Ch. 4.
8. Slavoj Žižek, "The Lesson of Rancière," in *The Politics of Aesthetics: The Distribution of the Sensible*, by Jacques Rancière (London; New York: Continuum, 2004). pp. 67–68.
9. Spillers, "Mama's Baby, Papa's Maybe," 67.
10. Alexander G. Weheliye, *Habeas Viscus: Racializing Assemblages, Biopolitics, and Black Feminist Theories of the Human* (Durham: Duke University Press Books, 2014).
11. Weheliye, 2.
12. Weizman, *Forensic Architecture*; Al Jazeera English, *Rebel Architecture - The Architecture of Violence*.

13. Mbembe, "Necropolitics," 13.
14. Jacques Rancière, "Politics, Identification, Subjectivization," in *The Identity in Question*, ed. John Rajchman (London ; New York: Routledge, 1995). p. 67.
15. Rancière. p. 67.
16. Bruno Bosteels, "Archipolitics, Parapolitics, Metapolitics," in *Jacques Rancière: Key Concepts*, ed. Jean-Philippe Deranty (Routledge, 2014), 80.
17. Amitava Kumar, *Bombay, London, New York*.
18. Anurag Kashyap, *Gangs of Wasseypur - Part II*, n.d.
19. Rima Mondal, "Stalled Show: How Kashmir's Cinema Halls Became Torture Centers," *Free Press Kashmir* (blog), July 21, 2017, http://freepresskashmir.com/2017/07/21/stalled-show-how-kashmirs-cinemas-became-torture-centers/.
20. Ylenia Gostoli, "Reviving the Art of Cinema in Gaza City," *Al-Jazeera*, March 26, 2016, http://www.aljazeera.com/news/2016/03/reviving-art-cinema-gaza-city-160324060451220.html.
21. James Baldwin, *The Devil Finds Work* (Verso, 2011).
22. Martin Jay, *Downcast Eyes: The Denigration of Vision in Twentieth-Century French Thought* (Berkeley: University of California Press, 1993), http://www.loc.gov/catdir/bios/ucal051/93000347.html; http://www.loc.gov/catdir/description/ucal041/93000347.html.
23. David Michael Kleinberg-Levin, *Modernity and the Hegemony of Vision* (Berkeley: University of California Press, 1993), http://www.loc.gov/catdir/bios/ucal051/93001523.html; http://www.loc.gov/catdir/toc/ucal041/93001523.html; http://www.loc.gov/catdir/description/ucal041/93001523.html.
24. Steve Rose, "Anurag Kashyap: Bollywood Is to Blame for India's Inability to Deal with Reality," *The Guardian*, February 28, 2013, sec. Film, http://www.theguardian.com/film/2013/feb/28/anurag-kashyap-gangs-of-wasseypur.
25. Rose.
26. Mirza Waheed, "India's Crackdown in Kashmir: Is This the World's First Mass Blinding?," *The Guardian*, November 8, 2016, sec. World news, http://www.theguardian.com/world/2016/nov/08/india-crackdown-in-kashmir-is-this-worlds-first-mass-blinding.
27. Anurag Basu, *Gangster* (Adlabs Films, 2006).
28. "Satya (1998)," accessed September 30, 2009, http://www.imdb.com/title/tt0195231/.
29. "Omkara (2006)," accessed September 30, 2009, http://www.imdb.com/title/tt0488414/.

Chapter Seven

Materialists in Love

In his lament and relief at the figure of the unreciprocated lover, Benjamin is not the only one among the Frankfurt School critical theorists to speak of love, even and especially as they criticize and reject the properties of bourgeois love that persists in the exploitation of capitalism and fascism and the criminal complicities of the culture industry. Adorno's search for a mode of suspended subjectivity requiring a special kind of love and sensibility beyond the comprehension of fascism is a case in point, as is his demand for an education that would unschool us in the coldness and hardness produced in the march toward Auschwitz which a Europe eager to move on from that terror was meant to overlook, and ironically even sustain, in its modes of teaching history and getting over it.

In our time, both these lessons are crucial, as is the fact that the unrequited shirks conscription into a particular form, refuses the blackmail of necessity as content without form, and is also unwilling to give up on love. Its propositions are on the order not of redemption, but of finding some possibility of still relating to others, in love. And the possibility not merely of an I, but a you—perhaps a we if we are lucky—by assuring that a you exists for me to be possible. The distance that Adorno seeks might be what needs to be overcome in this time: that might be the crucial difference between the love that is spared fulfillment and the one that is unrequited. The former is the love that seeks to stay away to protect itself that shies away from consumption given who it may next kill. The latter is the love that insists that perhaps a we is necessary, and that a we exists in some realm that may not be coextensive with the planes of existence legible within frames of sovereign politics. In that realm, perhaps time and space warp to bring us closer to the object of love but force a different way of knowing and being subjects.

The move from the unreciprocated to the unrequited, then, features not the loveless historian, but the one who loves in order to be close. Otherwise, the plunge away from politics into the ethical realm of dyadic relations—in a contemporary replay of the secularization episode—and the necessity to always confront one's beloved (and one's enemy) head-on and face-on, exhausts those of us who are always already finding ways to contort our bodies to be close but perhaps not confront, because what confronts may not be beautiful, and may not look back. Adorno and Benjamin, in different ways, are too nostalgic for that confrontation and perhaps a little too self-assured of their desirability for that confrontation (need a little more Rousseau and Nietzsche in the mix)—and someone like Fanon too convinced of the fallaciously indifferent desirability of the white master. I believe that we have to find other ways to round out this question of where one stands and what one can see from where one stands, something that is crucial to this book's positing of a shared world as a question. Might the unrequited find more ways of standing beside, behind, or in front of another as a shield, without any assurance that we will embrace or look into each other's eyes. Where Adorno stops, we must continue: a proposition of a world with others, not a retreat into wishful autonomy. A damaged life in the service of another life. It is also true that a kind of insistent materialism has to emerge from the margins and itself have a commitment to the unrequited—or else it is one that will most readily deliver the body in pieces, free of responsibility and charge, as if that is all that could be done. *As if that is all that could be done.*

BODIES IN PIECES

> What image am I offering your eyes now? The body of a woman cut into pieces; her limbs, dismembered and palpitating, sent to twelve Tribes; all of them, in the grip of horror, raising a unanimous clamor up to Heaven, crying out in concert; no, never has anything of the like been done in Israel until that day, since the day of our Fathers' exodus from Egypt. [. . .] Let us dare enter these details, and reassemble at the source of the civil wars that made perish one of the tribes, and cost so much of the blood of the rest. (First Canto)
>
> [. . .] the half-dead girl [. . .] (Second Canto)
>
> [. . .] without hesitation, without trembling, the barbarian dares to cut the body in twelve pieces; with a closed and sure hand he hits without fear, cuts the flesh and the bone, separates the head and the limbs. And, and after he has done sending the tributes of dreadful parcels he continues to Maspha, tears his clothes, covers his head with ashes/cinders, and bows himself down to measure when they arrive and cry out for the justice of the God of Israel. (Second Canto)
>
> . . .

Materialists in Love 165

[...]
Then the Levite, presenting in a dismal apparatus, was interrogated by the elders in front of the assembly on the death of the young girl, he spoke thus: "I entered into Gibeah city of Benjamin with my wife to pass the night, and the people of the country entered the house where I stayed, wanting to offend me and make me perish. I was forced to surrender my wife to their debauchery, and she is dead from what followed by their hands. Then I took her body, I put it in pieces, and I sent them to everyone in your borders. Lords, I tell the truth, do what one would see as just before the Most High." (Third Canto)

[. . .] Daughter of Bethlehem, I carry you good news; your memory will not remain without honor. In saying these words, he fell to his face, and died. His body was given public funerals. The limbs of the young woman were reassembled and put in the same sepulchre, and and all of Israel cried for her. (Third Canto)

[...] there are still virtues in Israel,
—Jean-Jacques Rousseau, "The Levite of Ephraim"[1]

Baghdad, one night. The end—the very end—of the river's course slopes gently between the city and the palace. Here, at the bottom of this wide river, the Tigris, rests a young woman's body. A body cut into pieces.
Algiers, 1994. Atyka, professor of French, a language she has chosen, that she enjoys teaching.
[...]
When she was twenty, born in the same year as Algeria's independence, decided to earn her degree in French.
"I'm surprised," her father told her. "You, so good in Arabic . . . I saw you in Arabic linguistics, in Islamic exegesis, a specialist in Muslim law . . . but what do I know?"
"Leave her alone," the mother said to him.
"It's obvious that she hears us laugh and argue in what? In French! It's we two that she loves in this language!"
[...]
"I am going to be a French professor. But you see, with truly bilingual students, French will let me come and go, not just in multiple languages—but in all ways."
[...]
"She remains nameless, alas," Atyka says to herself. "How can you name somebody who first shows up in pieces?"
The body, the head. But the voice? Where has Atyka's voice taken refuge?
The body of the woman cut into pieces. The body, the head. But the voice?
—Assia Djebar, "The Woman in Pieces "[2]

In his "The Body of Michael Brown," conceptualist poet Kenneth Goldsmith "remixes" and rearranges the official autopsy report of Michael Brown, the unarmed black teenager killed in the streets of Ferguson, Missouri, by a white police officer who is no criminal in the eyes of the law he enforces. The dead body that lay in the street for four hours or so, comes to the stage not only to be inscribed on by a reading of the autopsy (literally, self-seen, eyewitness) report, but to be rearranged, re-sutured, reordered as a body in the hands of a poet and presented to the world. Goldsmith's defense of this art was that he, like in his earlier work, "took a publicly available document from an American tragedy that was witnessed first-hand (in this case by the doctor performing the autopsy) and simply read it." The "poiesis," however, involved the following:

> I altered the text for poetic effect; I translated into plain English many obscure medical terms that would have stopped the flow of the text; I narrativized it in ways that made the text less didactic and more literary. [. . .] I always massage dry texts to transform them into literature, for that it (sic) what they are when I read them. That said, I didn't add or alter a single word or sentiment that did not preexist in the original text, for to do so would be go against my nearly three decades' practice of conceptual writing, one that states that a writer need not write any new texts but rather reframe those that already exist in the world to greater effect than any subjective interpretation could lend.[3]

It is worth wondering if it is the autopsy or the body that is publicly available, and what the relation between the public availability of the two is. Indeed, what becomes public first, or is the mode of publicity mediated by personal observation of a public murder (one signified in the presence of the murdered body) notarized by the state in the autopsy report? A personal observation turned public precisely because it is able to disavow this act as a witnessing of the self, only deeming it a witnessing by a self trusted by the state to see. The senses of the state, embodied in the policeman who sees in his target a demon beyond being killed, demand an investigation. His seeing, which ensures that scores of bullets will be required to kill a stationary target, flawlessly becomes something like the colonial mimicry that represents, exposes, and ironizes, liberating marginal elements in excess of the sovereignty intended to be affirmed. One wonders whose excess is this, the body's or the poet's (and whose to which end)? Goldsmith takes as fact that a publicly available—publicly available because of various degrees of publicity in death and beyond—body speaks for itself. For him, it is a text already existing in the world that only needs to be reframed and presented (importantly, not re-presented). By claiming that he did not alter a single word or sentiment of what is ostensibly self-evident and given, Goldsmith is unwittingly abdicating subjectivity in the garb of presenting what is beyond or prior to subjective interpretation. (What exactly *are* the rest of us doing, those who *turn* to the body when they do, and to what end and effect?) In disavowing his own subjective interpretation, Goldsmith normalizes and neuters himself disingenuously, refusing to take stock of the subjectivity that is wrought of the relation between himself and the other being conjured. A form of self-absolution even prior to any redemption of the murdered body, this is a dishonest suspension of Goldsmith's own subjectivity that still predictably uses the only body that exists—the body of the dead black boy—as shield, not subject, in a mimic of the absence of moral demands between those who are not subjects. I am not interested in arguments about the intention of the artwork, but the material effect that Goldsmith rushed to deliver the body on the heels of the law that delivered the body. I want to interrogate the politics of what it is we do when we show up with the body, or when we quickly turn to it as evidence, as either origin or terminus.

I ask this question because I am wary of the command that is being heeded when we present the body, or name the body in pieces. Is the body that is deemed to be prior to, the same as that which is declared to be beyond subjectivity (to draw an analogue to Goldsmith's claim about interpretation)? Who has access to this body? What does the body do when we ask it to show up for our sake? What problem does the body solve? What does it deflect and displace? And if one is to be true to the *auto*psy not only as personal observation, a seeing by the self, but also as a seeing of the self (a potent misreading), then what gets seen or exposed is the self that is seeing, and not just or even primarily what is being observed, or the observation of the personhood, eyewitness, self-seen. Not unlike Conrad's *Heart of Darkness* that clues us in to the heart of whiteness, not in playful or idealist inversion but in material, effective (as in *wirkliche*)—actual and actuating—constitution.

This form of producing at will the body of Michael Brown only once it has ceased to live, in a mimicry of the state power that first necessitated his body only as a necropolitical object of discipline, incarceration, murder, or war, recalls for me two things I would like to have account for each other. First, the twelved body of the concubine in "The Levite of Ephraim" that inaugurates state power as we know it, coalescing the body politic of the twelve tribes presumably in the name of the dead woman. And, second, the state's monopoly over legitimate physical violence that presupposes its capacity to produce and necessitate what will be treated to that violence: physicality, and forces us to ask exactly how and when the body appears in this history. Below, I present a few observations that thread these two to inform a historical and anticolonial materialism of the unrequited.

WARRING MATERIALISMS: BRUTISH OR LOVING?

No one in peace ever had the thought of turning to the body as evidence. Hobbes's turn to the allergic bodies in the body politic suggests that materialism is only ever a materialism of war. While Hobbes sees the bodies and their discrepant and dissonant languages as the source of war, might we consider that no one turns to the body without there being some war. It is not the body that causes the war or over which wars are fought, but war that causes and needs the body, and for which bodies can become the primordial validation or justification. The latter requires someone to tell that story rather than any other, a power conveyed abundantly both in Hobbes's insistence that it is deference to the logos of the state that brings sonorous peace, as well as in Rousseau's account of the perlocutionary and illocutionary force of the twelved body (only limbs, no head, not torso, no breasts, no womb) sent out to the tribes. So, turning to notions of sovereignty or justice as if the battle over the bodies, or the penchant to mutilate certain bodies, was nurtured in a vacuum, rather than bred through colonialism's legacy of virile war leaves us with an idea of a body as signifying a pre-political essence. The body is, in fact, summoned and produced only where there is war.

War certainly pervades other materialisms as well; when Marx, Rousseau, Nietzsche, Fanon speak of the body, it is already a political act, a declaration of war and resistance from the margins. When I compare each of them to Hobbes who can delineate and taxonomize the body, I wonder exactly what enables and disables each. What allows Hobbes to write about the body, and Rousseau to not write about the body as body? Rousseau is a materialist because he speaks about moving in and being moved by this world, of tools of being and moving parts, but he does not supply the same body as Hobbes does. While Marx's materialism speaks of atoms and bodies, it is nothing like Hobbes's who finally captures all the motives and motions within us, the blueprints for preferred (in)corporation. For one, corporeality contains; for the other, indexing the body serves as a frontier, a space, of uncontainment. Thus, fundamentally different forms. A materialism from the margins, if it has to be a warring one, has to be one of form. It has to remember that the body is not fundament but sediment, already a haunting when invoked *as* body; it behooves us to invoke it not as essence, but as a contentious form, always in relation to what summons it and who heeds that call.

Rousseau's retelling of the story of the Levite of Ephraim tells us something about how the body of the woman, especially when cut into pieces, inaugurates politics as we know it. It is not accidental that the philosopher who deconstructs modernity's social contract just while it is coming into being, rewrites the biblical story to locate the codifications—incorporations—of affective violence in the body politic as a result of the dismemberment of the body. Prior to the "peace-making," abducted or blackmailed, women from tribes willing to give themselves over to reproduce a people to come, marking the moment when the body becomes an element in this game, bodies which will be valued in certain ways, the body that was divided up and sent to various tribes marks a shift, a coming-to-be of modern politics, an honest portrayal of not the originary violence toward bodies, but the foundational violence that births and makes bodies once a judgment of some kind of value has been made. So, while it might be said that the first woman had to die in order for the body politic to be imagined, it can also be said that the body politic produces the body as we now know it. While Rousseau might be an apologist for conservative nationalist paternalism here, I see him narrating the production of the body that will haunt the rest to come, a sedimentation that is proof not only of the state's occasional violence but also of the very premises of its entire existence. This dismemberment and serving up of the body is what allows the bodies that we know to come into being—bodies whose meaning is premised on them becoming bodies for the state and capital, in wartime, and in "peacetime."

HISTORY AND LOVE:
DUELING ABUNDANCES, DISPARATE MATERIALISMS

When spaces that we occupy tighten around us, history or love often present themselves as enclosures of time that might still have room for us, even invite us in. When I began writing this book, austerity was not yet a thing, but in the face of what Sartre had taught me to call "interiorized scarcity"—typified in moments of rejection, exclusion, shame, humiliation, indignity, lack of reciprocity, cruelty, ignorance, hatred, indifference—I had mastered the art of summoning these two troves of time—history and love—as proof or promise of a righteous abundance. At its best, it is like when we pretend to be on the phone with someone as we walk down a street alone, or believe the healer who assures us that a throng of noble spirits watches over. Somewhere in the unhappy middle is the familiar superiority of ressentiment, the hurt that keeps compelling you to forgive but remains a hurt because it is your status as the sufferer that makes you more noble and compels you to forgive and so on. It is, after all, never a pain-free Jesus, and never griefless black bodies who have buried their slain, pleading to their God on behalf of those who know not what they do. At its worst, it is a sour grapes kind of coping mechanism—we never wanted it to begin with. Those excepted often claim their exceptions as destiny—history, memory, even inheritance—or will to love or suffer in a certain way. In the irony of ironies, history and love often signify zero-sum abundances—the unloved often get smothered with history—of nation, religion, race, family, and history, as homes conjured as needed, as points of departure and return. Those who claim love as their abundance, even if for a moment, might be able to skip conscription into the armies of History with all its certainties, and its march forward, perhaps even being spared a home in favor of a kind of homelessness.

Even in this accidentally spared fulfillment, love and history are very intimately related. In "Black churches taught us to forgive white people. We learned to shame ourselves,"[4] Kiese Laymon speaks of the burdens of love and shame historically borne by African Americans, often in a grotesque kind of re-memberment that, piece by piece, incarnates and cathects the black body as itself a material witness. He writes,

> We members of Concord were supposed to love white folks because they knew not what they did. We were supposed to heal them because they knew not who they were. We were supposed to forgive them because salvation awaited she or he who could withstand the wrath of the worst of white folks. We were supposed to pray for them, often at the expense of our own healthy reckoning.
> Grandma and her church taught me that loving white folks in spite of their investment in our terror was our only chance of not becoming them morally.

Laymon speaks of bodies that grow with the shame: a harvest of the church's taught love of white people and white supremacy, a desire to be chosen, shame for having desired and not being chosen, and shame for having desired and being chosen (as objects of sexual violence or Presidential honor). Poignantly and precisely, Laymon points to the space of the black church that accommodated these bodies—accommodated, palliated, incorporated, forced to love and to eat one's own shame. Its teachings of love that attached it to honor and memory were also, ironically, those that came from those preachers who in teaching these techniques of survival, also "pretended to know us better than ourselves." In doing so, these preachers silenced those whose forms of love—black love—taught Laymon "what could have been." This phrase is itself a working definition of love if we are to get one from Laymon, a definition worked through in spaces outside the church such as Home Mission. There was no set music at Home Mission, but those women, Grandma's friends, used their lives and their Bibles as primary texts to boast, confess, and critique their way into tearful song every single time. They revealed the partial truths of their lives, connected those partial truths to everyone in that room, wandered into some of the closets of those partial truths, and wondered if those partial truths held for women not in the room.

Not love that accommodates, captures, and encloses, but love that arranges, proposes, and saunters into other spaces, even creates a world. Certainly, in terms of desire and attachment, it seems like the taught love had no option but to attach to whiteness and to being desired by whiteness, a way of making sure that we knew what love to fall back on, as well as the shame, the costs of loving and not loving. Those spaces that were subsumed into and overpowered by the black church's love teachings were those which gestured to a love for each other, to choose each other, even what was hidden and unseen and distant, informing his inability to love the words that come out of the mouths of those who pretended to know us better than we did ourselves, a manner of loving passed down from the church to the parishioner in relation to whiteness, a deep unconfessed knowledge of who comes to kill. But they both exist, one because of the other, Laymon seems to suggest. While in the former, one might only wish to be spared fulfillment, the latter allows something to happen: maybe the partialities evade cathexis and the black body incarnate is precisely the one that is unrequited because it still holds on to the love.[5] Not in a way that perhaps could protect any of them, but that could still allow them to fall in love with each other, in a way, importantly, that white people never needed or never could, because they always had someone giving it to them. A love that maybe understands life and survival differently too. *A love "like our lives depended on it."*

It is such a nature of the unrequited rather than the unreciprocated, or rather unrequited because reciprocated (in the case of sexual violence, academic tenure, and Presidential office), that is evinced in the fact that Laymon's 2751 word essay uses the word love 17 times, only 4 times in relation to the taught love for white supremacy and white people. This is not a consolation—these, after all, are not the numbers Laymon wants to count—as much as it is a promise of what this love can build, what this love can produce, and who it must look away from. It is not a grudging love either, because needing to love each other is the only way to displace the desired subject of desire, and locate oneself as the subject of love and abundance who loves in order to propose a we, not to be incorporated in one that we were too afraid and too ashamed not to desire. *As if "our lives depended on it."*

> Grandma let go of my hand and rubbed the sides of her head. "Baby, I can't hear this right now," she said. "We remembered enough for today. I just can't. I'm sorry for not protecting you better. I don't even know what to do with the shame."
>
> I didn't know what to say. So I said nothing.
>
> Instead, my grandma and I held each other like our lives depended on it. We held each other because we are afraid of what happened at a black church in Charleston, South Carolina, afraid of the familiar thug who murdered us, afraid of the thugs who watched. We know those thugs sadly better than we know ourselves. Those people are cowards with blood in their eyes, absolution in their guts, and the wind at their backs. We have hoped to be chosen by them. We know that they are way closer to us than we let on. We let them in. We hold each other because we are in love. But not even that deep down, we are afraid and ashamed of where and who we've been with these people, and we are tragically hopeful that tomorrow our shame won't weigh so much.

We remembered enough for today. We hold each other because we are in love. The history itself relies on a kind of love, or else there would be no shame. The history that shames and jars asks for a certain kind of love. And the history that becomes a salve or refuge by being made into fetish objects like family and nation, among others, in which we find a home or salve for our current scarcities, also has made its transits through some kind of love. Those who need no history and no love are the ones who have taken it all already, and have no shame. Even Grandma is stumped by the impossible demand to love those who have no shame, what Laymon proceeds to characterize as "a hallmark of American evil, and really a fundamental part of the black American experience in this country."

Here memory and love meet, when history abandons or must be abandoned, memory more like Proust's *memoire involuntaire*. The pariah in history has a particular claim to this confluence of love and memory. The memory that interrupts history looks a lot like love, or acts as such. Laymon's remembering of what could be is either an act of love, or takes us back to it. When love is interrupted, it is often a sign that it is time to go find refuge in history and get accommodated in its many promised homes qua fetishes, as if that is what we were asking when we complained about not being loved. When the memory of black love interrupts the history of church love and its historical abuses by the oppressor, an abundance ensues. This abundance allows something to be imminently writeable, a sign that can signify anything and everything, a gift that does not stop giving, a kind of exhausting involuntariness that is almost compulsion to survive, live, continue to remember, be vouched for in this world.

Laymon and his Grandma hugging is love to counter history, love precisely where history must give up, love that allows history to leave even as it asks it to stay, as memory. The issue is certainly not whether Grandma can remember or not, but where she or Laymon see it as which kind of repose, who relies on it for what kind of home, and who gets to give memory and love what form in history. Lost in finding the final home is love itself. Whose fulfilled desire might that be on our behalf? Whose reserve of undeserved love and shameless life does it replenish? In the name of survival or protection, the black church and the white state are both invested in making black people perfect victims, one by scripting suffering and the other by conscripting love. The Home Mission left the story only partially complete, a place to return to and pick some pieces. And Laymon does.

Only out of love, one might construct history in forms that may be worth taking refuge in, temporarily, not to make them objects of love consummated, and injury perfected—the only promise and condition of the unrequited. Indeed, as Benjamin's hopeless lover would have it, what the historical materialist counts as history has already been constructed through a kind of love, so that this refuge is in love. While we may not choose that love or that suffering, there might be some choice in determining the forms in which it is cast—whether to bring closure and fulfillment to it or be spared its fulfillment in some way, whether to consider ourselves unloved, or yet to abandon those roles and attach to an unrequitedness. This attachment would be to the homelessness of the aptly named Home Mission—as a place for something new to emerge: a new kind of love, new subjects of love and capable of loving, and new objects worthy of our love regardless of whether they are able to return it or not.

IN THE BEGINNING WAS THE BODY?

Both in Laymon's invocation of love and hope, as honoring of the past and the future respectively, and in "Grandma" having remembered enough for today when "Kie" brings up other kinds of violences that have shaped the body, it is a sign that love is what re-collects something as it could be or would have been rather than simply as memory (what we know it was). In fact, love is that which must interrupt memory in favor of such an appearance. It interrupts not so that it can move on or distract with an image of time to come, but what an arrival of the time now would look like had we been together, and in order to allow the body to try to take stock of what it has accommodated as only it can. In contrast with the white killer who carries metabolic absolution in his guts, here there are parcels of undigested shame, voluminous bodies that inaugurate the idea of the body which produces value without volume, value *as* without-volume. Bodies that must be jetsam in order for value to happen, not the other way around. The history of matter and materiality in colonial capitalism flashes in the moment the Zong case gives the lie to any pretension that the body as body pre-existed value. What preceded value was body as cargo thrown overboard, and what followed this initiation of value was body as body, and body as labor that transsubstantiates the body with labor time. So, the black body, whether Kenneth Goldsmith or the black church incarnates it, is a body both because it can no longer produce, but also because it can only produce (and it only can produce). The body that appears as residue after conversion into labor time. This is the labor of bodies whose presence outlasts capitalism, and forces the question of the violence of colonization and slavery when we assumed all bodies had been converted into labor and processed forthwith. The body of the miner with black lung who has no job, and the body of the ghetto kid gunned down by the police, are not tragedies of the same degree or form, but reflect exactly what the effluences of capital look like. They are the penumbra that ensures the concrete outline of the efficient and productive society, the attachments and the love and the flesh that keep it in commission, keep it fed, keep it able to reproduce itself against the whiteness that fades into the backdrop of capital. So, this is not about the oppressed being invisible, or about representing an ontic vacuum, but the historical compulsion to immaterialize them that is always sated yet insatiable. These bodies confess and witness something else.

The hypermateriality of black bodies goes hand in hand with the immaterialization of black lives, with important lessons for those who turn to the body as an occasion for ethical rather than political work. Also, for all the poeisis that makes the body available, there is a labor that is being shirked in the act of just producing the body—the work of even just finding the pieces of what counts as the body, and ascertaining where the body must begin and end. Women's and slaves' bodies are not just or even primarily *kinds* of bodies but provide the template for how bodies become available and treated as bodies. Without the production of value that becomes possible in the Zong case, and which institutes the slave as body, we would not have an entire history of modern and contemporary materialism (in its vulgar, dialectical, or "new," forms) having ascertained the object or presupposition of its analysis. So, the black body becomes body because of what could be done to it, and because of what could not be undone. In that way, Goldsmith's chopping up of Michael Brown's body reminds us of the Levite after Zong. This ongoing primitive accumulation can then be seen as the act that puts the body together by being able to deem it destructible and destroy it. It brings me not to bodies on which histories and truths are inscribed, but those that get hung on to Truth, or thrown at History—Bachmann's fossils rather than Foucault's palimpsests.

What are the risks of turning to the body as the origin if we do not understand what is produced as body at any given moment in history? In trying to ask, then, if in the beginning there really was the body, I am following a suspicion I have had about who turns to the body as evidence of what. While who turns to the body as the object of exploitation is related to this, I am wondering if the materialist turn to the body, and the turn to a kind of onto-ethical politics via the body, arbitrarily programmes history to start once the body has become a body. I am interested in locating the politics, and potentially the anti-politics of the act that determines the body, or begins with the body thus determined, instead of explaining this presupposition. In Marx's vein, one might say, what concerns us is not only what the body must explain, but how the body must itself be explained. It is not the black or feminine body that should show up to confess to the political, but the political that must confess to these found bodies. Not in an act of justification, but of judgment, of politics. What forms bodies take, if already closed and foreclosed, must be dis-closed, since there is a relation between an anti-political closure of form and the turn to the body as the beginning. My investment in, and internal critique of, the materialist turn has specifically to do with the materialities that are conjured and normalized in a way that forgets exactly which bodies provided not the material (pace Foucault), but the very template for what we know to be the body, without asking what problem does the body solve for those of us interested in the possibility of politics?

THE LOVELESS LAMENTS OF THE PARTIES OF ORDER

The history of the body politic stars leaders such as Haroun Al-Rachid who finds the body of a woman cut in pieces at the bank of the Tigris. In the company of a Rousseau here and there, and the Levite, they shed tears on dead women's bodies, tears that supposedly emasculate them. Such is the emasculation that it necessitates yet another war, or is a step to one, or will be resolved by it, or effect some new extortion in its name. There is something to be said for the fact that what has always been seen as the justification for war, is only instituted as one. In Djebar's "The Woman in Pieces," Atyka's five-day retelling—of the story of the slain woman whose abode at the bed of the Tigris enables the state even to enact and profess its confessions of love and pity—is also her foretelling of the "sovereign" power that slays her.

So, it is a lie whenever we hear of someone fighting in the name of women's bodies or to avenge or defend them, since these are mere occasions to write the story of the state and nation only as those bodies lie unmourned and unburied, but still there, as purely poetic gestures that concretize what has already been happening. In Furetian terms, just as the French revolution does not happen when it actually appears, the body as a political object of evidence remains at the sediment of the Tigris, laying the foundations for something to appear, and when it does, it can be called the body, named as such in an act of naming that is politics, requiring that it always already be not a body but a body in pieces. The different kinds of cutting up of the body, and putting it together again, is all in service of telling a story of the body politic that could otherwise not be told, and ensuring that no other kinds of bodies are produced. The acts of destruction allow us to think of a contract in which we all participate to save ourselves, and secure our bodies. But not without someone being quartered as the premise of that body. *Love gave way to something else.*

The arranging and rearranging of the suffering that leads from the psychopathic meticulous twelving of the body of the woman by the Levite to the two different coffins for the head and the body—one more than the body found by Haroun at the bank of the Tigris—and the rearrangement of the pieces of Brown's body effected by Goldsmith in his poetic rendition, all give pause. The strange lovefilledness of the previous acts of violence sheds some light on how loveless the actual turn to the body is. When Goldsmith remembers Brown's body, he is already writing history, making the body, honestly showing the power whiteness has had to call the body into commission, into being, provoke it into an existence on call. So, that when Brown's body becomes the element of poetry, or his postmortem report only enables another act of making the body present, there is violence in the act of once again calling the body, controlling it, making it appear as it is desired, or actually with no question of desire at all. As if automatic, as if involuntary.

As if nothing else could be done. I want no part of a materialist turn that calls the body forth in that way, or turns to the body, as if it is always already there, for me. Only a kind of confidence in occupying space and geography that somehow feels foreign to me could inform such a calling forth—the feminine and colonial subjects I know and wonder about converge at what they cannot quite leave un-dis-closed, for their bodies mark that closure of form itself.

CODA: ALL THAT CAN BE DONE

If "this is all that can be done," is not the mantra of austerity politics, I do not know what is. This work has been written in a kind of impatience and despair at the manner in which that seems to be the ubiquitous slogan, even of the resistance, framed in a horrifying end of days rhetoric that again, dishearteningly, shows us the patho-theologies (or theo-pathologies) of our times. In times of austerity, when it is precisely fulfillment that is supposedly withheld, how might my atheological mystics of the Marxist or other orders be relevant? One might rightly ask: are they not precisely mandating and valorizing the kind of abusive abstinence demanded from some of us under organized austerity? What more can we deny ourselves? Whose needs and abilities are being factored in here (both in terms of love, but also in terms of refusal to consummate)? These questions still assume that the battles of austerity are being played on the terrain of quantity and content rather than quality and form: that the extraction of wealth, the disposability of bodies, and exploitation of labor on the global scale is a story that is continuous between those who are subject to it, versus those who are the subjects of this. Something beyond labor is being extracted to produce wealth; processes of conversion happen, extractions change forms in order to become wealth, and part of austerity is the flattening and making efficient of those pathways and assembly lines, with the presumption that translations are complete and effortless and the accounting perfect. This is where the old resort to excess also does not make sense, because it refuses to acknowledge that the power of the system and its continuation is at least partly owed to the normalization and generalization of forms of being, and ways of understanding and substantiating being. Until we see that it is life that becomes wealth, and death that becomes fervor, we cannot understand politics at the level of the form of our political being. The inscrutability of our desires and loves is one way out of preserving enough to build elsewhere, build alongside, do some falsework for solidarity and possibility rather than always addressing those who will only reproduce us and our labors in the way they know to, and the way they serve them. Are we all really fighting the same battle under the banner of austerity? Is Sabeen Mahmud fighting for the same love that someone else kills her with? Is there even a general equivalence here? Understanding austerity and its politics in terms of quantity and content rather than quality and form will always be a mistake, since there is nothing to then be debated and fought over in the face of a generalized absolutism of scarcity. There is absolutely no abstinence or withholding being demanded in my framing of the unrequited, but I also do not see most fulfillments promised or striven for to actually be fulfillments.

NOTES

1. Jean-Jacques Rousseau, "Le Lévite D'Éphraim," https://www.rousseauonline.ch/Text/le-levite-d-ephraim.php. Accessed 26 June 2018. Translated by Safi Alsebai and Coco Marcil collaboratively one afternoon between Richmond, Massachusetts, and Sofia, Bulgaria. Many thanks to them.
  Complete translation can be found in Jean-Jacques Rousseau, "The Levite of Ephraim" in *Rousseau on Women, Love, and Family* (UPNE, 2009), and in Jean-Jacques Rousseau and John T. Scott, *Essay on the Origin of Languages and Writings Related to Music* (Hanover: University Press of New England, 1998).
2. Djebar, *The Tongue's Blood Does Not Run Dry*.
3. Jillian Steinhauer, "Kenneth Goldsmith Remixes Michael Brown Autopsy Report as Poetry," *Hyperallergic*, March 16, 2015, https://hyperallergic.com/190954/kenneth-goldsmith-remixes-michael-brown-autopsy-report-as-poetry/.
4. Laymon, "Black Churches Taught Us to Forgive White People. We Learned to Shame Ourselves." All quotations in this section are from this text.
5. This brings up a conversation between Fred Moten and Hannah Arendt on the nature of the being desired and not desired as part of your subjection that Moten broaches toward the end of "The New International of Insurgent Feeling." In a corrective to Arendt's idea of the pariah (exemplified by Rahel Varnhagen as we have discussed in Chapter 3), Moten writes: "There is a particular kind of sub-political experience that emerges from having been the object of that mode of racial-military domination that is best described as incorporative exclusion that settler colonialism instantiates. It is not the experience of the conscious pariah, as Hannah Arendt would have it. Her misrecognition of this experience is at the root of her profound misunderstanding of black insurgency in the United States, which was not the unruly, sometimes beautiful, and ultimately unstable and pathological sociality of the ones who are not wanted, but was and is, rather, an unruly, always beautiful, sometimes beautifully ugly, destabilizing and auto-destabilizing sociality-as-pathogen for the ones whose desire precisely for that pathogen and its life-forming, life-giving properties is obsessive and murderous. This more than political, antipolitical, experience of the ones who are brutally and viciously *wanted* is something to which anyone who has any interest whatsoever in the very idea of another way of being in the world must constantly renew their own ethical and intellectual relation." This intervenes in a crucial way, along with Laymon, on the narrative of unlovedness, and the desires that have held us hostage (even our desire as the wanted that could never materialize in a system too afraid of our bodies). It *also* begs clarifying the nature of unwantedness in Arendt, if we look not at the pariah of "We, Refugees," unwanted by states until we make the state to want us—but the pariah which antedates that moment, in Rahel Varnhagen. Her labors of making a home in this world are of her love, and we would be well-advised to think how the oppressed, the one's subjectified and objectified by another's murderous desire, are home to love, in the very gesture to "another way of being in the world." Fred Moten, "The New International of Insurgent Feeling," Palestine Campaign for the Academic and Cultural Boycott of Israel, November 7, 2009, http://www.pacbi.org/etemplate.php?id=1130.

Chapter Eight

Invitations, Deferrals, and Refusals: The Many Hospitalities of Anticolonial Love

India shall be a nation! No foreigners of any sort! Hindu and Muslim and Sikh and all shall be one! Hurrah! Hurrah for India! Hurrah! Hurrah!

India a nation! What an apotheosis! Last comer to the drab nineteenth-century sisterhood! Waddling it at this hour of the world to take her seat! She, whose only peer was the Holy Roman Empire, she shall rank with Guatemala and Belgium perhaps! Fielding mocked again. And Aziz in an awful rage danced this way and that, not knowing what to do and cried: "Down with the English anyhow. That's certain. Clear out, you fellows, double quick, I say. We may hate one another, but we hate you most. If I don't make you go, Ahmed will, Karim will, if it's fifty-five hundred years we shall get rid of you, yes, we shall drive every blasted Englishman into the sea, and then"—he rode against him furiously—"and then," he concluded, half kissing him, "you and I shall be friends."

"Why can't we be friends now?" said the other, holding him affectionately. "It's what I want. It's what you want."

But the horses didn't want it—they swerved apart; the earth didn't want it, sending up rocks through which riders must pass single file; the temples, the tank, the jail, the palace, the birds, the carrion, the Guest House, that came into view as they issued from the gap and saw Mau beneath; they didn't want it, they said in their hundred voices, "No, not yet," and the sky said, "No, not there."

—E.M. Forster, *A Passage to India*[1]

He who can buy bravery is brave, though he be a coward. As money is not exchanged for any one specific quality, for any one specific thing, or for any particular human essential power, but for the entire objective world of man and nature, from the standpoint of its possessor it therefore serves to exchange every quality for every other, even contradictory, quality and object: it is the fraternization of impossibilities. It makes contradictions embrace.

Assume man to be man and his relationship to the world to be a human one: then you can exchange love only for love, trust for trust, etc. If you want to enjoy art, you must be an artistically cultivated person; if you want to exercise influence over other people, you must be a person with a stimulating and encouraging effect on other people. Every one of your relations to man and to nature must be a specific expression, corresponding to the object of your will, of your real individual life. If you love without evoking love in return – that is, if your loving as loving does not produce reciprocal love; if through a living expression of yourself as a loving person you do not make yourself a beloved one, then your love is impotent – a misfortune.|XLIII|
—Karl Marx, "The Power of Money in Bourgeois Society"[2]

INTRODUCTIONS; OR, THE NOT NOW COMPLEX

Are the closing lines of *A Passage to India* (quoted first above) a deferral of friendship, a utopian promise, or a resignation to the impotence of love normalized in the twin tragedies of empire and nation? And, might these possibilities be related to Marx's reference to the "fraternization of impossibilities," and "the embrace of contradictions" as powers circulating within capitalism propelling it through times and spaces—the grand set-up bound to end in a kind of disaster, so to speak, if it hasn't already? Is the fraternity and embrace necessitated by imperialism what traumatizes other fraternities and embraces out of possibility, or is it what we must accept as our only salvation in a world where other love has been ruled out? Both are potentially true: the former a justification for the ressentiment inherent in kinds of left and right fascisms; the latter a native tendency of a form of neoliberal consensus version of cosmopolitanism when all else fails. Despite appearances, both are oddly consistent with each other, perhaps a kind of a meta-contradiction fraternizing within our moment.

A refusal of friendship, a resistance to requital, and a desire interrupted by the elements, time, space, and senses, seem like failures to which we are destined in the society which Marx is attempting to ethnograph. He notes that one's existence in this society is not paltry in the sense of being, so to speak, simply friendless or with no one to embrace (or in contemporary parlance, see the imminent end of the world with!). Rather, the specificity of relations that locate oneself in the other and the other in oneself as a premise of politics, and the status of the beloved as a specific expression untainted by (or beyond) its interpellation as a fetish in the imperial, liberal, and neoliberal lifeworlds, certainly offers a different vision/account of society and of friendship, love, and intimacy within it. And, indeed, a different vision of political desire and action as well.

The juxtaposition of these two excerpts is an entry into this chapter's problematization of solidarity and alliance politics amid our moment's consensus on political sensibility and subjectivity. What kinds of friends, allies, and comrades does this moment compel, impel, spurn, enable, and disable? Which conditions and premises of acting politically, with others, become legitimized and invalid, sufficient and insufficient? Which conjunctures of ethics and politics become impossibly lost to us, and which present themselves as unavoidable? Is there something outmoded about the subject of politics that both representational and participatory, deliberative and radical, democracy flaunts? Is there an unchallenged consensus among seeming opponents within the field of democratic political theory that needs to be exposed, probed, and agonized over a bit more? How can political action and its prescriptions keep looking for the political subject that is outmoded and defunct, and what sort of conservative and reactionary role that reaffirms power is played by calls for certain kinds of activism, solidarity, engagement, publicity, and supposedly radical action in response to contemporary proclamations of crisis?

This chapter takes up the issue of the capacities for political relations, action, and existence that present themselves in the figure of the unrequited, and how it can inflect our thinking about solidarity politics and righteous commitments to certain visible forms of justice that assume and impute homogeneous objects of desire, appropriate sentiment, and prescribe ends. Rather than the notorious apathies of the citizenry that keep the discussion ensnared within quantitative and functionalist logics of feeling, responsibility, and democratic participation, I want to address a wholly political, transitive, allergy to solidarities and adhesions on demand, in search of a different kind of adhesion—because these reparative compulsions and what they are seeming to repair often seem to share some tendencies in their treatment of politics and normalize a similar political subject. This is the backdrop of my desperation in pairing these quotes, with a longing that all of us implicated in these embraces and fraternities take the risk of giving them up, even if just for a moment, to see what else may emerge, and to even reclaim and proclaim desire, indeed politics, apropos to this moment. Politics as a practice in grace and an exercise of the capacity to withstand and suffer, and to give up what we can on behalf of those who have nothing more to give up. This, in turn, requires an intimacy to know and be with, to think of closeness and community in space *and* in time. Sometimes it feels imperative to do so even when it risks alienating those most like us or most proximate in certain superficial terms, a risk worth taking when the cost of this destruction, earlier of (home)land, now of character, is writing no new story, and ending with no new victors. Maybe this gives away my own internal and external negotiations with figments of the unrequited subject that has been haunting this project.

In order to even begin to address some of these concerns, the chapter makes a few moves. First, it attempts to sketch out the nature of invitations to politics that need to be problematized for how they do or do not imbibe lessons from the history and present of colonial and imperial violence, and how they normalize a subject of politics that has also not lived through these times. Second, I turn back to E.M. Forster's *A Passage to India* and then forward to Leela Gandhi's *Affective Communities* to read the ethical and political calls each of them makes—as a way of understanding Fielding's invitation and Aziz's refusal. Gandhi's work on the anticolonialism of "immature" politics of subjects working across and against their national belongings, and of friendships between the metropolitan and colonial subjects, sheds some light on what the end of *Passage* portends and the relations that might still be able to save us. Third, I ask how Gandhi's discussion of friendship and hospitality would be inflected by the question of violence and terror of the kind we find, and with the globalization of cultural and affective landscapes. Finally, if her turn to the ethical is juxtaposed with Weber's thinking of the vocation of politics, then how might we build on her project in these different historical conditions. I end with a brief discussion of the political promise of the unrequited.

INVITATIONS AND THE INVITED

It is to this closing scene of *Passage* that my mind drifts every time I see myself saying no to a politics (and worse still, antipolitics) being waged on my behalf, at the same time working through all the ways I have had no ability to actually say no. In times of crises, I feel a kind of pull to withdraw, the question of alienation no longer a romantic or Hegelian one but inscribed in the very nature of things and spaces, of work, of life, of home. The moment someone else declares the urgency of an imminent end of the world, all the other yes-sayings are, in a way, compensated for by all the ways in which one recoils at those provocations, often fairly passive-aggressively: "oh, now you've got something to lose," "why now," "why don't you wait a little bit like the rest of us have." Perhaps a sign of addiction to a kind of politics that is only a way in and never a way out; in other words, learning to live on thresholds and inside walls, it is easy to see through someone's made-up urgencies. There is something sad about that, and I am not advocating it. I am just trying to pry into the emotional reserve that becomes regularized in the face of options that feel reactionary and which brims tempestuously with its own reactions when asked to: reassure the bearers of empty guilt—"no, please, not on my behalf"; join the joyride into messianism at someone else's pleasure; celebrate possibility always only on other people's terms; commiserate with yet another bout of left melodrama and left tragedy by those whose lives sadly need it; sit through exhortations to multitudinous love and narratives of disappointments inattentive to anyone else's love and disappointments; erase one's being in punishment for resisting the fascistic ressentiment of liberal identity politics of white and other varieties; tell your story again, to stop doing theory and write your story again, yes your story, you, there. What kind of isolation does one then choose? If the modes of politics being advertised are not one's own and never could be, is that reason enough to refuse or defer? Is the refusal or deferral in the name of an idealism of the perfect politics, or is it shaped mostly in a kind of refusal of that form of appropriation? Or is it about becoming more specific about the forms of intimacy one wants and values the more far gone things are, in the hope that we all might now learn? Moments of "crisis" can do more than make one succumb to any solidarity that is on offer: too many such partnerships feel unable to weather the demands of a time when, contrary to the generalized understanding of violence and death, what is befitting and needed is a particular kind of attentiveness to it. Far from finding the lowest common denominator in all our struggles, the wish can be for a very specific, honest, accounting of ourselves being and becoming in those struggles. This also means that, often at the end of the day, one is left homeless, but with strangely more understanding of and for whom that love is withheld from . . . and who never could return it *anyway*.

I am trying to understand the new varieties of non-elitist, not simply pessimistic, actually wholly "political," repulsions to a particular brand of fervent and moralistic calls to action, solidarity, unity, and identity that have crept into everyday experience just as the world apparently and understandably needs some saving. I speak of the burgeoning confessions and accusations of apathy that find so many young students. I speak of how the remedy is sought in a particular insistence on political action sponsored by simplifications and clarities that, just a little while ago, were deemed academically and politically suspect, and to political action driven by guilt in which I have no share but whose recipient and beneficiary is ostensibly someone like me. I suspect some of this has to do with a bafflement at how certain versions of prescribed "healthy" or "healthy-making" (reparative, redemptive) politics come with a complete blindness to how the political subject being acted on behalf of, or being inspired to action, is very different from the subject that is assumed in such prescribed politics. (And, by this, I do not mean some sociological or demographic set of facts, but constitutionally, in terms of its capacities and its incapacities, its overcomings and its failures.) When we proceed oblivious to the dissonance or at least a lack of resonance that these invitations represent, we are not merely being inaccurate but actively shunning another invitation to create a more just politics. It is not whether these calls yield "results" or not, because many will follow. However, their very outmodedness betrays a self-serving quality on behalf of the provocateur, and a complicity in a new form of docility and discipline. Then ensues an insistence on a known subject that we would much still like to have, please, so that "our" politics and "our" ends of worlds can stay in our control. Reliance on this redeeming subject is easy, but it is not benign. For one, it compels a rewriting of the "problem" of representational politics: that working with, for, and on behalf of others, only silences them if it is mere parity of interest or codified desire that brought us together, and that there is a way to give up that shortcut and use the moment of representation as an invitation to remake the time and space of politics anew together so that the relation itself shifts through that labor, and is no longer one of representation qua speaking or thinking for another.

What must be contended with is the ubiquity and pervasiveness of the subjects wrought in this general economy of violence, that have learnt to love and hate, trust and suspect, in this global political, economic, and sensuous regime. In addition, it must be acknowledged that despite the forms of forced miscegenations (used figuratively here) and the exchanges of population that define our times, there often is a loneliness necessitated by the onslaught of a kind of (anti)politics of the faithful and the fervent, a loneliness that resembles a deep sense of unrequitedness, a kind of casting out of entire ways of being and desiring, that is all the more meaningful and ironic given the modes of imperial and colonial love that were perfect antecedents to liberal multiculturalism and its attendant identity politics.[3] Reciprocity and intimacy are nonstarters when the frames of call and response in this mode of fellow-being and democratic participation are already set, or when a kind of blind Christian love in the mode of inclusion, acceptance, or reparation, lacks specificity and intimacy by its very nature. Something has come between us, I dare say, not least because the gestures of radical identity politics from the margins of the polity that could have taken us somewhere were sabotaged by expropriative liberal multiculturalism that evacuated its radicalism and its audacious politics of presence and futurity. The welcoming or accommodation of these potentialities into the order of institutions is what has come between those who were sitting on their fugal thresholds courting a different world to which the insurgent can testify—and some accounting for this among the impossible or no-longer we needs to happen. There is something that is missing, something sad as I re-read Fielding even claim that he and Aziz want the same thing. To this I now turn.

REGRETS ONLY—NOT HERE, NOT NOW

Even David Lean's mockery of homoerotic encounter in the film version of *Passage*[4] does a fine job of capturing this final moment, with Kashmiri shikaras (gondolas) replacing horses, of this deferral of friendship, unavailability of this time and this place for the union that has been foreclosed by a history of colonization and its toxic remnants in the lives of ordinary subjects. Interestingly, Lean's setting of this forfeiture and this foreclosure seems to be "magically realized" by Salman Rushdie's opening of *Midnight's Children* in the politics of memory, forgetting, absurdist sensuality, and carnivalesque ressentiment, as Saleem Sinai—the son of a doctor not unlike Aziz in *Passage*—comes of age in those same shikaras, "handcuffed to history," gliding on the lakes of Kashmir.[5]

This correspondence, even if purely a stretch, is one of the "hundred voices" that still can be heard from beneath, the unfortunate witnesses to failed friendships and their aftermath in a region speckled with madness, hatred, and misplaced unforgivingness that have lost their way and are wielded too proudly and insecurely to allow for this realization. I almost feel compelled to read back into Aziz's depiction, an embarrassed, insulting, fury and violent half-kisses foolishly denying only himself to himself, missing all along that his rejection of Fielding is only a paltry symbolic gesture of consolation in face of the abandonment and betrayal that he has already suffered. Add two decades from this moment to the partition and freedom—a naughty and pernicious ritual of betrayal given what it has produced—and one visualizes the masters having a good laugh at the self-congratulatory self-destruction they gifted. We have shown how well we can hate ourselves. Add another few decades to see how this story has unfolded, and one sees far and wide more madness than Manto could narrate, and more terror that leaves one not sure if disgust or grief is requisite, and an inconsolability sets in when not being able to quite decide on one, we project our inability on to others who know even less what to say.

What is the relation between this refusal, postponement, or deferral on the one hand, and the consents we seem to have given to so much continuing imperialist necropolitics on the other? Consents to the market, global humanitarianism, religious fundamentalism, nationalism, order-maintaining institutions, and so on that, despite appearing contradictory on the surface, do not seem to quite thwart each other, in some kind of wicked replaying of the underhanded pacts between church and state, fascism and liberalism, freedom and dependency, and so on, that seem to continue to plague us. What is the relation between the hatred for one another and the hatred of oneself that thrives just as the old oppressors seem to have been forgiven and overcome, perhaps even become saviours overnight? What is the relation between the shared desire for the friendship and the inability to consummate it?

Of late, I have been unable to take Fielding seriously, or sympathetically. For I have often wondered how to separate him from empire: why assume him being driven out into the sea is at all a punishment, a deprivation of some sort? Isn't it what "they" wanted at this time? Why give that power to Aziz when it was never his to begin with? The "magnanimous" overture that

Fielding makes continues to stump me, since it is one to which I must have an answer when I am included in some community of desire. And when I feel troubled by my resistance, often unable to say it aloud, worrying that my rejection would become a rejection of me, I often think of Aziz's sorry character. Is it hatred that keeps him? Is it the judgment of others? Is it revenge for the Quested episode—something that showed that no ethical offering or demand for truth could wipe off the hurt and insult of having been put on trial anyway, for being the one who was so easy to be cast out, othered, severed? A revenge indeed pretty much in line with ressentiment in Nietzsche, where a particular high valuation of oneself has to be presumed in any value given to self-abnegation, asceticism, or sacrifice. What might be the reason someone like Aziz says no?

Fielding's suggestion of shared desire—at least of the object of desire—is a familiar trope: it gathers within it any claim to difference in time and space, and smoothes over different relations and ways of wanting. Indeed, that is its very charm. And if love, as I have defined it, inheres both desire and attachment, then the objections made by the skies and the earth at the end of *Passage* are objections both to taking the known passage, and to the attachment. The objection is a tacit invitation to embrace what lies in the way of the requital in order for there to be the possibility of a new attachment, new passages.

The foreclosure of this particular desire and attachment—here, in this moment—is not the foreclosure of all desire, all attachment, a fact that gets lost in the habits mastered as inhabitants of colonized lifeworlds. There is certainly a filiality folded into the lack of requital, because it bears the mark of an expectation of intimacy, however unfulfilled, something not merely written over by other valid and valuable ethical relations and prescribed and policed political performances.

COSMOPHILUS: FRIENDSHIP AND HOSPITALITY

Leela Gandhi's *Affective Communities: Anticolonial Thought, Fin-de-Siècle Radicalism, and the Politics of Friendship*[6] offers a compelling account of and argument for these other ethical relations, as an antidote to the curse at the end of *Passage*. While, as discussed in the previous section, Forster's moment portends a particular narrative of anticolonial historicity as it has unfolded, Gandhi has a very important, revisionist take on this. For her, the end of the novel beckons us to turn to the promise of friendships that were fulfilled, that this lack of permission in this time and space was actually countered by a commitment to utopianism, to friendship as itself utopian—at once not of this time and place, and the resistance to which was only possible in this time and place. She draws on friendship as a antifoundational foundation, a kind of Kantianism manifested in a range of social experiments and empiricisms at the turn of the century. This is a project which, in its turn to ethics to salvage politics, resembles Weber's far-reaching plea in "Politics as a Vocation" but ends in an entirely different place. It makes a full turn to politics of subjects with each other rather than a resignation to the state as uncompromisable locus, and to the tragic ethical individual who can "do no other."[7]

Affective Communities speaks of the kinds of alliances and companionships that come about in subversion of modes of resistance that are dominant at a given time, in locations that are unexpected and would be "too suspect" in light of these modes. Gandhi brings the metropole and the colony in the same frame, resisting the binaries but also resisting the pieties of a kind of perfect politics and the charms of an idealist disinterest in the question of boundary, distinction, and power. She turns to friendship and utopianism—beautifully seeing them as connected—as versions of what were deemed "immature" politics and which lay the blueprint for thinking about cross-cultural understanding, boundary-crossing solidarity, and transnational anticolonial politics. Instead of the popular turn to the speechless subaltern being ventriloquized back into history, she broadens the scope within which to consider anti-imperialist thought and practice. She does so not only by bringing in a cast of British anticolonial sympathizers in the metropole, but by focusing on the relation between the metropolitan and colonial subject as historic and worth investigating.

One might read Gandhi's book as a series of character studies of individuals who unlearned (or at least gave up) some of the privileges of imperial domination, suspended certain convenient comforts and securities in order to be close to and ally with the oppressed, and launch a critique of imperialism and the Enlightenment thought ensconcing it. This has much to offer to those of us who have been focusing on issues of speaking for oneself/the other—representation understood in this way—as the primary diagnostic and remedial space in progressive politics. While she certainly focuses on personal capacities and ethical strengths, it is important to note that they are called upon and fostered within certain relations and relatednesses. Some of these capacities entail making the choice to be in "a world without taxonomy," risking the "psychic derangement"[8] that occurs upon dislocating the self, after the disavowal of epistemological and ontological safeguards that come with the Enlightenment and its political projects. This, I think, is most crucial in shifting the emphasis to a more materialist, relational, and substantive analysis of political binds, and the ethics that underpin and suffuse them.

Gandhi posits the other side of the impossibility on which I have chosen to focus, and offers a counter-history of the relations that are damned at the end of Forster's novel. She shows how numerous embraces of contradictions happened, in a response to the totalizing moralities and political scripts of colonizers and revolutionaries alike. Countless friendships contorted themselves to walk through the gap, and enabled the emergence and overcoming of this fate by the ordinary actions of minor subjects who risked impossible identifications, rejected the comforts and redemptions promised by the formulaic politics of property and propriety codified in liberalism and nationalism, and still found a way to make something otherwise. In an interesting take on the question of "maturity" as invoked by Weber as he draws out his picture of the desirable politician, Gandhi tracks friendships between the colonizer and the colonized. These were exemplary for overcoming the curse of national attachment, and engaging in "immature" anticolonial politics anchored in the ethical domain, as the only possibility of the survival of politics otherwise overwritten by some vanguard of history or another.

Gandhi's argument leaves out an important complication. In reading into the "not there, not yet" injunction the possibility of a utopianism, must we assume some shared political conceptions and shared conceptions of politics? Is it appropriately utopian, and within the realm of friendship rather than love, just because it is accepting of, tolerant of, even premised on, the divergence in those? The ethical turn's mapping of a shared ground for new modes of resistance and political judgment (to counter what Arendt might call prejudice) sets aside the more trenchant question of the relation between divergent conceptions of politics. With the common bond of anticolonialism, the underlying ruptures in politics are either bandaged or never broached by focusing on the shared object. This is important because while Gandhi's characters do go some way in showing how we actively navigate exclusions from the "proper" political domain, they stop short of dealing with the divergent implications for politics, its conduct, and its form, that hold this motley crew feebly together. For Gandhi, this might fall in the realm of the radical insufficiency that must be inhabited in these friendships, as a positive existential and political choice, not deluding oneself about the kind of apotheosis that lies at the end of the story. She writes:

> The expenditure is more existentially profound, involving the potentially "agonizing" risk of self-exile which haunts any ethical capacity to become (to suffer oneself to become) foreign to "one's own" and, above all, to oneself. Derrida's notes on ethics-as-hospitality are apposite here: "the stranger, here the awaited guest, is not only someone to whom you say 'come,' but 'enter' ... come in, 'come inside,' 'come within me,' not only toward me, but within me: occupy me, take place in me.[9]

This hospitality broaches the self in a way that flouts the solipsism inherent in both communitarianism and liberalism, exposing their farcical binary, since both succumb to the temptation of the individual, and flaunt an idealism that is unable to probe truly the root of this "self" and "identity" in relations. They stubbornly hold on to an idealist figment that might come immanently undone once the constitutive and contingent relations are parsed and become privileged as objects of inquiry. In the realm of ethics and politics, this would translate into a kind of "subject-agent open to forms of sociality exacerbating the condition of its insufficiency," and "a community that was never itself." She writes:

> The ethical agency of the host-friend relies precisely on her capacity to leave herself open, in Blanchot's terms, to the risk of radical insufficiency. Poised in a relation where an irreducible and asymmetrical other always calls her being into question, she is ever willing to risk becoming strange or guestlike in her own domain, whether this be home, nation, community, race, gender, skin, or species. So too, the open house of hospitality or the open heart of friendship can never know guests-friends in advance as one might a fellow citizen, sister, or comrade.[10]

Gandhi links a utopian mentality (not here, always here) to a genuine cosmopolitanism (all here, never here): "open to the risky arrival of those not quite, not yet, covered by the privileges which secure our identity and keep us safe."[11] In place of an abstract, solipsistic, and sensually stunted cosmopolitanism, she inaugurates cosmophilus, "the way to puncture those fantasies of security and invulnerability to which our political imagination remains hostage." She concludes, "Let us say yes to the possibility of who might arrive. . . ."[12] In doing so, Gandhi places much-needed ellipses at the end of *Passage*, seeing in it the unfinished, yet to come, deferred interracial friendship between Aziz and Fielding.

HERE, NOW: REREADING FORSTER AFTER GANDHI

The last few paragraphs of *A Passage to India* have been the source of much conversation over the years, or at least their message seems to have traveled. Does this final exchange foretell the inability to forgive that seems to be at the root of the colonial exit from India? But, if the history of the subcontinent is any proof, the hatred of "each other" to which Aziz refers has far outlived the hatred he promises the English rulers. Few will argue who has eventually been consented to: the consensual relation between the former colonizers and their subjects grows and thrives at least within the confines of the colony itself, and within the bloody imagination of the nation that continues to "come into being" fuelled not by any withheld forgiveness of the former masters but soaked in the hatred among subjects.

Does the deferral of this union enable the kind of hatred of "one another" that Aziz owns up to the degree that has plagued the region since winning "freedom"? Can the reality of postcolonial states that have "failed" for all but the richest and the most resentful be connected to the narrator's mockery of

India's fall from grandeur to become a "state" like many other irrelevant entities celebrating their hard-earned and still precarious monopoly over the legitimate use of physical violence? I certainly do not want to sound like I begrudge the British for leaving us to kill each other because we were not "ready or able" to be free (a strange kind of sympathetic reason at times for failure to "democratize"). Even less do I want to go down the path of suggesting that we made a mistake rejecting the only friends who could have saved us from ourselves, which is the refrain one sees in the continuing romance of the metropole, in the sickening warmth bestowed upon the former rulers in moments of bourgeois mirroring among compatriots of the bourgeois class, in the liberal and/or fascist apologism of ex-colonials that constantly betrays the refugees and the occupied, and in the uncannily similar cosmopolitanism of the global financial and humanitarian elite. I am more concerned about the way in which we can actually see what that last scene prefigures, how it can be read, and whether it can be translated into the possibilities of solidarity in the current moment.

It is important to note the ways in which the strange promise of hatred in the present and of friendship in another time and space has been fulfilled or not. Aziz says that we must be left to deal with our own hatreds. Regardless of who the recipient is, these hatreds are incorporated into the necropolitics of the postcolony (Mbembe transposing Bataille's account of the accursed share.) Following that transposition of Aziz's promised hatred into the worldly realities and inner lives of postcolonial subjects left in the rubble of contemporary fascisms and imperialisms, what becomes of the promised friendships? Does the ethical imperative to hospitality look different once one starts to account for who is always the hospitable one? Is there room for grief and mourning in the friendships of Gandhi's well-meaning defectors? Or is that too much to ask for? Not only the outcome of hatred, but hatred itself deserves grief. When my people are dying at their own hands thousands of miles away, even fewer grieve for them than those that protest drone strikes. It is like the silence that settles in a room when people are not quite sure how to grieve or mourn for those whose "irrational" deaths they do not understand. Since it is beyond thought, we must not know how to mourn; we just do not know why and what to mourn. Right there, Gandhi's requirement of giving up taxonomies that make us safe might yet require having to cultivate other senses that replace that old habit.

The issue is not only what kinds of intimacy does our era of violence allow, but also what it makes us ask for. Not only whether another is loveable, but also how, under what conditions, and what portion of that love must be, in this moment, a capacity to mourn all that has gone unloved. Not only what kinds of refusals are set in motion and enabled, but also what kinds of yes-sayings are disabled, at least for now—as the only self-respecting response to this consensus on death, and not quite being able to mourn it.

Thus, the context of contemporary violence and terror compels us to illuminate differently the problem and conditions of friendship and solidarity. The sharing of a goal is insufficient. Ethical reconciliations do not hold (that) much water in the face of discrepant notions of politics wielded by subjects differently affiliated with the accursed share, on different sides of the compulsion and obligation to sense different times and space, and situated differently in relation to the risk of radical insufficiency as outsiders to hegemonic notions of love, terror and location. Together these define for me a different imperative—ethical, aesthetic, political—to unrequitedness.

SHIFTING TIMES OF MATERIALIST POLITICS

There is something truly refreshing about Gandhi's reading of the utopian promise fulfilled by those who were on different sides of attachment to country or identity, who walked across, and who made the alliances and friendships that kept redoing and remaking the political and its limits, perhaps finally or hopefully freeing it from the bounds of the polis reflexively set where the state's monopoly over legitimate violence ends. The move to the space of quiet friendship and cosmophilus, while attractive, leaves something unacknowledged and unasked for. The ethical world obtaining in the context of violence and pulverizability at least suggests a different kind of attention to the tired body, to the non-utopian body, to the body whose very possibility is forsaken and deferred, to the body that does not always leave one's home but at the same time is most threatened in it, even to the body that left home and claims to find it everywhere as a polite gesture of friendship and acceptance of any hospitality granted it.

What do friendship and solidarity mean to someone whose life is affected by violence, or whose grief, one must say, lives in another register, illegible to the friend or compatriot? If we aren't to become apologists for the state once the question of violence comes up, what is the way to think about what is possible today? If the state as the locus for this love is let go of, but violence and a certain proximity to destruction remains, then what is it that moves, wields, and redeems politics? The answer is not in merely an other-centred, non-solipsistic, subject-agent a la Gandhi, which keeps us mourning the unavailable subject (sending identity politics and legalisms in a nervous frenzy). It also will not be found in the range of bourgeois anxieties and pathos folded into Kwame Anthony Appiah's or Martha Nussbaum's cosmopolitanisms.[13] It could possibly lie in the consideration of a subjectivity being defined by its exceptions to time and space, factoring in the subject who grieves, out of a kind of love, for a love unfathomable and sidelined by the other politics performed in the reliable key of sufficient requitals or destructive austerities.

Building on Gandhi's discussion of anticolonial friendships and the hospitalities that underwrite them, speaking of a politics of the unrequited would require factoring in the issue of violence and terror that she sets aside. I understand her work not to be disregarding the question of violence per se but somehow able to separate out the possibilities of materialist politics from the reality of violence, given the incontrovertibly nonviolent legacy of politics she upholds. So, in faithfulness to her project, I think that a hundred years on from the end of that century, a materialist politics that does not contend with the issue of terror, and thus of love, and does not deal with the universalization of a kind of cruelty within which "healthy" nonviolent politics (so to speak) are framed, is really no materialist politics.

If a century ago, the ethical turn served as a guarantee for any politics to survive, it is important to acknowledge that any such valid ethical turn (let alone political one!) today cannot be allowed wishful exceptions from the issue of postcolonial and neoliberal necropolitics of austerity, violence, terror, and destruction. To not have to contend with the destinies of politics born of a ground soaked in senseless terror and violence, and a normalization of disregard, suspicion, brutality, cruelty, is not an option. Far from giving up on solidarities and shared political desire, I wonder if this is basically a finessing of the additional labor that must be performed in a world that is going berserk. This bonus labor needs to tread a new path of appreciating how essential form is to content. It has to factor in wounded bodies and apathetic ones, the righteous indignant and fascist of the left and the right, and the wrong of human rights and non-state humanitarian elitism.

The troubling continuities between the urgencies of liberals and fascists, and in more radical discourses on the left and right, can be traced to temporalities that are domesticated and naturalized in the liberal and social scientistic discourses of class, race, and gender, and other identities—of those that for now seem relevant to politics per se—that are again affirmed in contemporary politics of redemption and hope. Such are the invitations that are sent to us, sharing elements that might render them unacceptable. Still unwilling to give up on the possibility of an anticolonial and materialist politics that does not reaffirm the temporalities and attendant spatialities of the former and current colonizers (sometimes recast as "friends" and "saviors") but instead disrupts them by the modes of sensing and suffering that underpin and nourish those, I suggest that we consider recovering and re-sensing politics itself first, in order to recover a *we*.

WE, INVITED, INVITING

A prose poem by Palestinian playwright Amir Nizar Zuabi wrenchingly "reports" that all of Gaza has moved underground.[14] We are told that this marks the completion of the mission that took ten years and seven operations. The piece sports a "we" as the subject of these actions: the are ones digging, producing "mirror images of the land that has been abandoned." Since there was no where else to go out of the Strip, where even abandoning it was a desire in the midst of blockades and their crowdedness and hunger, this is what those trapped have accomplished. The claim is that this is a turning back on life—a forgetting, an abandonment that found its equal. But not without effort, a great deal of life was spent in digging the earth, and producing a Gaza underground. The writer reports, "We buried ourselves alive."

The entire city is not of the dead, but of those who are buried alive. This digging down is also a digging not into the earth, but into time as well. A digging onto the sediments of time, of history, perhaps one hopes for a moment prior to this one, for a time where one realizes also that those digging are not victims or the most despairing, because they find messages that ask for revenge on their behalf. Zuabi writes, "the loamy Gaza soil has been the ally of despair and the despairing." Loamy because of the tears of the living. Remnants.

As they dig deeper, the blockade comes undone, revealing a logic of time and space that far underpins, and thus transcends in time and space, the definitions and borders of the upper world. But these are borders of time as well, enclosing not linear chronologies, but entire ways of existing, entire worlds of memories and absences that started to define at some point in time who would live, and who would die, and in what way. The shared despair that once all sought refuge and now one's refuge overwrites another's; the perfect victims have become the perfect perpetrators. This deep in the heart of the earth, one finds no need to be a refugee, because they are all refugees, where the times and the persecutions and the abandonments—and the murders and the inheritances—that separate, do not exist. This is not some claim to a kind of initial oneness or unitariness, this is not the oceanic feeling being disrupted by civilization, or Eden forever messed up by the violence of Adam's children. The very crucial and critical gesture is to the despair that unites, to the pain that does not make hypocritical claims to being of more value than another's.

The "report" then goes to the hope that if this work of those buried alive continues, by virtue of the fact that they are alive, that the land will be perforated, made "like honeycomb," made "flimsy as silk," perhaps it will collapse in of itself, and that all will mix together, . . . and "we'll know that we were saved from the living death in which we are trapped, and now we'll join the life of above, and with them build a new land." But what would happen once they start to believe that they can can rebuild, if they return to the life of the above? Perhaps they will discover that the land above killed itself, was left behind and emptied out. That it existed only because they had been there. That its sustenance even through our death owed something to the expelled.

Reading, Being, With

It is impossible to read with Zuabi and not start writing *with* him, and the inelegance of retelling it in the third person is already a sign. It is a "we" that is almost like the *you* of a *kafi* or *qawwali*—no claim on behalf of something known, no *I* as prior (but also not excluded, not any more nor any less than in the you)—but the fanatic, the lover, or the devotee referring to the object of their devotion prior to, and in place of themselves. So, a kind of expression of love not as description or location or tether, but as a kind of dislocation, displacement, release, in the act that makes us a we—be it love, grief, or digging with all you have got.

The proclamation of the we is not a claim to an identity, contra Rancière, premised on claiming the wrong, and it is addressed to no one—largely because those who are speaking are not actually existing, but are making others speak through them.[15] Zuabi, reminiscent of James Baldwin in some of his letters, never addresses his "people" with a proper name. Those proper names always conferred by others, bearing relations to others inside them, only make room for Baldwin to claim what he is *not* in relation to someone in order to assert one's humanity (e.g., Raoul Peck's reading of *Remember This House* in "I am Not Your Negro").[16] He also keeps the "proper" phrases of politics out of his writing—and it is also Baldwin who proposes a relation, an unacknowledged, yet-unrequited relation to the master race and its (our) freedom. A people under siege are a people who have been named. At the same time, the we in Zuabi's poem intersperses many other proper names, each a relation to a world far beneath the world under this one, and far behind in history as well, so that the we is a gesture as much to a community that has existed, as one that that might exist, as one that exists dispersed in other lands and times, as one that may never. The we becomes an open, capacious temporality, and a gesture to a relation as open as one feels invited to. It is a claim of a wrong, but it is a claim that far surpasses the name "proper" to the wrong, and takes the we to a different temporal and spatial dimension. The other does not exist except in their actions of evacuating the population of a besieged city, telling everyone to leave while blocking all exits. There is no detailing of the wrong, no explication. The siege is hospitality par excellence. (After all, Zuabi speaks of a tray with tea and biscuits crashing and everything mixing together indiscriminately.) One cannot settle this wrong, and the wrong to the aggressor is that "we" are still alive when we should have been "settled" by now. The right of return being invoked here is "subterranean," as he speaks of digging "along the length and breadth of the land whose refugees we are." No claim to an ownership of the land, no language of loss or expropriation. Whose history is this? Whose murder did we inherit?

The self-fashioning of the we is itself an act of love, tying what is sensible and visible and what is not to what we want to make close. Not reducible to time or space alone, it forces seeing concepts like community and authority as intensely related to each other internally. What are the loves that produce us as a we—a we with hope, with a right to return, with a promised land—that allows us to murder and be murdered? Hope, in Zuabi's poem, is very importantly contained by its impossibility. That is, hope is possible only when we can exclude the reality of how the lives of those on whose behalf we hope are spent, when what they do with their time becomes increasingly irrelevant and not even a good enough spur to a lovers' quarrel. It is the curses they bear that energize the work of the wounded and the living.

"We dig out of despair, not hope," assures Zuabi. Either calling the bluff on the topos of sovereignty (not my concern or the most exciting read), or refusing to be corralled into, tethered to, or besieged by it, the digging deep is reminiscent of Marx's hidden abode of production underneath the noisy sphere of the distribution of commodities, and also of the worlds Nadeem Aslam conjures in *The Blind Man's Garden*, a novel about lives of two Pakistani boys, and numerous others, caught in the war in Afghanistan.[17] Life happens in layers and sediments on top of each other, with sovereign borders, checkposts, and bridges always too far from where one is supposed to be, no matter where exactly they might be—in Pakistan, the next city over, or in Afghanistan, over the border, in another universe. In the novel, prize horses are "buried" alive for safekeeping by their owner who does not want to let them be taken away by anticolonial troops in the 1857 war of independence, but then erupt/irrupt back from their grave. The sky, the garden, the dungeons in which young boys are tortured and raped, all seem to have a kind of ordinary, accepted, unsurprising stratification—not necessarily corresponding to any discrete metric of life or death—in a novel where life and death are importantly such mysteries that never get solved and are never really the stories that are being told. The writer tells us at points that there was no time to discuss how someone had died. There is too much love to bother with those questions. And the novel leaves us not knowing whether someone returns. Because at some point, the manner in which people live and die—and love—has changed. Both Zuabi and Aslam construct heterologic and heterotopic poetics that stage a different meaning of emancipation and equality. Redone thus, emancipation becomes premised on emancipating the objects of our desire from ourselves, and equality becomes a stand-in for a provocation to a shared world, waiting to be verified, reciprocated, requited. More invitation than declaration. An invitation is an acknowledgment of an inequality of some sort, except when it is an offering of love.

Unwilling Ends

When the usual crises of the world are invoked, I tend to dismiss the endisms that destroy any possibility of politics, which only reify a modern narrative of history in its insistence on an impending or inevitable end, and more pettily, for the relief it might bring to the wrong people (often those who are always scripting others' ends and the impending end of the world may think they will never have to pay for it). Having left home to be recolonized in the west is already an experience that forestalls the sense of there just being one world that would ever begin and end. The ends of worlds that we have witnessed, and those that we continue to feel viscerally, prove that the problem of these end times is certainly not a problem for those who have always been in worlds that represent disaster and damage for the rest of us. On an emotional level, the world as a definitive space-time eludes those who, having left home, deal with destinations and terminations on a regular basis, confronting an end in every departure, and an end in every arrival. This is when time itself becomes a space of refuge, allowing worlds to co-exist and not eliminate each other at will, as long as you can hold them in some way and defy the rationalities that expunge worlds that do not fit, or the possibility of existences that do not necessarily preclude others. It is here that the questions of ends, beginnings, and necessity, get transposed into those of presence and absence, appearance and disappearance, in time instead of space. It is here that the time in and of different spaces compels us to think about time and worlds in a fundamentally different way. And when thinkers go in search of the outside of time, for the moment of emergency where law is suspended and can be re-invoked as justice by those who have nothing, I am left to wonder how there is nothing special about this state of emergency for those spaces who are defined as states of emergency, margins which are always outside of time of the sovereign state and whose existence is premised on that exclusion. In this moment of grand crisis and of the acceptance of the destruction of the subject of politics, there is much to learn from those whose time has always been an effluent to time, whose life has been an effluent to life, cast in the terms of emergencies to which no one responds without more violence, whether physical, linguistic, material, or ideal. The subject who inhabits the margins both within and of the metropole, needs to be looked at for ways of re-inaugurating and challenging the normalized politics of liberalism and capitalism, and their familiar oppositions as well. This includes unsettling the very fundamental homogeneity of the desire for sovereignty that paints all terror with the same brush and then waits for a miracle for deliverance. Be it individual subjects or entire states as embodied failures that now bring the failure of western liberal democracies into sharp, and tragicomic, relief—such as all these countries are going through a complete cynical takeover of the state system by unapologetic creators of these crises—we might have something to learn about politics yet and take notes for what an anticolonial materialist politics might look like if we are to have one (a politics, and a world).

OF THRESHOLDS FROM WHICH NO ONE LEAVES EMPTY-HANDED: THE UNREQUITED AND THEIR ORDINARY REDEMPTIONS OF POLITICS

Beyond any other contemporary undertakings of the question of anti-imperialist politics, *Affective Communities* aligns with those treatments of the notion of the political that deem the agon over the meaning of the political to be a veritable arena of politics itself. To those of us who have looked to Weber, Gandhi mounts an important challenge that deals with the question of maturity in a Weber who, despite his lament over disenchantment, is tragically only able to accept a particular ethics as a mode of maturity. Gandhi helps us re-read the *Vocation Lectures*. Weber juxtaposes disenchantment with the question of leadership and sense of proportion, and turns to the ethical individual as a means of preserving even just a world for politics to exist it, not politics itself. Gandhi very clearly does not see the ethical as an antipolitics, but as a counter to the political asceticisms that obtain in the cleansed political ontologies of Marxism and liberalism. I read her invocations of immature politics and of utopianism qua friendship as ways to re-enchant the world Weber has all but given up on. By looking at minor subjects, their minor interrelations and their minor politics (in various senses of minor) she is able to make an argument for resistances that keep politics on its toes, vital, unwilling to be given up on, and an important site for questioning the temptations of identity politics, nativisms, and nationalisms in a range of anti-imperial struggles.

A few directions for future work and investigation are indicated here (that I must defer out of necessity). Is a kind of minimalist defence of politics (not unlike Weber's) still lurking in Gandhi's avowed rejection of ascetic politics? Is the labor of the hospitable metropolitan subject the same as the labor of the hospitable colonial subject, given the actual and ongoing conditions of the encounter? Where is the choice in either situation, and whose power is to see guest-friendship as optional? Gandhi sticks with the politics of friendship and of the guest-as-stranger to which we must stay open rather than opting for the clearly exploitative and one-sided demand for the consummation of desire and the desperate need for "recognition" that obtains in a bloody dialectic of love and death in colonialism and what follows it. With that crucial distinction in mind, is this ethical imperative able to withstand these limits without encrusting and fixing its subjects? Is it able to recognize that the body of the hospitable "other" gets tired, and that the subject position that adheres might be too predictable and part of a disciplining of politics we are unwilling to disrupt and challenge? Might the ethical turn, instead of loosening the hold over the subject-agent, inflict an awful self-sameness that compels one to see no difference between a refusal and a deferral at the end of *Passage*? How can we posit a kind of sociality that is the grounds for the fact that the ethical burden does not always fall on the same people all the time? Might the impossibility of friendship impel a new kind of politics?

The answer, for me, lies in the domain of how and what one senses are the stakes of political life, and how and what one confronts frustrated desire or spurned or impotent love. In the epigram from "The Power of Money in Bourgeois Society," Marx equates love that is unable to make itself the beloved as a misfortune, at the same time as he suggests that this fate was part of the condition of society.[18] Any desire for this state of abstract, unspecific, love on the one hand, and of the unrequitedness on the other hand, to be overcome without a transformation of the social conditions that necessitate such relations is part of that misfortune. In other words, unrequitedness is a fundamental feature of life here and now that must be contended with as such, as part of the system of social relations in which one lives. All requitals need to be vetted in this light. The lack of reciprocity and unrequitedness is also, I think, in reference to the kind of political action one undertakes, and the journey to transforming the conditions that will make reciprocity and requital possible must take on the full burden of this lack of reciprocity and requital. The object of love ought to be seen for where it is a fetish and where an object rich in specificities most of which stay beyond the reach of our words. The meaning of reciprocity and requital changes when we are able to be honest, even if not exhaustive, about who, how, and what it is that we love and desire. The beloved, then, needs to be an honest beloved, freed from the shrouds of fetishism—because, under present conditions, only fetishism allows for requital and for romanticizing its loss, having abstracted so much from the particularity and allowing the object to pretend to be something other than an image of our projected needs frozen in time and space. The call, minimally, is to not fetishize oneself as a lover, or court the affirmations of someone else's love that treats us as fetish—but to hear the call in others' existences and struggles, and in the presence of the remains of loves past, for us to keep being. . . reader, witness, friend, comrade, lover (and maybe for a different reason than before).

Being other than a fetish or a fetishist "in love" requires dealing with the issue of space and time in a different way. The temporalities naturalized across the urgencies of liberals and fascists on the one side, and in more radical discourses on the left and right, on the other call for a subject to match, a subject who will love and be loved as a fetish, as a naturalized container of experiences pasteurized and evaporated into essences, interests, and destinies. This is liberalism's amazingly cynical revenge on democracy, affirmed in contemporary politics of redemption and hope. The conscription of experiences of oppression and marginalization for politics in a manner that is taxonomized, functionalized, contained in time and space, and thus empirically incontrovertible, counter-intuitively fuels the notion that requital is at hand anytime now, and will only return us to the selves identified as such—otherwise the requital is, well, no requital. The temporality that does not undo the attachment but only imagines a constant present in which the struggles of a constant history are being waged makes us blind and insensible to new provocations and calls.

The unrequited of our times are subjects who articulate, and are articulated in, the convergence of experiences of love, terror, and marginality to hegemonic spatiotemporal regimes. In this moment of global imperial, neoliberal, anti-political consensus, they engage in a politics of love and suffering, forming and deforming regimes of times, space, and sense to which they are forcibly betrothed. In doing so, they churn out life despite its impossibilities, perhaps life that is illegible or dis-sensual to the normalized understandings of love, terror, and located-ness. The unrequited are those who, beyond the conquest and devastation of land and body, are dealing with the murder of character and sensibility—all acts of great rapacious, presumptuous, intimacy—and struggle with the regimes of time and space that perform the farcical obligation to desire them (either through colonialism or through liberal multiculturalism) without quite loving them. They show, in their repeated acts of living and loving, that love, and not hope, is the appropriate double for this suffering. There are those who, perhaps like Leila in the wilderness, live in and with terror, even allow it to live inside them, withholding consent and love, certainly any kind of redemption or requital of that love—even going as far as seeing in love the only dissensus necessary to give politics another life and body.

These subjects hold out a promise of politics in this time against the destruction, abandonment, or evacuation of politics by those who have given in to the temptations of the loves on offer and convinced themselves that what is on offer and what they got is, indeed, love. These include both the unloved who seek salvation, and those who are scared of not being the beloved and the saved even if only in the histories they feverishly write. Surrounded by the anti-political consensus that binds these, the unrequited are left to safeguard what is left of politics, whether by sitting silently next to unburied bodies in the streets for days in the dead of winter like the mothers of disappeared Baluchis or Pashtuns or Kashmiris, or, like Leila and Qes, by turning back to reanimate dead animals decorating the oppressor's palace. Wouldn't their love otherwise be forever tainted by the memory of having chosen something as meager as their own life?

The unrequited subject is marked both by its history of being implicated in the love that consummates in colonialism and infuses the lifeworld of the colony to this day, and by now bearing a kind of unreciprocated, struggling, or impotent love. This is because the possibility of intimacy and mutuality, indeed even just solidarity with others in this moment, is already shaped by how intimate with terror we are, how we acknowledge that, and how our ability to be close, to feel, and to trust another with our ignorance, knowledge, violence, vulnerability, silence, and grief—indeed the very possibility of proximity and engagement necessary to politics—get framed in this scenario. The familiar idea of politics, of subjects knowing and wielding their identities, interests, political action, and words like flags, tridents, hashtags, and daggers, might be more excluding of possibilities of listening to and being with ourselves and others, and sensing and producing politics in this moment, than we think.

NOTES

1. Forster, *A Passage to India*. pp. 361–62.
2. Karl Marx and Fredrick Engels, "The Power of Money," in *The Economic and Philosophic Manuscripts of 1844* https://www.marxists.org/archive/marx/works/1844/manuscripts/power.htm, Accessed 26 June 2018 .
3. This loneliness as unrequitedness is clearly different from the organized loneliness/isolation of totalitarianism that Arendt narrates. But they both relate to a structure of austerity in some way, where liberalism requites with visions of community that supplant the desire indexed in the loneliness with something else, whereas totalitarianism produces a internalized deprivation that can only be requited with the subsumption of community into authority, and the isolation, and death of everyone else. It is unclear to me at this point in history if these are differences of degree or form.
4. David Lean, *A Passage to India* (Sony Pictures Home Entertainment, 2001).
5. Salman Rushdie, *Midnight's Children: A Novel*, 25th Anniversary edition (New York: Random House Trade Paperbacks, 2006), 3.
6. Leela Gandhi, *Affective Communities: Anticolonial Thought, Fin-de-Siècle Radicalism, and the Politics of Friendship* (Duke University Press, 2006).
7. Weber, *The Vocation Lectures*. p. 92.
8. Gandhi, *Affective Communities*. p. 7.
9. Gandhi, 30.
10. Gandhi, 31.
11. Gandhi, 31.
12. Gandhi, 32.
13. Martha C. Nussbaum, *For Love of Country?*, ed. Joshua Cohen, 1st ed. (Boston: Beacon Press, 2002).
14. Amir Nizar Zuabi, "The Underground Ghetto City of Gaza," Haaretz, August 3, 2014, https://www.haaretz.com/opinion/.premium-1.608653. All quotes in this section before the break are from this piece.
15. Rancière, "Politics, Identification, Subjectivization." p. 68.
16. Raoul Peck, *I Am Not Your Negro,* 2017, reading James Baldwin's *Remember This House,* an incomplete last work in which Baldwin arrests the fundamental mythos of American "democracy" that entails the white man to produce a category of (non-human) being that denies humanity, binding the white man and the black man in that relation about which Baldwin became increasingly hopeless over the course of his life, especially after the murder of Martin Luther King, Jr., and Medgar Evers, having always asserted the undeniability of relation at the heart of the possibility of an otherwise.
17. Nadeem Aslam, *The Blind Man's Garden*, Reprint edition (New York: Vintage, 2014).

18. Karl Marx and Fredrick Engels, "The Power of Money in Bourgeois Society," in *The Economic and Philosophic Manuscripts of 1844 and the Communist Manifesto*, trans. Martin Milligan, 1st edition (Amherst, N.Y.: Prometheus Books, 1988), p.135–40.

Epilogue:
The Classroom, A Community of Longing

Jaise veerane mein chupke se bahar aa jaye
As spring comes to the wilderness, surreptitiously

Dear Jean-Jacques,

    This is and is not a love letter. It is about the loves you have mediated in those who have had illicit and torturous love affairs with you all their lives and then inspired this in generations of students and thinkers and dreamers and revolutionaries. As a teacher, when I more fully understand the importance of the good infection I have deemed you to be and the love to which your work has clued me, it seems as if the love is tested most and becomes most precarious when it is time to pass it on, teach it, teach with it. Your work has made me vulnerable to many other infections in my life beyond and besides you, and here's hoping that I can make an attempt at locating that love in a way I have never had to, to push my words to different kinds of materiality within institutions of power, culture, and education where one's attachment to you gets at once affirmed and tested, energized and thwarted. I have come some way from my pride at the inscription by my teacher on a copy of his book about you, where he placed me in your company by addressing me in his inscription as "another 'dreamer of democracy.'"[1] Understanding how the truth of love requires its own fictions, I know very well how much work both you and I, and all in between, have put into sustaining this relationship that you are most likely not even aware of, or wouldn't be in if ever we had really inhabited the same spatio-temporal nook. As I, in being a writer and teacher, go on with my task of furnishing the spaces for the sensibilities I would like to nurture, here is me turning back to you, and to some texts of yours I am still perhaps too heady and romantic to read carefully or for their mundane implications, for fear of losing you or finding something that I could not defend, to actually celebrate the fact that you have given me something that completely preempts that fate! I have found my way to you, and through you, many times, and will do so once again.

One of my favorite books written about you stole the line I wanted to write in my ode to you and your dreams and torments for the world you lived in, and the dreams and torments they infect. The line went, "For as long as I can remember, I have been a Rousseauian."[2] How easily it rolls off the tongue, as if those could be my words. Not that you were the only one to have inspired such a *community of longing* as you represent, but it is quite noteworthy that there is something assuring about the wish to have written what you wrote, to have written what others I have fallen in love with by association with you have. Being a Rousseauian is not a matter of being a disciple—far from it—but it does require a form of belief, I think, in this case a belief in what it could mean to be with someone, to be from and of someone or somewhere, and to be suspended within associations that do not scare or frighten. Thus every act of reading and learning someone is ultimately an act of learning to be with them, with the possibility of discovering a way of being close that can only rejoice at rather than regret someone else having said what you meant to say. This possibility has haunted me and I hope it haunts my students—right on the other end of the form of misanthropy that can set in when sensitive people try to insert themselves into worlds, and still try to remain true to who they are even when the knowledge and confirmation of who they are is perpetually deferred. This elixir is what I have felt keeps those of us going who consider the classroom sacred not because it is not touched by the world but because it is where one can attempt to have faith and to love in ways that perhaps require a necessary suspension of the kind of arrogant reality and, indeed, all the naturalized arrogant claims of the real and the empirically true that, ironically, remove the role of the potent forces, of history, of structures, of institutions, and their politics in framing our relation to and understanding of the real and our location as subjects and objects.

When these forces are accepted into our spaces, and the classroom takes its exception from History but not from time, we invite back into it possibilities of thinking in ways that do not foreclose the question of what it is to be human, and who we are as subjects and objects inscribed within the social and political structures of our ordinary and extraordinary lives, so that the very meaning of acting and being in the world stands a chance at change. This form of intimacy with the present and with the absent, this longing and not an abstract hope, is necessary to political and sentimental education required for a becoming-with that does not smother into homogeneity but produces subjects not of their time and space. It becomes even more curious for me to be talking about this intimacy, because it is also this space of being a teacher where I have felt most compelled to love *and* to be misanthropic, to be marked as an outsider who is an insider into the worlds we may like to know more about but not be in, where I have seen spaces reveal themselves to be far truer to the brutal idea of American exceptionalism and white capitalist patriarchal supremacy than their express imperatives or manifestoes would suggest. It is also where I have felt I will die, not unlike Atyka, slain by those who had your love, or where friends will politely hand me over to the fascists saying they never got what I was doing in the classroom anyway. In this community of longing (and not be-longing), one has to struggle to explode the complacency of the apolitical and the non-political for whom the community is immanently secure. They also cannot comprehend that the strength of a community, like any relation, is to be able to put its premises in question and withstand that questioning. What is taught is the occasion for a community of longing, not of extraction of knowledge or truth, instrumentalization and functionalization, or the final interpretive climax as if we had never known the joys of waiting for the beloved.

A submission to this conscription is often irreversible, as our times are teaching us.

Even before the more popular naysayers, Rousseau, yours has been the pedagogy of suspicion and love at once—where, as outsiders to a certain history, we do not swear a kind of immunity, but can actually see at what moments we have created the conditions that made us subject to certain desires for subjection. This is what unifies you and Adorno, feminists and anticolonials, who are willing to look at themselves by taking a bit of a leave of themselves.

I think it was the war class so many years ago that was my first effort at framing a course that talked about something that was not yet dead. What realities are not yet done with, where is the subject of our inquiry so intractable, and so pervasive? It was here that I realized more and more the permeation of the classroom by the kinds of responses that were the hardest to let go—the worried activist student who wanted to know what to do, the quick theorist who defended abstraction without quite knowing what abstraction is. And then there were those in the middle who were able to take me out of the picture entirely: what kind of answers did they want me to give them that I wasn't giving, and would my inadequacy be the same if I looked different? What kinds of failures haunt those of us who, resist as they can and may, carry the burdens of presences they cannot let go of. As an outsider, it took me a long time to realize that the residues in the classroom were accumulated from long before me, and that sometimes the ghosts that enter the room with all of us there in the moment are not strong enough to fight the others off. One of the hauntings that has often threatened to devour and exhaust us is the history of the kinds of invitations students have been given: the invitation to remain a child, to citizenship they do not have a role in defining, to being protected from politics, to receive meaning rather than make it, to receive love like charity rather than an honor, to not receive love at all. Those who historically have the experience to be secure with ideas are systematically removed from the helm of affairs since they are made to carry the burden of everyone's voyeurism of the concrete—while those whose experiences and sentiments have gaping holes which the available people of color and women, etc. have to fill, are the ones who are assigned the role to think the big thoughts. There is a remarkable comfort in some of these roles, even where least expected. Perhaps because there is a hierarchy of injustices to fight, and this division of labor seems useful to some in that fight.

Grappling with your own paradoxes regarding the self and different ways of making the self present that one finds in your reveries, in your confessions, and their deeply theatrical nature (despite/because of your critique of theater itself), I have reconciled with the fact that the way to understand what you want from this critique is to push a question of asking how, given the inability to turn time back, could one deal with one's yearning for a different present, and for a kind of presence and materiality that tempts a different fate for experience, sensing, suffering, being, and becoming, with and for others, that contemporary life keeps making distant from us. Shouldn't we at least be able to entertain, perform, the possibilities to tempt them to become real? Shouldn't the self that is resilient be able to leave itself to find itself in others before returning to itself? Beyond mourning the loss of this availability that one finds symptomatized in the creation of this thing called "culture," a fetish not unlike many things we produce and then forget to relate to or make claims on, I do wonder whether it is indeed possible that this impossibility of turning back sends us building those tentative, fledgling, communities that are fuelled, but not foreclosed by, imagined ones.

The space of study with others—often called the classroom—is one of those. Perhaps this courtship, this love of the absent despite its literal unavailability, has something to do with the reason I teach and with what the classroom always anticipates, and holds the promise of location for. My labor in that space looks to the theater not as a display or exhibition or a performance of those things that we must always want, but as an example of how we learn and amass the modes of subjectivity society assigns us, given the spaces already configured for us, and the stages already set for us by forces within and beyond us. It is thus that the theater brings home the understanding that the promise of a democracy in its unfulfilled nature, of a kind of politics as yet unrendered in the languages and performances taught us and taught by us in an explicit way, is premised on the setting of structures, temporal and spatial, for different relations within these locations, to afford us modes of speech and response, sensing and suffering, and thus subjectivity and citizenship. Teaching politics, I feel, is ultimately a holding of this suspicion close to one's heart.

Finding my own way as an outsider to most places, including this country, has necessitated repeated claims of home that have been made possible within precisely the kinds of institutions that you foresaw to be the breeding ground of a form of inequality premised on the differential allocation of skill, talent, ability, and knowledge recognized and rewarded by systems of power that are by their nature not democratic, but sometimes try to be. These very spaces hold on to the elitism that you have completely abhorred, but are also the spaces of promise where anything close to the communities that are resilient enough to challenge their own senses, sensibilities, their notion of citizenship, etc., might come to be and exist, and give a kind of home to so many of us whose torments would otherwise completely deface us, and commit us to the form of privations that is not at all healthy for the performance of the society to come, and for a society that can imagine itself otherwise than it is. Maybe the university is the place where certain other academic fictions need to prolong themselves like Intizar Hussain's dream or a terrible TV soap depending on the day, or are ghettoized so that they do not permeate the world whose unquestioned submission those in power are counting on for their own life. So, it is a bind.

Concentric and undulating institutional and existential spaces construct the possibility of an enterprise of knowledge and transformation that closely learns from the imperative to treat students to an education of sentiment without an education in the sentimentality and sensibility of the times, that make them feel and relate to presences "on-demand." This work requires a constant understanding, renewed and reworked, of our own relation to power within and outside the classroom, where we cannot help but think about the equal importance of being *and* not-being who we are, and about the fact that situated knowledges also involve being unsituated. Protecting and conserving something we love happens simultaneously with, and is not threatened by nor always presupposes, understanding what it is that is being protected.

When I arrived here, I immediately recognized it as a place that in its size, promise, beauty could well embody the locations that charmed your life, that provided the settings, both real and wishful for your work. But it is only now that I realize the truth and trenchant dualities of all spaces; I had initially asked myself whether this would be your nightmare or your dream. But it is both, like all your reveries suggested. I don't want to know for certain anymore. What can that certainty do for anyone, whether those who rest or resist, those who believe and those who naysay, those who persevere and those who have never even had to negotiate the demands spaces make beyond the demands they can make on spaces? The important thing, learnt from history, is that of the silly flukes that put us on what now seem to be our paths, and on the possibility of a kind of redemption present in precisely those unfulfilled possibilities that got missed but still linger somewhere waiting to be acknowledged and picked up, held close to the heart, not necessarily to be fulfilled this time either.

You have always advised a kind of training in time in order to challenge history. Words know this well, always in the throes of that strange lag between utterance and materiality which I count on my students to embrace. The little worlds of study are like spaces of love, then, since they require certain patience with words and images—not merely, or at all, in tolerating them when they are bad—but in giving them the space to build, to manifest themselves, to allow those to be insights into our materialities, ways to enter others, and ways to barricade some others completely, in the name of those we love. These are spaces of struggle too, because in this moment in history we come to them with broken hearts, and we are answerable to them. And how is one to educate the hearts when they are broken? Is it unfair to ask this much of them? But aren't they the only ones who can deliver? What are the presences we are compelled to and compelled by, and how do we create spaces and availabilities within these spaces that can enable us to respond to, relate to, and do justice to these presences?

When I tell someone I have a materialist politics, they do not quite understand it. And they did not get it when I tried to argue all those years ago that yours was as well. Maybe that gives me a rare moment of security. It is a politics that, simply put, is interested in our capacities as human beings who are able to build relations and communities and are able to sense things and suffer our own and another's suffering. In that sense, it is about forms of being accountable to the kinds of presences the making material of which is also part of the politics. So, in some ways, a materialist politics understands the deep connections between ways of knowing and ways of being, as activities of being alive, and of honoring the dead, and of ways of knowing that conflict with being and thriving and nurturing; and then it is also something that sees politics as not reducible or equal to every other thing, but that requires ethics and aesthetics—questions of judgment in a personal realm in various ways to be keenly linked to forms of judgment and enactments in the realm of human bodies, souls, communities, and institutions. I, and you would understand this, am not really in the knowledges I am supposed to be a reservoir for, but the beginning foretold a different kind of mediation. In the classroom, I have to mediate my own presence in the knowledges I mediate for my students—for usually the roles of people like me are those of objects of knowledge or the subject from which we must abstract in order not to complicate things too much. I am sure many of my colleagues cringe at leaving you or Emerson in my hands; maybe the thought crosses their mind that I do some grave injustice coming to you in order to read how awful the injustices of western culture and its imperialism are, or being fashionably postmodern. But that is enjoyable too: the unsuspected alliances one can make on the basis of not what one's party politics are but what experience means, where the self goes, how bloated it is, what is the connection of a certain mode of knowledge to fascism and its various iterations, and so on. So, there is an abiding community possible only because we can attempt to reframe its tenets and the conditions of its possibility.

This invoked community varies in form and composition depending on how removable or detachable our knowledges, or the inquiries of the classroom, are from the current mediations of contemporary news and realpolitik, etc. To put it in another way, certain kinds of life which knowledge has not conquered forces really tough moments of being out of sorts, as well as the worst moments of a stubborn sticking to totems that would otherwise be more easy or relaxed. This is a question of fidelity to the living and to the dead. The anxiety one experiences of a mind at work that has learnt not to deal with the object of knowledge as alive, mutable, and making demands on oneself—rather than finding the self all too important in being able to come through this relation, this encounter, with war, alive—is scary. And how easily the world is able to render war a category that can be empiricized and quantified and how easily social scientists can study it, or people respond to the demands of their own self-preserving sense of goodwill. Some other faith is involved here, a closeness and a trust that does not force a taking of stances, and passing judgment as if a reality is over and done with, or worse still, rendering it "dead" like Marx said the empiricists did.

Part of the absence I am peeved by is the absence of politics, the vacation of the public space, and spaces of education from all politics but of the kind one calls bureaucracy or opinion. It is not in the presence of politics but in its absence that spaces become unsafe, for there is nothing to rely on, no spirits to call on, since all witnesses have been laid off. A teacher of politics cannot possibly be party to this vacation of politics—a politics whose ontology and epistemology is materialist and historical is not an ideological form, but refers to the mode in which one starts living the worlds as if something was at stake. To be able to not merely respect but honor, and to feel safe not when no one asks anything of us, but when someone trusts you enough to ask. To contain the weariness of those of us who have always to tell their story, who have always to root their "opinion" in their particular "perspective." What monstrous certainties and knowledges are bred when the modes of love and pathos that have to be performed, for those who have yet to learn any other kind, are those of possession, surveillance, and control?

Reason's ability to work only through imagination, is very crucial to me, as it is to you. Thus my joy that, quite similar to the feeling I get when I read your *Second Discourse*, on insisting on a relation to matter and to experience that is irreducibly political in the choice of *form* it takes, and fights over it. It isn't to render the object merely accessible to students, but to make it available to them, to make them available to themselves and to each other, and to construct spaces where comportment would be more important than an ability to imagine a kind of transformative power that could easily co-exist with a thoughtlessness, an easy conscripting of our capacity to love, and a utilitarian relation to existence whether our own or others'. That is a requital we do not wish for. It is one that must be spared fulfillment.

Amid so many willed and unwilled, consensual and unconsensual ends scripted for us, the question of autonomy and anonymity remains timelessly valid. Where does the imposition of an empty liberal space full of ordinary power and cowardly self-protections (failing proposition, you know it as well I do!), become way more demanding than a place full of violent opposition, of conflicts that have integrity and rigor? If both the feeling and the object have taken the form they have in this space of existence, how am I to trust either, or myself for that matter—if at all my own education in and into this world is not a done deal yet? How am I supposed to trust the self enough to preserve it, and how am I supposed to trust anything but that?

After all, you know, how can one explain how one loves?

Yours.

A.

the page prepared
like one lays out the *chandni* for *saf-e-matam*
and then they came and said
how come you grieve
the love
when you should be the one dying

deaths foretold
are so silly
this is no prophecy
just a report
making sure someone knows
how many were smoked inside that cave
and out

fiction became prophecy
when the soldiers and the medics
and other officers of death in life
stop keeping books
stop sounding notes
memory comes in the way
you know

the page dressed
with its neat printed words
lines that might as well be
like rows of mourners
ready to go
follow
rhythmically

but then all of a sudden
the rhythm falls
you know what happens
when the chants fall with it

NOTES

1. Thank you, Jim Miller. James Miller, *Rousseau: Dreamer of Democracy* (Yale University Press, 1984).
2. Thank you, Tracy Strong. *Jean-Jacques Rousseau: The Politics of the Ordinary* (Rowman & Littlefield, 2002), p. xxvii

Bibliography

Abbas, Asma. *Liberalism and Human Suffering: Materialist Reflections on Politics, Ethics, and Aesthetics*. 1st ed. New York; London: Palgrave Macmillan, 2010.
——. "From the Love Studio." *Hypatia: A Journal of Feminist Philosophy*. Special Issue: Feminist Love Studies Winter 2017, Volume 32, Issue 1.
——. "In Love, In Terror, Out of Time." In Razack, Sherene and Suvendrini Perera, eds. *At the Limits of Justice: Women of Colour on Terror*. University of Toronto Press, 2014.
Adams, David. *Colonial Odysseys: Empire and Epic in the Modernist Novel*. Cornell University Press, 2003.
Adorno, Theodor W. *Aesthetic Theory*. Edited by Gretel Adorno and Rolf Tiedeman. Minneapolis: University of Minnesota Press, 1997.
——. *Negative Dialectics*. Routledge, 1990.
Adorno, Theodor W., and Brian O'Connor. *The Adorno Reader*. Wiley-Blackwell, 2000.
Al Jazeera English. *Rebel Architecture - The Architecture of Violence*. Accessed December 3, 2017. https://www.youtube.com/watch?v=ybwJaCeeA9o.
Andre, Chris. "Aphrodite's Children: Hopeless Love, Historiography, and Benjamin's Dialectical Image." *SubStance* 27, no. 1 (1998): 105–28. https://doi.org/10.2307/3685719.
Arendt, Hannah. *Love and Saint Augustine*. Edited by Joanna Vecchiarelli Scott and Judith Chelius Stark. 1st edition. Chicago: University of Chicago Press, 1998.
——. *Rahel Varnhagen: The Life of a Jewess*. The Johns Hopkins University Press, 2000.
——. "We Refugees (1943)." In *Altogether Elsewhere: Writers on Exile*, edited by Marc Robinson, 1st edition, 110–19. Winchester, MA: Faber & Faber, 1994.
Asad, Talal. *Formations of the Secular*. Stanford University Press, 2003.
Aslam, Nadeem. "Leila in the Wilderness." In *Granta 112: Pakistan*, edited by John Freeman. London: Grove Press, Granta, 2010.
——. *The Blind Man's Garden*. Reprint edition. New York: Vintage, 2014.
Babbitt, Irving. *Rousseau and Romanticism*. Houghton Mifflin Company, 1919.
Bachelard, Gaston, M. Jolas, and John R. Stilgoe. *The Poetics of Space: The Classic Look at How We Experience Intimate Places*. Beacon Press, 1994.
Bachmann, Ingeborg. *Malina: A Novel*. New York: Holmes & Meier, 1990.
——. *The Book of Franza & Requiem for Fanny Goldmann*. First English Language Edition. Evanston, Ill.: Northwestern University Press, 1999.
Badiou, Alain, and Peter Hallward. *Ethics*. Verso, 2002.
Badiou, Alain, and Simon Critchley. Ours is Not a Terrible Situation, March 6, 2006.
Baker, Robert. "Crossings of Levinas, Derrida, and Adorno: Horizons of Nonviolence." *Diacritics* 23, no. 4 (Winter 1993): 12–41. https://doi.org/10.2307/465305.

Baldwin, James. *James Baldwin: Collected Essays*. Edited by Toni Morrison. New York: Library of America, 1998.

———. *The Devil Finds Work*. Verso, 2011

Bargu, Banu. *Starve and Immolate: The Politics of Human Weapons*. New York: Columbia University Press, 2014.

Barker, Jason. "To Have Done with the Other." Ghent University, Belgium, 2005.

Bassam, Sulayman Al. *The Arab Shakespeare Trilogy: The Al-Hamlet Summit; Richard III, an Arab Tragedy; The Speaker's Progress*. Bloomsbury Publishing, 2014.

Basu, Anurag. *Gangster*. Adlabs Films, 2006.

Bataille, Georges. *The Accursed Share: An Essay on General Economy, Vol. 1: Consumption*. Translated by Robert Hurley. 1st edition. New York: Zone Books, 1991.

———. "The Sorcerer's Apprentice." In *The College of Sociology, 1937-1939*, edited by Denis Hollier, 223–32. University of Minnesota Press, 1988.

Beardsworth. "A Note to Understanding of Love in Our Age."

Beiser, Frederick C. *Early Political Writings of the German Romantics*. Cambridge, U.K.; New York: Cambridge University Press, 1996.

Benjamin, Walter. "My Great Fear Is That We Have Much Less Time at Our Disposal Than We Imagined," August 2, 1940. http://harvardpress.typepad.com/hup_publicity/2015/09/walter-benjamin-last-letter-to-adorno.html.

———. *The Origin of German Tragic Drama*. London; New York: Verso, 1998.

———. *The Writer of Modern Life: Essays on Charles Baudelaire*. Edited by Michael W. Jennings. Translated by Howard Eiland, Edmund Jephcott, Rodney Livingstone, and Harry Zohn. Cambridge, Mass.: Belknap Press, 2006.

———. "Theses on the Philosophy of History." In *Illuminations: Essays and Reflections*, 253–64. New York: Schocken Books, 1988.

Bhardwaj, Vishal. *Haider*, 2014.

Bhattacharya, Sabyasachi. *Mahatma and the Poet: Letters and Debates Between Gandhi and Tagore 1915–1941*. National Book Trust, 1997.

Biddick, Kathleen. *Make and Let Die: Untimely Sovereignties by Kathleen Biddick*. Punctum Books, 2016.

———. "Unbinding the Flesh in the Time That Remains: Crusader Martyrdom Then and Now." *GLQ: A Journal of Lesbian and Gay Studies* 13, no. 2 (May 14, 2007): 197–225.

Boehmer, Elleke, and Stephen Morton. "Introduction: Terror and the Postcolonial." In *Terror and the Postcolonial: A Concise Companion*. John Wiley & Sons, 2009.

Bosteels, Bruno. "Archipolitics, Parapolitics, Metapolitics." In *Jacques Ranciere: Key Concepts*, edited by Jean-Philippe Deranty, 80–93. Routledge, 2014.

Bradley, Rizvana. "Poethics of the Open Boat." *ACCeSsions* 2. Accessed December 4, 2017. https://accessions.org/article2/poethics-of-the-open-boat/.

"Caché (2005) - IMDb." Accessed December 6, 2017. http://www.imdb.com/title/tt0387898/.

Campbell, Timothy, and Adam Sitze. "Biopolitics: An Encounter." In *Biopolitics: A Reader*, edited by Timothy Campbell and Adam Sitze, 1–40. Durham: Duke University Press Books, 2013.

"Charleston Church Shooting: Nine Die in South Carolina 'Hate Crime' - BBC News." Accessed December 3, 2017. http://www.bbc.com/news/world-us-canada-33179019.

Chibber, Vivek. "Why We Still Talk About the Working Class." *Jacobin*, March 15, 2017. http://jacobinmag.com/2017/03/abcs-socialism-working-class-workers-capitalism-power-vivek-chibber/.

Ciccariello-Maher, George. *Decolonizing Dialectics*. Duke University Press, 2017.

Cladis, Mark S. "Redeeming Love: Rousseau and Eighteenth-Century Moral Philosophy." *Journal of Religious Ethics* 28, no. 2 (January 2000): 221–51. https://doi.org/10.1111/0384-9694.00045.

Coulthard, Glen. *Red Skin, White Masks: Rejecting the Colonial Politics of Recognition*. University of Minnesota Press, 2014.

Critchley, Simon. "Demanding Approval." *Radical Philosophy*, June 2000. http://www.lacan.com/critchley.htm.

Da Silva. "Fractal Thinking." *ACCeSsions* 2 (April 27, 2016). https://accessions.org/article2/fractal-thinking/.
Dallmayr, Fred. "The Politics of Nonidentity: Adorno, Postmodernism-And Edward Said." *Political Theory* 25, no. 1 (February 1997): 33–56. https://doi.org/10.2307/192264.
Debord, Guy. *Society of the Spectacle*. Zone Books, 1994.
Dialogics. "Michael Hardt: On Love."
Dinshaw, Carolyn, Lee Edelman, Roderick A. Ferguson, Carla Freccero, Elizabeth Freeman, Judith Halberstam, Annamarie Jagose, Christopher S. Nealon, and Tan Hoang Nguyen. "Theorizing Queer Temporalities: A Roundtable Discussion." *GLQ: A Journal of Lesbian and Gay Studies* 13, no. 2 (May 14, 2007): 177–95.
Djebar, Assia. *The Tongue's Blood Does Not Run Dry: Algerian Stories*. Seven Stories Press, 2006.
Du Bois, W. E. B. *Darkwater: Voices from Within the Veil*. Mineola, N.Y: Dover Publications, 1999.
———. *The Souls of Black Folk*. Edited by Henry Louis Gates, Jr. and Terri Hume Oliver. New York: W. W. Norton & Company, 1999.
Edelman, Lee. *No Future: Queer Theory and the Death Drive*. Duke University Press, 2004.
Edensor, Tim. *Industrial Ruins: Space, Aesthetics and Materiality*. Oxford U.K. ; New York: Bloomsbury Academic, 2005.
Esposito, Roberto. *Categories of the Impolitical*. Translated by Connal Parsley. Translation edition. New York: Fordham University Press, 2015.
Faiz, Faiz Ahmad. "Mujh Se Pehli Si Mohabbat (Love, Do Not Ask)." In *Poems by Faiz*, translated by V. G. Kiernan. London: Allen and Unwin, 1971.
Fanon, Frantz, and Adolfo Gilly. *A Dying Colonialism*. Translated by Haakon Chevalier. New York: Grove Press, 1994.
Fanon, Frantz, Jean-Paul Sartre, and Homi K. Bhabha. *The Wretched of the Earth*. Translated by Richard Philcox. Reprint edition. New York: Grove Press, 2005.
Feral, Josette. "Kristevian Semiotics: Towards a Semanalysis." In *The Sign: Semiotics Around the World*, edited by R.W. Bailey et al. University of Michigan Press, 1980.
Ferber, Michael. *Romanticism: A Very Short Introduction*. 1st edition. Oxford; New York: Oxford University Press, 2010.
Feuerbach, Ludwig. *The Essence of Christianity*. Amherst, N.Y.: Prometheus Books, 1989.
———. *The Fiery Brook: Selected Writings*. Translated by Zawar Hanfi. 1st edition. London; New York: Verso, 2013.
Forster, E. M. *A Room with a View*. Penguin Books, 2011.
———. *A Passage to India*. Penguin Classics, 2005.
———. *Howards End*. Mineola, N.Y: Dover Publications, 2002.
———. *The Hill of Devi*. San Diego: Harvest Books, 1971.
———. *Where Angels Fear to Tread*. Vintage Books, 1959.
Freeman, Elizabeth. "Introduction." *GLQ: A Journal of Lesbian and Gay Studies* 13, no. 2 (May 14, 2007): 159–76.
Freud, Sigmund, and Hugh Haughton. *The Uncanny*. Translated by David McLintock. New York: Penguin Classics, 2003.
Gandhi, Leela. *Affective Communities: Anticolonial Thought, Fin-de-Siècle Radicalism, and the Politics of Friendship*. Duke University Press, 2006.
Gaur, Ishwar Dayal. *Martyr as Bridegroom: A Folk Representation of Bhagat Singh*. Anthem Press, 2008.
Ghosh, Rituparno. *Chokher Bali*, 2003.
Gostoli, Ylenia. "Reviving the Art of Cinema in Gaza City." *Al-Jazeera*, March 26, 2016. http://www.aljazeera.com/news/2016/03/reviving-art-cinema-gaza-city-160324060451220.html.
Gržinić, Marina. "From Biopolitics to Necropolitics: Marina Gržinić in Conversation with Maja and Reuben Fowkes." *ARTMargins*, October 9, 2012. http://www.artmargins.com/index.php/5-interviews/692-from-biopolitics-to-necropolitics-marina-grini-in-conversation-with-maja-and-reuben-fowkes.

Gržinić, Marina, and Šefik Tatlić. *Necropolitics, Racialization, and Global Capitalism: Historicization of Biopolitics and Forensics of Politics, Art, and Life*. Reprint edition. Lanham, Md.: Lexington Books, 2016.

Hamilton, Omar Robert. "Refugee Stasis." *N+1*, May 18, 2017. https://nplusonemag.com/online-only/online-only/refugee-stasis/.

Hanif, Mohammad. "Of Dogs, Faith and Imams." *New York Times*, July 25, 2015. https://mobile.nytimes.com/2015/07/25/opinion/sunday/mohammed-hanif-of-dogs-faith-and-imams.html.

Hardt, Michael, and Antonio Negri. *Empire*. Cambridge, Mass.: Harvard University Press, 2000.

Haver, William. "Queer Research." Edited by Sue Golding. Routledge, 1997.

Hussain, Intizar. *The Death of Sheherzad*. Noida: HarperCollins India, 2014.

"If You Fold a Paper in Half 103 Times It'll Get as Thick as the Universe." Accessed December 3, 2017. https://sploid.gizmodo.com/if-you-fold-a-paper-in-half-103-times-it-will-be-as-thi-1607632639.

Ivory, James. *A Room with a View*. Criterion Collection (Direct), 2015.

Jay, Martin. *Downcast Eyes: The Denigration of Vision in Twentieth-Century French Thought*. Berkeley: University of California Press, 1993. http://www.loc.gov/catdir/bios/ucal051/93000347.html; http://www.loc.gov/catdir/description/ucal041/93000347.html.

Kashyap, Anurag. *Gangs of Wasseypur - Part II*, n.d.

Khanna, Ranjana. *Algeria Cuts: Women and Representation, 1830 to the Present*. 1st edition. Stanford, Calif.: Stanford University Press, 2007.

Kleinberg-Levin, David Michael. *Modernity and the Hegemony of Vision*. Berkeley: University of California Press, 1993.

Kojève, Alexandre, and Raymond Queneau. *Introduction to the Reading of Hegel*. Cornell University Press, 1980.

Kotef, Hagar, and Merav Amir. "(En)Gendering Checkpoints: Checkpoint Watch and the Repercussions of Intervention." *Signs* 32, no. 4 (2007): 973–96.

Kristeva, Julia. *Time and Sense*. Translated by Ross Guberman. New York: Columbia University Press, 1998.

———. "Word, Dialogue and the Novel." In *The Kristeva Reader*, edited by Toril Moi, 34–61. Columbia University Press, 1986.

Kumar, Amitava. *Bombay, London, New York*.

Kushner, Tony. *Angels in America: A Gay Fantasia on National Themes*. New York: Theatre Communications Group, 1995.

Laymon, Kiese. "Black Churches Taught Us to Forgive White People. We Learned to Shame Ourselves." *The Guardian*, June 23, 2015. https://www.theguardian.com/commentisfree/2015/jun/23/black-churchesforgive-white-people-shame.

Lean, David. *A Passage to India*. Sony Pictures Home Entertainment, 2001.

Lebron, Chris. "Time for a New Black Radicalism." Opinionator, 1434970944. //opinionator.blogs.nytimes.com/2015/06/22/time-for-a-new-black-radicalism/.

Levinas, Emmanuel. *Totality and Infinity*. Springer, 1979.

Limone, Noa. "Chronicling Walter Benjamin's Final Hours." *Haaretz*, July 9, 2012. https://www.haaretz.com/chronicling-walter-benjamin-s-final-hours-1.449897.

Lukacs, Georg. *The Theory of the Novel*. 1st edition. Cambridge, Mass.: The MIT Press, 1974.

Malabou, Catherine. *The New Wounded: From Neurosis to Brain Damage*. Translated by Steven Miller. 1st edition. New York: Fordham University Press, 2012.

Manto, Saadat Hasan. *Mottled Dawn; Fifty Sketches and Stories of Partition*. 1st edition. Penguin Books,India, 2004.

Marder, Elissa. *Dead Time: Temporal Disorders in the Wake of Modernity*. 1st edition. Stanford University Press, 2002.

Marx, Karl. *Critique of the Gotha Program*. Edited by Bi Classics. Translated by Friedrich Engels. CreateSpace Independent Publishing Platform, 2017.

———. "The Difference Between the Democritean and the Epicurean Philosophy of Nature." In *Activity in Marx's Philosophy*, edited by Norman D. Livergood. The Hague: Martinus Nijhoff, 1967.

Marx, Karl, and Fredrick Engels. "Critique of Hegelian Dialectic and Philosophy as a Whole." In *The Economic and Philosophic Manuscripts of 1844 and the Communist Manifesto*, translated by Martin Milligan, 1st edition, 141–69. Amherst, N.Y: Prometheus Books, 1988.

———. "Estranged Labour." In *The Economic and Philosophic Manuscripts of 1844 and the Communist Manifesto*, translated by Martin Milligan, 1st edition. Amherst, N.Y: Prometheus Books, 1988, 69–84.

———. "The Power of Money in Bourgeois Society." In *The Economic and Philosophic Manuscripts of 1844 and the Communist Manifesto*, translated by Martin Milligan, 1st edition, 135–40. Amherst, N.Y: Prometheus Books, 1988.

May, Todd. *Political Thought of Jacques Rancière: Creating Equality*. Edinburgh University Press, 2008.

Mbembe, Achille. "Necropolitics." Translated by Libby Meintjes. *Public Culture* 15, no. 1 (March 25, 2003): 11–40.

McGann, Jerome J. *The Romantic Ideology: A Critical Investigation*. Chicago: University of Chicago Press, 1983.

McLaughlin, Kevin. "Benjamin's Barbarism." *The Germanic Review: Literature, Culture, Theory* 81, no. 1 (January 1, 2006): 4–20. https://doi.org/10.3200/GERR.81.1.4-20.

Miller, James. *Rousseau: Dreamer of Democracy*. Hackett, 1984.

Mondal, Rima. "Stalled Show: How Kashmir's Cinema Halls Became Torture Centers." *Free Press Kashmir* (blog), July 21, 2017. http://freepresskashmir.com/2017/07/21/stalled-show-how-kashmirs-cinemas-became-torture-centers/.

Moten, Fred. "Notes on Passage: The New International of Sovereign Feelings." *Palimpsest* 3, no. 1 (2014): 51–74.

———. "The New International of Insurgent Feeling." Palestine Campaign for the Academic and Cultural Boycott of Israel, November 7, 2009. http://www.pacbi.org/etemplate.php?id=1130.

Murdoch, Iris. *A Severed Head*. Reprint edition. Harmondsworth, Middlesex: Penguin Books, 1976.

Murray et al., ed. "Face to Face with Agamben; or, the Other in Love." In *The Work of Giorgio Agamben*, n.d.

Nair, Nandini. "I Want to See More Clearly: Interview with Amitava Kumar." Hindu Business Line, 4 September 2015 https://www.thehindubusinessline.com/blink/read/i-want-to-see-more-clearly/article7611846.ece.

Nelson, Deborah. "The Virtues of Heartlessness: Mary McCarthy, Hannah Arendt, and the Anesthetics of Empathy." *American Literary History* 18, no. 1 (2006): 86–101.

Nietzsche, Friedrich Wilhelm. *On the Genealogy of Morals and Ecce Homo*. Translated by Walter Arnold Kaufmann. New York: Vintage Books, 1989.

Noys, Benjamin. "Encountering Badiou." *Polygraph*, no. 17 (2005).

Nussbaum, Martha C. *For Love of Country?* Edited by Joshua Cohen. 1st ed. Boston: Beacon Press, 2002.

"Omkara (2006)." Accessed September 30, 2009. http://www.imdb.com/title/tt0488414/.

Orr, Leonard. "Intertextuality and the Cultural Text in Recent Semiotics." *College English* 48, no. 8 (December 1986): 811–23. https://doi.org/10.2307/376732.

Parshley, Lois. "The Life and Death of Sabeen Mahmud | The New Yorker." Accessed December 3, 2017. https://www.newyorker.com/news/news-desk/the-life-and-death-of-sabeen-mahmud.

Peck, Raoul. *I Am Not Your Negro*, 2017.

Price, Joshua M. "The Apotheosis of Home and the Maintenance of Spaces of Violence." *Hypatia* 17, no. 4 (2002): 39–70.

Proust, Marcel. *The Captive & The Fugitive: In Search of Lost Time, Vol. V*. Edited by D. J. Enright. Translated by C. K. Scott Moncrieff and Terence Kilmartin. New edition. New York: Modern Library, 1999.

Rancière, Jacques. "Aesthetics against Incarnation: An Interview by Anne Marie Oliver." *Critical Inquiry* 35, no. 1 (2008): 172–90. https://doi.org/10.1086/595633.

———. *Disagreement: Politics and Philosophy*. Translated by Julie Rose. Minneapolis: University of Minnesota Press, 1998.

———. *Hatred of Democracy*. Translated by Steve Corcoran. Reprint edition. London New York: Verso, 2014.

———. "Politics, Identification, Subjectivization." In *The Identity in Question*, edited by John Rajchman. London; New York: Routledge, 1995.

———. "Ten Theses on Politics." *Theory and Event* 5, no. 3 (2001).

———. *The Flesh of Words: The Politics of Writing*. Translated by Charlotte Mandell. 1st edition. Stanford, Calif.: Stanford University Press, 2004.

———. "The Thinking of Dissensus: Politics and Aesthetics." In *Reading Rancière*, 1–17. London ; New York: Continuum, 2011.

Rancière, Jacques, and Davide Panagia. "Dissenting Words: A Conversation with Jacques Rancière." *Diacritics* 30, no. 2 (Summer 2000): 113–26.

Rancière, Jacques, and Slavoj Žižek. *The Politics of Aesthetics: The Distribution of the Sensible*. London ; New York: Continuum, 2004.

Razack, Sherene. *Casting Out: The Eviction of Muslims from Western Law and Politics*. University of Toronto Press, 2008.

Riffaterre, Michael. "Intertextuality vs. Hypertextuality." *New Literary History* 25, no. 4 (Autumn 1994): 779–88. https://doi.org/10.2307/469373.

Rose, Steve. "Anurag Kashyap: Bollywood Is to Blame for India's Inability to Deal with Reality." *The Guardian*, February 28, 2013, sec. Film. http://www.theguardian.com/film/2013/feb/28/anurag-kashyap-gangs-of-wasseypur.

Ross, Kristin. "Translator's Introduction." In *The Ignorant Schoolmaster: Five Lessons in Emancipation*, by Jacques Rancière. Stanford, Calif.: Stanford University Press, 1991.

Rousseau, Jean-Jacques. *Rousseau on Women, Love, and Family*. UPNE, 2009.

Rousseau, Jean-Jacques, and Donald A. Cress. *Discourse on the Origin of Inequality*. Hackett Publishing, 1992.

Rousseau, Jean-Jacques, and John T. Scott. *Essay on the Origin of Languages and Writings Related to Music*. Hanover: University Press of New England, 1998.

Rushdie, Salman. *Midnight's Children: A Novel*. 25th Anniversary edition. New York: Random House Trade Paperbacks, 2006.

Said, Edward. *Out of Place*. New edition. Granta Books, 2000.

Said, Edward W. *Orientalism*. 1st Vintage Books edition. New York: Vintage, 1979.

———. "The Essential Terrorist." *The Nation*, August 15, 2006. https://www.thenation.com/article/essential-terrorist/.

Santner, Eric L. *On Creaturely Life: Rilke, Benjamin, Sebald*. New edition. Chicago: University of Chicago Press, 2006.

Sartre, Jean-Paul, and Arlette Elkaïm-Sartre. *Critique of Dialectical Reason*. Verso, 2006.

"Satya (1998)." Accessed September 30, 2009. http://www.imdb.com/title/tt0195231/.

Schmitt, Carl. *Theory of the Partisan: Intermediate Commentary on the Concept of the Political*. Translated by G. L. Ulmen. New York: Telos Press Publishing, 2007.

Schmitt, Carl, Tracy B. Strong, and Leo Strauss. *The Concept of the Political*. Translated by George Schwab. Enlarged edition. Chicago: The University of Chicago Press, 2007.

Schroeder, Brian. "The (Non) Logic of Desire and War: Hegel and Levinas." In *Philosophy and Desire*, edited by Hugh J. Silverman, 45–62. Routledge, 2000.

Schutz, Alfred. "On Multiple Realities." *Philosophy and Phenomenological Research* 5, no. 4 (June 1945): 533–76.

Shakespeare, William. *The Oxford Shakespeare: Hamlet*. Edited by G. R. Hibbard. Reissue edition. Oxford, England; New York: Oxford University Press, 2008.

Sharoni, Simona. "Compassionate Resistance: A Personal/Political Journey to Israel/Palestine." *International Feminist Journal of Politics* 8, no. 2 (June 1, 2006): 288–99. https://doi.org/10.1080/14616740600612962.

Silverman, Hugh. "Twentieth-Century Desire and the Histories of Philosophy." In *Philosophy and Desire*, edited by Hugh J. Silverman, 1–13. Routledge, 2000.

Sinclair, Charlotte. "Arundhati Roy: Why Happiness Is a Radical Act." *Vogue*, July 27, 2017. http://www.vogue.co.uk/article/arundhati-roy-interview.

Spillers, Hortense J. "Mama's Baby, Papa's Maybe: An American Grammar Book." *Diacritics* 17, no. 2 (1987): 65–81. https://doi.org/10.2307/464747.

Spivak, Gayatri Chakravorty. "Can the Subaltern Speak?" In *Marxism and the Interpretation of Culture*, edited by Cary Nelson and Lawrence Grossberg, 271–313. Urbana: University of Illinois Press, 1988.
Steinhauer, Jillian. "Kenneth Goldsmith Remixes Michael Brown Autopsy Report as Poetry." *Hyperallergic*, March 16, 2015. https://hyperallergic.com/190954/kenneth-goldsmith-remixes-michael-brown-autopsy-report-as-poetry/.
Stewart, Susan. *Nonsense: Aspects of Intertextuality in Folklore and Literature*. Johns Hopkins University Press, 1989.
Strong, Tracy. *Jean-Jacques Rousseau: The Politics of the Ordinary.* Rowman & Littlefield, 2002.
Tagore, Rabindranath. *Chokher Bali*. Translated by Sukhendu Ray. New Delhi: Rupa Publications, 2005.
———. *The Home and the World*. Penguin Classics, 2005.
Tagore, Saranindranath. "Tagore's Conception of Cosmopolitanism: A Reconstruction." *University of Toronto Quarterly* 77, no. 4 (December 31, 2008): 1070–84. https://doi.org/10.1353/utq.0.0305.
"The Assassination of My Friend Is Not Just a Personal Loss — It's a Loss for Pakistan." Accessed December 3, 2017. https://mic.com/articles/116616/the-assassination-of-my-friend-is-not-just-a-personal-loss-it-s-a-loss-for-pakistan#.5AjC9i8X4.
"The Other Half: For Many Kashmir 'Half-Widows', Remarriage Ruling Means Little | The Indian Express." Accessed December 4, 2017. http://indianexpress.com/article/india/india-others/the-other-half/.
Umar, Baba. "The Dilemma of Kashmir's Half-Widows." Accessed December 4, 2017. http://www.aljazeera.com/news/asia/2013/09/dilemma-kashmir-half-widows-201392715575877378.html.
Waheed, Mirza. "India's Crackdown in Kashmir: Is This the World's First Mass Blinding?" *The Guardian*, November 8, 2016, sec. World news. http://www.theguardian.com/world/2016/nov/08/india-crackdown-in-kashmir-is-this-worlds-first-mass-blinding.
Weber, Max. *The Vocation Lectures*. Edited by David Owen and Tracy B. Strong. Translated by Rodney Livingstone. Indianapolis: Hackett Publishing Company, Inc., 2004.
Weheliye, Alexander G. *Habeas Viscus: Racializing Assemblages, Biopolitics, and Black Feminist Theories of the Human*. Durham: Duke University Press Books, 2014.
Weizman, Eyal. *Forensic Architecture: Violence at the Threshold of Detectability*. 1st edition. Brooklyn, NY: Zone Books, 2017.
Woolf, Virginia. *Mrs. Dalloway*. Mariner Books, 1990.
Zaman, Naziha Syed Ali and Fahim. "Anatomy of a Murder." Herald Magazine, July 31, 2015. http://herald.dawn.com/news/1153209.
Žižek, Slavoj. *Living in the End Times*. Verso, 2011.
———. "The Lesson of Rancière." In *The Politics of Aesthetics: The Distribution of the Sensible*, by Jacques Rancière. London; New York: Continuum, 2004.
Žižek, Slavoj, Eric L. Santner, and Kenneth Reinhard. *The Neighbor: Three Inquiries in Political Theology*. Chicago: University of Chicago Press, 2006.
Zuabi, Amir Nizar. *I Am Yusuf and This Is My Brother*. London: Methuen Drama, 2011.
———. "The Underground Ghetto City of Gaza." Haaretz, August 3, 2014. https://www.haaretz.com/opinion/.premium-1.608653.

Index

absence, 21, 22, 51, 70, 89, 95, 105
abundance, 22, 113, 119, 142, 169, 171, 172
accursed share, 117–119
Adams, David, 65
Adorno, Theodor, 43, 48–50, 53–55, 163–164
Agamben, Giorgio, 51
agency, 14, 22, 36, 189
agonism, 145
Algeria, 48, 68, 111, 150, 165
alterity, 28, 38, 42, 43, 44, 49, 51
anthropology, 108, 116
anticolonial, 6, 48, 52, 77, 138, 153, 161, 186, 188, 192
anticolonialism, 182, 188
Arendt, Hannah, 57n36, 72–75, 177n5, 200n5
Asad, Talal, 52
Aslam, Nadeem, 141, 195
attachment, definition of, 21
austerity, 10, 19, 22, 169, 176, 200n3; necropolitical, 112, 116

Bachelard, Gaston, 60, 75
Badiou, Alain, 51–52
Baldwin, James, 14, 88, 143, 194
Bataille, Georges, 27, 54, 119, 134
beautiful stranger, 50, 54
beauty, 30, 49, 54
becoming, 42, 46, 48, 75, 91, 159, 205

belonging, 28, 35
beloved, 1, 13, 16, 17, 19, 29, 44, 93, 164, 180, 198, 205
Benjamin, Walter, 10, 16–18, 95, 112, 163–164, 172
betrayal, 2, 7, 69, 82, 97–103, 108
Bhardwaj, Vishal, 97, 158
black church, the, 13, 14, 165–174
body, 10, 14, 64, 88, 94, 121, 135, 149, 164–176, 191
Brown, Michael, 165–167, 174, 175

camp, refugee, 81, 99
Charleston, 13–14, 171
checkpoint, 98
cinema, 70, 97, 103, 153–158
classroom, the, 203–210; authority, 7, 105, 136, 195
colonial odyssey, 65, 68, 76, 82
colonialism, 23, 27, 36, 46, 48, 62, 65, 66, 68, 70, 72, 73, 90, 135, 136, 138, 199; settler, 10, 60, 61, 62, 71, 76, 77, 78, 80, 106, 113, 116, 153, 155, 160, 177n5, 194
colony, 3, 36, 46, 60, 113, 118, 121, 129
commitment, 7, 9, 16, 28, 90
community, 7, 99, 115, 136, 147, 189, 194, 203–210
cosmopolitan modernity, 10, 17
cosmopolitanism, 56n13, 69–70, 153, 180, 189

crisis, 48, 76, 82, 103, 138, 183, 197

dead love, 23, 27
death, 6, 10, 18, 26, 27, 48, 79, 82, 98, 112–124, 130–161; death-world, 117
decisionism, 145, 149
decolonial, 6, 23, 47–48, 52, 77
democracy, 6, 36, 102, 120, 143, 146–147, 151, 158, 206–207
desire, 7, 9, 19, 21, 23, 24, 26, 29, 30, 32n18, 38, 39, 42, 43, 47, 49, 55, 61, 63, 68, 73, 78, 82, 101, 102, 105, 124, 127, 137, 155, 161, 170, 171, 177n5, 181, 184, 185, 192, 195, 198
dialectic, 37, 42–50, 53–55, 65, 76, 77, 91, 127, 159, 197
difference, 7, 38
disappearance, 1, 17, 38, 73, 92, 93, 96, 98–99, 103, 105, 106, 196, 199
dissensus, 10, 21, 121, 124, 125, 146, 148, 149, 153, 199
Djebar, Assia, 106, 175
domestic violence, 64, 75
domestication, 9, 23, 24, 27, 28, 61, 64, 75–79, 159, 192
double, the, 23, 32n25, 42, 66
dream, 18, 60, 87–89, 95, 108, 158
Du Bois, William Edward Burghardt, 41, 66

education, 163, 203–210
emancipation, 48, 148, 150–151, 195
emergency, states of, 136, 196
empire, 67, 116, 121, 134, 135, 157, 180, 186, 187, 204, 209
empiricism, 9, 10, 16, 41, 42
England, 64–66
equality, 26, 45, 141, 143, 147–151, 195
ethics, 7, 8, 18, 21, 43, 49, 50–54, 117, 122, 146, 164, 177n5, 186–192, 197–198, 208
excess, 19, 40, 50, 118–119, 127, 134, 142, 166, 176
exclusion, 9, 25, 35, 37, 38, 90, 136, 151, 177n5, 188, 196
experience, 6, 16, 17, 21, 22, 23, 24, 36, 39, 40, 41, 42, 45, 48, 52, 53, 55, 68, 72, 85n31, 90, 92, 93, 95, 108, 118, 129, 135, 137, 142, 146, 155, 158, 172, 184, 206, 209

fanatic, 5, 22, 41, 102, 104, 194
Fanon, Frantz, 6, 10, 40, 43, 45–48, 55, 68, 116, 119, 137, 164, 168
fascism, 6, 7, 22, 24, 49, 68, 73, 78, 91, 99, 101, 104, 106, 108, 112–115, 138, 147, 157, 163, 180, 183, 185, 190, 192, 198, 209
Forster, Edward Morgan, 6, 10, 40, 47, 59–68, 153, 179, 182, 187, 188, 189–191
freedom, 27, 30, 32n18, 46–48, 97, 103, 106, 124, 138, 149, 185, 189, 194
Freud, Sigmund, 42, 51, 71
friend(ship), 66, 68, 145, 180–192, 197–198
fugitivity, 9, 39, 61, 62, 79, 81
fugue states, 9, 79, 81, 82, 98, 106
future, 13, 23, 92, 93, 104

Gandhi, Leela, 182, 187–192, 197
Gaza, 153, 193
ghost, 71, 98, 110n26
grief, 2, 99, 169, 185, 190, 191, 194, 199
Gržinić, Marina, 112, 116, 120

haunting, 9, 40, 71, 83, 102, 105, 130, 168, 206
Hegel, Georg Wilhelm Friedrich, 21, 42–51, 55, 57n27, 134, 182
historian, 10, 17, 85n31, 164
historicism, 18
history, 2, 8, 14, 15, 22, 24, 40, 48, 50, 65, 66, 68, 72–74, 79, 81, 88, 92, 93, 94, 97, 98, 99, 101, 108, 120, 134, 138, 142, 148, 151, 159, 169–175, 187–189, 193, 199, 206, 208
home, anticolonial conception of, 60–83
hope, 16, 23–24, 26–27, 105, 142–144, 192, 195, 199
hospitality, 6, 14, 18, 62–64, 76–78, 81, 105–106, 142, 188–189, 190, 194, 197; of hauntings, 3, 102
humanitarianism, 25, 29, 61, 76, 85n35, 190, 192
Hussain, Intizar, 87, 158, 207
hypermateriality, 174

Index

identity, 28, 37, 42, 43, 45, 49, 67, 69, 79, 89, 99, 150, 189, 191, 194; politics, liberal, 20, 29, 36, 42, 63, 68, 72, 91, 108, 183–184, 197
ignorance, epistemologies of, 64
imagination, 6, 16, 17, 38, 42, 46, 48, 56n13, 59, 70, 71, 76, 78, 81–82, 94, 101, 108, 121, 136, 157, 161, 164, 189, 198, 210
immaterialized, 4, 20, 123, 148
imperialism, 4, 50, 52, 64, 67, 88, 115, 180, 182, 185
inclusion, 4, 8, 24, 26, 37, 51, 62, 91, 96, 108, 184, 186
India, 47, 65, 67, 69, 87, 88, 97, 99, 106, 153, 155, 156, 159, 179, 180, 182, 189–190
institutions, 4, 5, 18, 39, 42, 43, 60, 78, 82, 91, 136, 184, 203–208
intermateriality, 39–41, 49, 51, 55
intertextuality, 40
invitation, 3, 11, 62, 67, 169, 182–184, 186, 192, 194, 195, 205, 206
irreconcilability, 68, 90, 95, 104

journey, 42, 64–66, 81, 88, 101, 198
judgment, 21, 45, 49, 92, 102, 131, 137, 169, 174, 188, 209

Kant, Immanuel, 42, 147, 187
Kashmir, 97, 101, 143, 153, 158, 185, 199
knowledge, 4, 8, 18, 25, 29, 31, 36, 41, 42, 51, 57n27, 71, 90, 92, 98, 99, 103, 123, 141, 143, 148, 151, 155, 163, 199, 204, 205, 209
Kojève, Alexandre, 43, 55
Kristeva, Julia, 40, 93

labor, 4, 6, 9, 23, 25, 26, 37, 38, 46, 47, 48, 51, 61, 63, 72, 74–76, 78, 83, 91, 96, 113, 118, 121, 145, 155, 161, 173, 174, 176, 177n5, 184, 192, 197, 206; of suffering, 9, 26, 27, 35, 137, 138
Laymon, Kiese, 14, 170–173
legitimacy, 45, 57n27, 82, 167, 190, 191
Levinas, Emmanuel, 43–45, 49–51, 54
liberal democracy, 8, 147, 151, 199
liberalism, 4, 6, 9, 14, 20, 23, 24, 25, 26, 28, 29, 36, 37, 41, 42, 51, 61, 64, 68, 69, 82, 91, 105, 108, 113, 115, 116, 118, 128, 138, 147, 149, 155, 185, 188, 190, 197, 199
lifeworld, 6, 9, 51, 70, 77, 128, 137, 156, 158, 180, 186, 199
longing, 38, 52, 72, 82, 90, 93, 99, 101, 102, 103, 106, 159, 181, 204, 205; community of, 204, 205, 206
love: dead, 23–24, 27; definition, 7, 21–22, 30, 31, 160
lover, 10, 16, 18, 22, 32n25, 72, 94, 104, 141, 142, 163, 172, 194, 195, 198

madness, 2, 38, 68, 98, 101, 103, 105, 185
Mahmud, Sabeen, 1–2, 14, 177
margin(ality), 3, 6, 8, 9, 26, 31, 36–55, 60, 62, 66, 76–77, 78, 91, 95, 106, 118, 119, 136, 137, 138, 157, 158, 159, 160, 164, 168, 184, 196
Marx, Karl, 10, 25, 51, 71, 90, 91, 94, 96, 134, 149, 168, 174, 176, 195, 197, 198, 209
materialism, 10, 22, 23, 27, 119, 124, 132, 138, 145, 149, 164, 168, 174, 176, 192, 197, 209; anticolonial, 8, 9, 108
materiality, 25, 39, 42, 45, 55, 67, 77, 78, 83, 93, 120, 130, 148, 153, 173, 203, 206, 208
Mbembe, Achille, 114–115, 118–125, 133–135, 137, 144–145, 148, 149
memory, 22, 40, 57n30, 71, 83, 88, 89, 95, 101, 103, 106, 108, 109n10, 172, 173, 185, 199
metapolitics, 147
militancy, 17, 18, 97, 103, 105
minor poetics, 60–61, 76
minor politics, 197
minor subjects, 188, 197
misogyny, 19, 30, 47, 63, 106, 137
misreading, 103, 167
modernity, 42, 61, 62, 63, 64, 65, 68, 75, 78, 82, 91, 103, 108, 135, 144, 169; cosmopolitan, 10, 112
mourning, 3, 99, 103, 106, 127, 129, 134, 175, 190, 191, 206
muslim, 1, 17, 79, 101, 108, 121, 133, 165, 179

Index

nation, 22, 25, 78, 117, 137, 142, 172, 175, 179, 182, 189; -state, 63, 64, 77, 119, 137
nationalism, 46, 67, 69, 77, 101, 104, 108, 119, 158, 169, 185, 188, 197
nativism, 61, 77, 197
necessity, 27, 37, 62, 74, 79, 81, 96
necrocapitalism, 116, 121
necropolitical austerity, 10, 112, 116
necropolitics, 22, 113, 114–117, 119–125, 133–135, 144, 148, 152–153, 167, 185, 190, 192
need, 10, 19, 21, 26, 39, 43, 45, 46, 47, 62, 68, 104, 108, 112, 121, 134, 144, 159, 168, 172, 176, 198
neoliberalism, 3, 15, 18, 22, 39, 63, 98, 112, 116, 119, 148, 161, 180, 192
Nietzsche, Friedrich, 25, 142, 164, 168, 186
non-violence, 7, 28, 130
novel, the, 144, 159

object, 8, 15, 16, 17, 21, 23, 24, 31, 37, 39, 42, 43–55, 61, 71, 74, 83, 92, 96, 103, 116, 128, 138, 143, 146, 151, 159, 172, 186, 188, 189, 194, 195, 198, 209
occupation, 62, 73, 77, 85n35, 97, 98, 99, 106, 149, 190
Odysseus, 68, 99–101
odyssey, colonial, 65, 68, 76, 82
ontology, 9, 23, 24, 25, 27, 38, 43, 45, 88, 92, 104, 122–124, 129, 131, 150, 152, 161, 187, 197, 209
orientalism, 68, 69, 128
otherness, 7, 35, 42, 44, 48, 51, 52, 130; See also difference

Pakistan, 1, 98, 106, 129, 154, 158, 195
Palestine, 83, 98, 117, 138, 149, 158, 177n5, 193
pariah, 35, 36, 39, 79, 82, 172
partition, 69, 70, 87, 98, 99, 153, 185; of the sensible, 132, 147, 148, 153
pathos, 40, 51, 52, 57n31, 119, 132, 191, 209
plasticity, destructive, 123, 131–132
poetics, 18, 22, 31, 60, 76, 89, 92, 95, 148, 150–151, 152, 195
polis, 39, 75, 77, 78, 82, 106, 121, 158, 191

politics, definition, 4, 8, 20, 28
post/colony, 115, 118, 124, 125n13, 136, 158
postcolonial, 6, 52, 61, 112, 131, 137, 155, 190
postcolony, 10, 61, 79, 112, 113, 116, 119, 125n13, 133, 134, 148, 153, 157, 190, 192
power, 21, 28, 29, 32n18, 42, 64, 65, 67, 74, 85n35, 92, 103, 105, 124, 143, 148, 167, 168, 175, 177, 181, 186, 187
prayer, 17, 101, 103, 106, 108
presence, 7, 8, 21, 27, 38, 41, 51, 55, 71, 89, 90, 92, 94, 99, 102, 105, 134, 138, 142, 146, 152, 153, 173, 176, 205, 207
production, 4, 6, 14, 15, 17, 21, 28, 32n18, 38, 42, 44, 46, 49, 60, 63, 75, 76, 95, 105, 115, 119, 127, 129, 133, 134, 138, 159, 167, 168, 173–174, 175, 176, 195, 206; aesthetic, 10, 17, 90, 94, 118, 132, 143–150, 153, 161, 163; cultural, 153, 155; knowledge, 5

race, 19, 38, 57n39, 63–64, 135, 144, 145, 169, 194
Rancière, Jacques, 22, 31, 102, 118, 119, 121, 122, 124, 132, 133, 134, 143–148, 149–153, 194
reading, 90, 103, 138, 149, 155, 158, 161, 188, 194, 204
reality, 4, 6, 7, 63, 69, 89, 98, 118, 128, 132, 143, 153–155, 156, 204, 209
reconciliation, 5, 21, 28, 49, 55, 78, 90, 91, 95, 98, 103, 104, 106, 121, 155, 191
refuge/e, 9, 36, 39, 61, 63, 68, 76, 79, 80, 82, 98, 101, 103, 158, 172, 177n5, 190, 193, 194, 196; camp, 81, 99
relation (s), 5, 6, 7, 8, 9, 10, 18, 20, 21, 26, 27
representation, 9, 25, 26, 27, 51, 105, 158, 161, 167, 184, 187
requital, 9, 15, 16, 19, 24, 36, 67, 73, 83, 180, 198, 199, 210
ressentiment, 18, 169, 180, 185, 186
romance, 21
romanticism, 42, 49, 70, 95, 96, 104, 137, 182
Rousseau, Jean-Jacques, 42, 164, 165, 168–169, 203, 210

ruins, 79, 82, 91, 95, 101, 105, 106

safe space, 75, 76, 79, 80, 159, 209
Said, Edward, 57n27, 69, 88–89, 95, 128
Saleh, Ahmad, 79–81
scarcity, 3, 18, 19, 22, 82, 112, 117, 118, 119, 127, 142, 169, 172, 177
Schmitt, Carl, 32n25, 115, 129, 145
secular time, 65, 84n12
secularism, 14, 17, 79, 105, 122, 142, 164
sensible, the, 4, 10, 94, 99, 118, 119, 121, 129, 132, 133, 144, 145, 146, 147, 148, 149, 153, 154, 155, 158, 161, 195; partition of the, 132, 147, 148, 153
sensorium, 24, 26, 40, 45, 92, 98, 101, 137, 153, 155, 158
sensuousness, 9, 24, 25, 28, 39, 88, 90, 92, 93, 94, 96, 99, 102, 106, 118, 131, 133, 142, 146, 184
settler colonialism, 10, 60, 61, 62, 71, 76, 77, 78, 80, 106, 113, 116, 153, 155, 160, 177n5, 194
sex, 23, 32n18, 38, 42, 63–64, 79, 105, 119, 141, 170, 171
sleep, 70, 88, 89, 129
solidarity, 7, 9, 22, 28, 29, 93, 102, 177, 181, 183, 187, 190, 191, 199
sovereignty, 18, 20, 30, 81, 90, 103, 105, 106, 108, 112, 114, 115, 120, 122, 124, 125, 129, 132, 133–136, 138, 144–145, 149, 151, 163, 168, 175, 195–196
Spillers, Hortense, 63, 149
standpoint theory, 9, 36, 41, 51
state, 1, 2, 3, 9, 18, 26, 46, 60, 62–64, 71, 74, 79, 104, 106, 115, 116, 118, 129, 135, 136, 138, 144, 145, 158, 167, 168, 169, 172, 175, 190, 191, 197; of emergency, 136, 196; of exception, 102, 105, 122; failed, 117, 190; fugue, 9, 79, 81, 82, 98, 106; nation, 63, 64, 77, 119, 137; statelessness, 76
storytelling, 16, 89, 141, 143
student, 46, 183, 203, 204, 206, 207, 210
study, 8, 10, 21, 29, 55, 60, 209
subject, 8, 9, 10, 14, 15, 16, 22, 25, 28, 29, 39, 41, 42, 43, 45, 46, 49, 50, 53, 55, 70, 71, 91, 95, 96, 105, 112, 117, 118, 123, 128, 131, 133, 134, 136, 159, 173, 177n5, 182, 184, 188, 191, 193, 197, 199
subjectification, 92, 95, 101, 146
subjectivity, 5, 20, 24, 42, 47, 51, 56n13, 61, 63, 66, 74, 108, 163, 167, 207; political, 14, 22, 23, 25, 28, 31, 40, 78, 93, 99, 119, 121, 132, 148, 152, 181, 182, 184, 197
suffering, 23, 25, 26, 27, 29, 41, 45, 75, 113, 119, 121, 122, 128, 132, 138, 144, 158, 172, 176, 199, 208; labor of, 9, 26, 27, 35, 137, 138
suicide, 106, 134, 138, 143, 151
supremacism, 6, 38, 68, 108, 112, 123, 170, 171

Tagore, Rabindranath, 40, 69–70, 160
temporality, 24, 39, 40, 53, 62, 63, 66, 74, 75, 78, 90, 91, 92, 93, 95, 96, 97, 105, 112, 135, 137, 142, 158, 161, 194, 199
terror, 6, 16, 26, 62, 117, 119, 127–128, 130, 132, 137, 138, 141, 185, 192
terrorism, 24, 27, 102, 103, 125, 128, 131, 135, 136, 144
theology, 116, 120, 122, 124, 135, 136, 176
time, 21, 23, 26, 53, 66, 67, 73, 84n12, 88–99, 102–103, 108, 113, 121, 136, 137, 138, 142, 146, 147, 151, 156, 193–195
topography, 8, 9, 22, 36, 38, 39, 63, 78, 90, 91, 147, 158
trauma, 3, 4, 39, 42; empire 118, 131–132, 142, 180
truth, 22, 38, 51, 57n31, 143, 144, 157, 161, 170, 174, 186, 204, 205
travel, 59–66, 64, 68, 76, 80, 81

uncanny, the, 71, 99
Unheimliche, das, 71, 78, 81
University, the, 18, 207
unloved, 8, 14, 16, 19, 37, 38, 47, 63, 83, 99, 106, 141, 169, 172, 177n5, 190, 199
unrequited, concept of the, 6, 8, 9, 16, 19, 27, 35, 46, 47, 55, 81, 83, 99, 103, 106, 158, 163, 164, 177, 184, 192, 194, 199

value, 15, 24, 106, 144, 145, 153, 173
victim, 18, 23, 24, 36, 99, 108, 129, 131, 193; perfect, 3, 27, 172

violence, 5, 6, 10, 17, 18, 32n22, 47, 50, 51, 63, 64, 81, 82, 85n35, 105, 106, 117, 119, 127, 128, 130, 131–132, 134, 135–137, 144, 158, 167, 173, 176, 182, 183, 184, 191, 192, 193; domestic, 64, 75; non-, 7, 28, 130; political, 131, 135

war, 119, 143, 149, 151, 157, 167–169
Weber, Max, 18, 115, 187, 188, 197

Weheliye, Alexander, 149
whiteness, 46–48, 63, 68, 99, 164, 167, 169–173
will, 7, 15, 21, 22, 44, 48, 66, 79, 105, 108, 180, 210
world, 28–29, 99; death-, 117

Zuabi, Amir Nizar, 83, 192–195

About the Author

Asma Abbas is associate professor of politics and philosophy at Bard College at Simon's Rock, Great Barrington, Massachusetts, and the dean of academics at the Indus Valley School of Art and Architecture in Karachi. She is also founder and member of Hic Rosa, an art, education, and politics collective. This is her second book, following *Liberalism and Human Suffering: Materialist Reflections on Politics, Ethics, and Aesthetics* (Palgrave Macmillan, 2010).

www.ingramcontent.com/pod-product-compliance
Lightning Source LLC
Chambersburg PA
CBHW050903300426
44111CB00010B/1355